Enjoying Majorca

The Island of Majorca

Enjoying Majorca

By Pamela Legge

With illustrations by Claire Baker

G G Baker & Associates

Published by
G G Baker & Associates
PO Box 81
Windlesham,
Surrey GU20 6NN

A catalogue record for this book is
available from the British Library

ISBN 0 906635 21 7

Printed and bound in Great Britain by
Biddles Limited, Guildford, Surrey

Contents

Introduction 7
1 Second Class to Majorca 11
2 Life in Deià 22
3 Letters from Majorca 30
4 From One Posada to Another 38
5 Majorca Revisited 53
6 A New Home 69
7 Early Days 84
8 Friends and Neighbours 101
9 A Cinema under the Stars 119
10 Saints and Sinners 129
11 Fiestas 143
12 Flora and Fauna 171
13 Rules and Regulations 185
14 Around the City of Palma 197
15 Too Much Talk 217
16 Recycled Rubbish and Desperate Doggies 230
17 A Party at Porto Cristo 235
18 The Hinterland 240
19 Information and Entertainment 249
20 Food and Wine 259
21 The View from Randa 271
Appendix 1 Dates of Festivals and Fiestas 280
Appendix 2 A Brief History of Majorca 282
Index 284

Index to Illustrations

Cover Deià from the south

Page

9 Girls in traditional dress

10 The village of Deià

15 The Cartuja, Valldemossa

18 Belvedere at Son Maroig

23 The cala at Deià

29 Almond blossom, Calvià

34 Letter from Robert Graves

39 The bus for Deià, 1954

48 The Hotel Formentor

51 The road to Formentor

52 Mirador de Ses Animes

57 The Hotel Coronado

74 The mountain of Galatzo

78 In the churchyard, Deià

81 Tia Maria in flight

83 A china water fountain

89 Starting on the garden

91 Pool terrace completed

95 The oil wagon

112 Tia Maria on the prowl

120 The film projector

128 Palma Cathedral

142 Homage Tower, Bellver

145 Masks used in fiestas

151 The Majorcan bagpipe

154 Statue, Santa Margalida

160 Judging at Binissalem

165 Traditional dancers

168 Es Cavallets

170 A hoopoe

192 The sheep at Calvià

196 Paraires Tower, Porto Pi

199 The Almudaina Palace

205 Arab arch in Palma

216 The Torrent de Pareis

221 The road to Colobra

226 Roman bridge, Pollença

245 The road to Alaró

264 A lobster at Portixol

270 Typical wind pump

274 Cala Figuera

279 Es Pontas rock bridge

Introduction

What is Majorca really like? Over six million tourists visited the island last year and many of them must have realised that there is something beyond the beaches, bars and clubs of the popular resorts, but remarkably few ventured very far from their hotels.

This book attempts to convey the enjoyment I have experienced living in a Majorca that I have come to know as a place steeped in history and rich in culture. Many of its fascinating customs have been observed since King Jaime I came to conquer the Moors in 1229. The fine palaces in Palma and the vast manor houses in the country still stand as evidence of a very sophisticated society, rich in money and talent, which included internationally respected merchants, cartographers, philosophers and evangelists.

I have tried to present a light-hearted but factual account of what it is like to live on the island which offers such a choice of excellent restaurants, concerts, historic buildings, fiestas and breathtaking scenery that no-one could ever be bored. If I have tended to ignore the holiday resorts and the major tourist attractions it is because they are already well documented in other publications, many of which are available free from the tourist offices. I have concentrated on places of interest, customs and events that are not widely publicised elsewhere.

My Majorca is usually as sunny as the brochures portray it, but I also know that the wind can blow hard enough to strip tiles from the roof; I may have to spend a morning sweeping up yellow pollen that has been shed by the thousands of pine trees behind the house; and occasionally the swimming pool can turn brown with fine dust carried in rain from the Sahara.

I also know that the Majorcans are a friendly, honest people who welcome the stranger and are always delighted to explain the mysteries of their culture. Much of the material in this book has been gathered by simply standing next to a Majorcan at a fiesta, expressing an interest in what is going on and hearing first-hand about the historical significance of the event.

My other sources are too numerous to mention in full, but I would like to pay special tribute to the superb facilities provided by IBATUR, the Balearic Institute for the Promotion of Tourism, whose literature has been invaluable, especially for information about forthcoming events.

I am also indebted to Carmen and George Bowden for allowing me access to their extensive library of books, some of which were written when the tourist industry was still in its infancy. They have also greatly assisted me with spelling in both Spanish and Majorcan. I have borrowed considerably from the superb book written by George's American mother, Dina Moore Bowden, when covering the life of Fray Junípero Serra who was born in Majorca and who is known to all Americans for his work in California.

Two other books I have frequently consulted are the translation of George Sand's *Winter in Majorca* by Robert Graves, in which his footnotes contain very well observed comments on life in Majorca, and the comprehensive biography of Robert Graves by Martin Seymour-Smith.

I have listed most towns as they are shown on the popular Firestone map of the island. Because both Spanish and Majorcan are in widespread use, there is considerable variation in how the name of a town may be recorded and, because Majorcan is a spoken rather than a written language, the placing of accents is very much a matter of personal choice. Deià for example is often written as Deiá or even Deya while Andratx frequently appears as Andraitx. To the natives the island is, of course, Mallorca but I have used Majorca throughout the book, and for the title, as I believe that it is still the more familiar spelling for most readers.

The illustrations by Claire Baker are largely based on photographs that I have taken over the years, but some are from life. I am indebted to her for her ability to convey with no more than a pen and ink the sparkle and beauty of Majorca which I find difficulty in expressing in thousands of words.

Majorca has suffered from several unflattering reports in the British press and on television. I hope that this book will create a better awareness of the incredible scenery and fascinating character of an island paradise where only a few small and well-defined areas are enlivened by wet T-shirt contests and where film crews have to cruise around for days before finding a genuine lager lout to portray in their biased accounts of life on Majorca.

1. Second Class to Majorca

Sinking back into my corner of the compartment on the Dover boat train, I glanced at the four Oxford undergraduates with whom I would be travelling to Majorca. It was by mere chance that I had heard about their holiday plans through a mutual friend and our first meeting had only taken place a week before, but they had generously agreed to allow me to join their party; the only proviso being that I must make an instant decision. It was an unexpected opportunity to have an inexpensive holiday so I had seized it, little knowing how much the island would later feature in my life.

My parents had raised no objections because the mother of one of the boys was to travel with us accompanied by her two younger children. It was only when I met the four at Victoria station on the day of our departure that I learnt with astonishment that she had already flown with them to Palma the day before.

One of the undergraduates was an American called Tommy Matthews, the son of the editor of Time magazine. His father was a long-time friend of Robert Graves, the author and poet who lived in Deià on the north coast of Majorca. So it was to Deià that we were going, to meet the Graves family, in that summer of 1952.

Our journey down through France by train was uneventful but very uncomfortable. Not for us the luxury of the Blue Train; our limited budgets dictated that we must forego even a couchette, so we sat bolt upright as the train trundled slowly through France, stopping at many stations on its way to the Spanish border. Our discomfort was only slightly alleviated by vendors who came to the windows to sell food, drink and straw pillows to those who were not brave enough to descend from the train in case it left without them.

My spirits rose once we reached Perpignan because it was our first link with Majorca. Although it is now part of France, it was formerly the capital of the kingdom of Jaime I of Catalonia who liberated Majorca from the Moors in 1229. He was a good and powerful king who initiated a programme of colonisation which brought many settlers from Catalonia to the island and he is possibly best remembered for introducing a new Constitution, the *Carta de Poblacio*, which guaranteed liberty, equality and autonomy. He was caught in a storm at sea and vowed that if he survived he would raise a great church in Palma and he kept his promise by initiating the work of constructing the Cathedral which was to continue for several hundred years, resulting in one of the world's most beautiful Gothic buildings.

Perpignan was the last town before the French railway line terminated at Cerbère. We had to walk across the border, carrying our luggage up a dusty mountain track to the Customs post which had a distinctly unfriendly atmosphere. It was small and barely furnished and the slightly scruffy officers silently indicated that we were to lift our suitcases onto the benches where they were opened and thoroughly inspected. Our passports were taken from us and it was over half an hour before they were returned. Tommy, who was the eldest of us and who had effectively become the leader of our party because he had made the journey before, collected them and we were free to go.

It was getting late and the train for Barcelona did not leave until the morning; so we found a small *hostal* in Port Bou where we could stay the night. I was allocated quite a large room with a double bed, but it was a little disconcerting to find that there was no key to the door. The unfortunate boys, however, had to share a very small, sparsely-furnished room resembling a school dormitory which was almost completely filled by four iron bedsteads.

In the dining area of the *hostal* bar, we had just started to enjoy our first proper meal for forty-eight hours when we noticed that we were being watched by two grim-faced officers of the *Guardia Civil,* the Spanish police. After a few moments they approached us and, even though we knew that we had done nothing wrong, we began to feel a little uneasy. In their dark green uniforms with black belts, shiny black coal-scuttle hats, and guns in their holsters, they looked slightly menacing as they demanded our passports. Tommy handed them over and the taller of the two officers examined them carefully, singled out mine and said: 'I regret *señorita* that this is not in order.' Thoughts of having to return alone through France flashed through my mind and I was not far from tears when Tommy came to my rescue by asking them what was wrong. 'When you arrived we charged for only four persons but we have discovered that you are five and this passport has not been stamped.' said the officer. We handed over the small additional amount and the police left the *hostal* wishing us a pleasant meal and an enjoyable holiday.

On arriving at Barcelona early in the afternoon we found that the ferry to Majorca did not leave until midnight and that the crossing would take twelve hours. We passed the time in true Spanish style, sitting at a café on Las Ramblas and watching the world go by until we could board the ship. Our tickets, which were the cheapest available, only entitled us to hard benches on the open deck.

With a strident blast of its siren the ship edged away from the quay. It was fairly warm at first, but by four o'clock in the morning the chill air began to seep through our light clothing and, although we took it in turns to shelter under a small tarpaulin attached to one of the bulkheads, the cold and damp soon found their way underneath and we were glad when the sun rose and the temperature gradually increased.

We were all feeling somewhat travel-weary but our spirits rose when the island came into view and we sailed around its western end to enter the bay of Palma. This is the ideal way to approach Majorca for the first time, the initial impression of a sparkling sea, dark green pines and a clear blue sky gradually filled with detail as we entered the immense bay and saw the city with its back-cloth of purple mountains. As we drew closer we could make out the features that never fail to impress every visitor; the ornately buttressed Cathedral beside the Almudaina Palace on the waterfront and, crowning a hill to the left, Bellver Castle sharply outlined by the bright sunshine above its green nest of trees.

The ferry fussed its way into the harbour and, as soon as it had docked, we disembarked and made our way to where the bus for Deià was preparing to leave. This vehicle was of considerable age and featured a relatively short wheelbase and a long bonnet, so that the driver sat approximately mid-way between the front and rear wheels. To accommodate more people, the bodywork, with curved sides and wide running boards, continued for some way behind the driving compartment, resulting in a substantial overhang at the rear. An elaborately ornamented gallery was fixed around the roof to serve as a luggage rack.

Our fellow passengers were returning home after shopping in Palma and there was a great deal of noise because the bus journey was valued as an opportunity to catch up with local news. All the Majorcans knew one another and conversations were conducted from side to side and front to back of the bus, usually simultaneously. Eventually the driver emerged from a nearby café. He was a typical Majorcan with dark hair and brown eyes in a jolly face; not very tall but with a long body and rather short legs, whose wide and powerful shoulders gave him a somewhat square appearance. The regular passengers greeted him by name and thereafter included him in their chatter. He took his seat and, after a few abortive attempts, coaxed the engine into life. With a crunch of gears we commenced our journey and progressed without further incident until we approached Valldemossa about eighteen kilometres north of Palma.

The previously straight road started to twist and turn from the plain up to the town situated in the hills over 400 metres above sea level. The long overhang of the bus resulted in the passengers at the rear being suspended over a sheer drop on some of the sharper bends causing as much excitement as a ride at a fairground. A hush descended as the next hairpin bend approached; then the passengers cheered as it was successfully negotiated, the driver turning and grinning broadly to acknowledge their applause.

The bus wound its way through the narrow streets, climbing all the way, until it came to rest in the tree-lined square in the centre of the picturesque town outside the Carthusian Monastery of San Bruno known as *La Cartuja.* Originally a palace, it was given to the Order of the Carthusians in 1399 who rebuilt it in 1717 in the plan of a cross. The monks were expelled in 1835 and the building, in a semi-ruinous state, then passed into private hands.

Valldemossa spreads across the top of a mountain, the surrounding hills being stepped by extensive terracing. Old stone-built houses line narrow winding streets often with no space for any pavement. The front doors open directly into the *salón* as there is seldom any hallway and the shuttered windows open inwards. Majorcans tend to leave their *persianas* closed to provide privacy and coolness in the summer but this sensible habit results in whole streets sometimes having a rather deserted air. When a house has been converted into a shop, the exterior is often unchanged so it is only by peeping through a fly-curtain in the doorway that a busy *carnicería* or *panadería* is revealed.

In the monastery, the old monks' cells, really small suites of rooms, were once rented out to visitors; the most famous tenants being Chopin and his mistress the writer George Sand, who was actually the Baroness Aurare de Dudevant. The couple came to Majorca in 1838 when Chopin was suffering from consumption, then an incurable disease. She was prompted by a desire to continue her love-affair with the composer away from the eyes of Paris society and an intention to finish two literary works, one of which was her *Spiridion.* He came to escape critical comment regarding their liaison and also to work on his Preludes.

Only part of their stay, during the exceptionally cold and wet winter of 1838-39, was spent in Valldemossa but the town has cleverly exploited its connection with Chopin and no visit to the monastery is complete without paying to see the rooms they rented and the Pleyel piano that Chopin imported with much difficulty from Paris. George Sand brought her children with her; Maurice, her son, who was then fifteen and Solange, her daughter, who was only eight. She also took her maid Madame Amélie although she makes no mention of the fact in her book *Un Hiver à Majorque*, Winter in Majorca, preferring to leave her readers with the impression that she nursed her patient and cared for her children unaided. Despite an uncomplimentary account of the Majorcans whom she describes as unfriendly, deceitful, dirty and ignorant and the foul weather which she almost certainly exaggerates, it is sold in large numbers and many languages throughout the island, especially in Valldemossa.

From Valldemossa our bus ran along the coast past the viewpoints of Mirador de Ses Pites and Miramar. Our elevated seats gave us breathtaking views of the dramatic rocky coastline to the left; while inland to the right the fields were divided by dry stone walls and dotted with ancient olives, their trunks contorted into fantastic shapes. These olive groves are sometimes attributed to the Roman occupation of Majorca, but it is more probable that they date from the tenth century when the island was ruled by the Moors. Further inland the mountains of the Sierra del Teix towered above the fields with peaks rising to over 1000 metres. Sheep and goats roamed the lower slopes, many wearing bells which emitted a distinctive clonk like a cracked gong which carried for a considerable distance.

About six kilometres after Valldemossa we noticed a white marble belvedere some way down the slope to our left in the grounds of Son Marroig, the former home of Archduke Luis Salvador of Austria who was known locally as S'Arxiduc. It is now a museum containing relics of his work as a leading naturalist and historian who succumbed completely to the charm of Majorca. He devoted much of his life to the production of many books on its history, geography, flora and fauna; the most famous being *Die Balearen.* A peninsular called Sa Foradada forms part of the estate and a path enables visitors to walk to where it terminates with a rock in which a hole has been pierced by the sea.

The road continued along the rocky coastline for another four kilometres to Deià, a village which has attracted many artists and

writers. It is built on a hill rising to over 200 metres and its narrow cobbled streets wind up from the main road that skirts its southern edge. The sand coloured houses with pantiled roofs huddle together up the slopes leading to an old church with a square belfry at the summit.

The driver assisted us from the bus and brought our luggage down from the roof. Tommy Matthews walked to meet Robert Graves whom he had spotted coming towards us and, after they had greeted one another, Tommy introduced us to Robert; so my first meeting with this great man was while I was sitting on my dusty case, totally exhausted from the long journey and absolutely filthy.

Robert was then 57, tall, erect and well built with unruly grey curly hair under a battered straw hat, piercing blue eyes, bushy eyebrows and a full-lipped mouth. His Irish face was deeply tanned with a trace of stubble around the chin. The first words he addressed to me were 'You must come to a party tonight.' Tired though I was, I gladly accepted and he then walked with us to a small *hostal* called the Miramar where we were to stay.

The *hostal* was run by a charming Majorcan couple who expended endless energy ensuring that it was clean and that the guests were contented. It was modest to the point where one could have passed it without realising that it was there because it displayed no sign, but it offered outstanding value. My room, on the first floor in the annexe, was large and adequately furnished. The bathroom was outside, leading from a small patio at the back of the building and was spotlessly clean with freshly whitewashed walls and a basin with running water.

As we were on half-board, we all gathered later in the cool shady dining room which opened on to a small terrace at the back. By then there were eight of us at the table as we had met up with the mother and her two young children who had flown over earlier. She took an instant dislike to me and within a few days the feeling was mutual. She had a somewhat similar effect on Robert who later christened her 'Mrs Thing.'

After a simple but satisfying dinner, one of the boys played the guitar that he had brought with him all the way across France and Spain. It had travelled well and he surprised us with his mastery of flamenco music. Later Tommy and I set off for the party to which Robert had invited us and followed other partygoers down some terraces to a clearing, sheltered by umbrella pines, where everyone was gathering.

After the heat of the day, the thick springy carpet of pine needles gave out a heavy resinous perfume when disturbed by our feet. It was almost dusk and as the sun faded the moon came up looking like no moon that I had ever seen in England. Majorcan moons are larger than life and Majorcan moonlight is almost bright enough to read by.

Robert introduced us to some of the other guests and it was then that I met Will Price for the first time. He was an American who had suffered badly in World War II when he was a marine in the Pacific. His ship had been torpedoed and he had been adrift in an open boat for several weeks, watching his companions die one by one before he was rescued. This experience had affected him both mentally and physically and he wore bandages on his arms to cover scars from severe sunburn.

Will and Robert had become great friends. Robert was excited by a proposal from Will that they should jointly work on a script for a Hollywood film which would be produced by Will and funded by another American named Forrest Judd. Will had been an assistant producer in one or two minor American films and he and Judd had persuaded Robert that he could be a success in Hollywood if he wrote the script which was to be based on one of the stories from the Arabian Nights.

I was to learn later that Will's girl friend, nicknamed 'Kitten', had only recently returned to London. Her departure had not been her own choice because she had become a definite embarrassment and Robert had paid to have her shipped off the island. In his excellent biography of Robert Graves, Martin Seymour-Smith provides the background to Kitten's sudden exit from Majorca. He states that '*Kitten became a problem. She drank triple brandies, and many of them; often she would order them by house telephone while lying stark naked on the bed in the room she shared with Will, causing considerable agitation to the waiters (most of whom were young men unfamiliar with such matters).'*

By a curious coincidence I knew her by sight because some months before we both had bed-sits on the same floor of a house in Kensington. I remember one night while I was waiting outside the bathroom, which had been occupied for a very long time, a man suddenly emerged, bare except for a raincoat draped over his head, and streaked into Kitten's room before my startled gaze. I do not know whether it was Will because I never saw his face!

Will was a great raconteur and fascinated me with stories about his experiences in Hollywood producing films. He also told me about his broken marriage to the actress Maureen O'Hara which had affected him deeply and left him very depressed. By then we were sitting a little apart from the main group who were having a riotous time. I noticed that he was becoming maudlin and I began to suspect that he might have me in mind as a replacement for the departed Kitten. When I finally convinced him that this was not to be, he completely lost control and started pelting me with pine cones and clumps of earth but fortunately Robert saw what was happening and came to my rescue. Since it was then about two in the morning and the party was already starting to break up, he took charge of the rather inebriated Will and guided him safely back to his hotel.

Tommy and I made our way alone up the terraces towards the village. The outlines of the olive trees were exaggerated into grotesque patterns by the moonlight until their branches looked like arms outstretched to catch us. I was still a little shattered after my experience with Will and nearly jumped out of my skin when a sheep gave a graveyard cough from behind a wall. It was a considerable relief to reach the comfort of my room at the *hostal* after what had been a very long day.

2. *Life in Deià*

The morning after our arrival we all headed for the beach and, as we passed the Graves's house, *Canelluñ*, which is situated a short way outside Deià on the road to Lluc-Alcari, Robert came out to greet us. He invited us in to meet his wife Beryl, a very attractive woman in her thirties with dark hair and striking deep blue eyes, who was expecting their fourth child. He decided to come with us in order to show us the way to the *cala.* I can still picture him looking like a Greek God, running down the olive-covered terraces until he reached a small cliff from which he dived straight into the sea.

Although we were much younger, we were not nearly as athletic and made our way down a track through the olive groves, only occasionally scrambling down from one terrace to the one below until we eventually reached a wide stretch of sand in a lovely cove surrounded by high cliffs.

This was idyllic! I took myself off to a secluded corner because I wanted a little time on my own to enjoy the beauty of Majorca. I had been grateful for the company of my companions during the journey, but three of the boys were in their first year at university and I found their undergraduate banter rather wearing. Tommy was older and much more mature, but they were his friends while I was still almost a stranger, so he spent most of his time with them.

I sat on a rock in the sunshine with the dark blue sea lapping softly below my feet, the ultramarine heaven above and the scent of pines perfuming the air. For the first time for many months I felt completely content and happy. Majorca fully deserves its epithet 'the island of calm' but those who only visit the tourist areas are unlikely to experience the peace and tranquillity that can still be found in hundreds of places off the beaten track.

At the side of the beach there was a little bar run by a family of fishermen who had lived there for generations. They were extremely friendly and told us that we could have lunch at modest cost so long as we had whatever they were cooking that day. It was never elaborate, often just a simple *paella* with saffron flavoured rice and fish, but it was a sustaining meal and their rough but drinkable wine cost the equivalent of a few pence per glass. After a hot day by the sea, we would clamber like mountain goats back up to the road. The direct route lay up and over successive terraces and in places a stone or two had been dislodged to provide a foothold; one of the boys would climb up as best he could and then assist the rest of the party.

Later that week I went with the boys to a bullfight. We took the bus to Palma and walked from its terminus in Calle 31 de Diciembre to the *Plaza de Toros*, joining large numbers of Majorcans heading in the same direction and enjoying the contagious excitement of the crowd. None of us had been to a bullfight before and I treated the outing in the same way that I would have approached a visit to the theatre.

There were three choices for entrance tickets at the bullring: those for seats in *sombra*, shade, were the most expensive; those which started in the sun and became shady later were *sol y sombra;* but we bought the least expensive, *sol*, which were in full sun. The interior of the bullring was really a series of steps and we sat on one with our feet on the one below; to add a little comfort we rented cushions. It is said, with more than a grain of truth, that the *corrida* is the only event in Spain that starts on time.

I enjoyed the colour and spectacle of the initial parade and the thrill when the first bull appeared, but when the *picadores,* astride horses well protected by padding, began to stab their lances between the neck and shoulders of the bull to weaken it, I was overcome by nausea and almost fainted. Spaniards view the performance as an art form with a strict ritual. The bull would be killed anyway; at the *corrida* it has an honourable death. To them the importance lies in the skill displayed by the *matador* and his assistants in tiring the bull and lowering its head until the moment comes when he can perform the kill.

Tommy quickly took me down to an area underneath the stands where there was a large bar with tables and chairs. Having fetched me some water and satisfied himself that I could be left, he returned to his seat and I took stock of my surroundings, realising that I would have to wait there for about two hours until my companions rejoined me.

There was only one other customer in the bar, an American in marine uniform, who came over to me and explained that he too had been forced to leave the *corrida* as he had been violently sick. I looked at his tough craggy frame and immediately felt much better. If a marine could not take it there was at least some excuse for me. We sat and chatted and he started to pour out his troubles. Our conversation was interrupted by occasional roars from the crowd in appreciation of the art of a *matador* and boos for the *picadores* when the crowd thought that they were weakening a bull too much. I gathered that he had joined the marines on impulse and could not stand the pain caused by long separations from his family in Arizona. He was not a good sailor and was ill whenever the sea was even slightly rough and I came to the conclusion that he had probably chosen the wrong career. Both of us agreed that this would be our first and only bullfight.

The boys were excited by their first *corrida* and after collecting me they decided that we would return to Deià in style by taxi. We all crammed in and entertained the driver by singing popular songs. By the time we reached Deià he had mastered most of the tunes and some of the words and as he left us we heard him burst forth with 'Ees too darn ot'!

Later that week Tommy and I were invited to the wedding of Jan and Martin Seymour-Smith who were working for Robert. On the wedding eve, a small dinner party for the bride was held at *Canelluñ*. It was a very merry affair with everyone laughing, joking and reminiscing when, without warning, the bride-to-be threw her glass across the room and it crashed into the wall shattering into a thousand pieces. She had succumbed to pre-marital nerves and collapsed into hysterical tears. In the shocked hush that followed Robert came to the rescue by taking her gently by the hand and saying: 'Well, if you can't break a glass the night before your wedding, when can you?' The party then continued as if nothing had happened. The remark was typical of Robert who frequently showed such kindness and concern for his friends and would never hesitate to intervene if he could assist them.

The following day the wedding took place at the British Consulate which was located on the first floor of a fine old house at No 11 Calle Almudaina, behind the Cathedral. We entered through a wide arched doorway into a typical Majorcan courtyard and ascended an impressive open stone staircase to the first floor.

For her wedding the bride looked radiant, with no sign of her emotional outburst the evening before. Mr John Lake, the British Consul, performed the wedding service and his wife had supervised the decoration of the large room with an abundance of white flowers and it looked magnificent. Rows of chairs had been set out for the guests and the French windows along one wall were opened to provide access to a long terrace where drinks would later be served.

About mid-way through the wedding service, Robert, seated immediately in front of me, turned round and in a deafening stage whisper asked: 'What do you think of this; quite different from an English wedding?' I murmured a reply as the ceremony continued. After the marriage we moved outside to the terrace where toasts were drunk to the bride and groom; also to the Consul and his wife who were thanked for attending to the arrangements. Until 1975 the British Consul was able to marry British citizens in Majorca but this is no longer possible.

We then set off for a Majorcan lunch, a meal that can commence at any time up to three in the afternoon during the week and even later on a Sunday. We walked down to a restaurant in the port where a long table was set outside for the wedding feast. It was a prolonged affair and the hot afternoon turned to evening as we sipped our wine and relaxed in the balmy air while the lights of Palma appeared around the bay.

All too soon, the end of my holiday approached. I had fallen in love with the Majorcan scenery and perhaps even more with the Mediterranean way of life that is only partly typified by the much quoted *mañana* syndrome which implies laziness. The Majorcans are far from lazy; in fact they are very industrious and things get done remarkably quickly, but their attitude to work and other everyday activities, such as eating, drinking, conversing and bringing up their children, is significantly more relaxed than that of the British. In short, they have the knack of getting more out of life and do not need much wealth to do so.

I was therefore delighted when Robert asked me if I would be willing to stay on and use my secretarial training to assist him and Will with their new film script; I would not be paid anything but Robert would settle my hotel bill when I left. I suspected that the offer was more for my benefit than his but immediately agreed because I was enjoying every minute of my time in Majorca and it was wonderful to have the opportunity to delay my return to London.

Robert told the couple at the *hostal* that I would be staying on. As the summer visitors had mostly departed by then, I was moved from the annexe into the main building where I was given what must certainly have been the best room in the house. It was large and beautifully furnished with massive old mahogany pieces. This had a predictable effect on Mrs Thing who was incensed by my good fortune and made no attempt to hide her resentment of what she regarded as preferential treatment by making several quite hurtful remarks.

The evening before her departure we were all having dinner when there was a tremendous thunder-storm, with flashes of lightning every few seconds. She betrayed her feelings by saying: 'What a frightful storm, I would be terrified if I had to go to bed alone in that huge room of yours with all that heavy furniture waiting to fall on top of me.' Tommy assured me that lightning had never been known to cause damage in Majorca; this restored my confidence and I slept remarkably well that night happy in the knowledge that Mrs Thing was returning home the following day.

The story that lightning is harmless in Majorca was a white lie, Majorcan storms can be sudden and violent and I now know of many cases of damage by lightning strikes, including a bolt that hit the church in Capdella and almost destroyed the tower. The road was blocked with rubble for several days but the building was later reconstructed with voluntary assistance from the crews of ships belonging to the US Sixth Fleet.

In those days moral attitudes were far more puritanical than today. While walking alone along the road leading down to the beach I met an old Majorcan and greeted him with a bright '*buenos días.*' I expected him to respond with a smile but instead he just glared at me and then spat on the ground. I was upset by the incident and mentioned it later to Robert, who told me that I had probably offended him because I was wearing shorts. At that time tourists in Palma were liable to be apprehended by the police and taken back to their hotels if they were considered to be unsuitably dressed and two piece bathing suits were forbidden on the beaches. In C'an Barbara, swimmers were segregated by a partition extending some distance into the water; men swam on one side and women on the other. Today attitudes have changed so much that there are several nudist beaches and on many of the others women can be seen topless.

On the morning that I was to start my secretarial activity, I walked to the *Posada*, another house in Deià owned by Robert, where he and Will were working. Throughout the weeks that followed Robert was careful never to leave me alone there with Will. Their plans had already changed slightly; Will had a long-standing ambition to write a play based on Susanna and the Elders and they decided to make a start on it. Initially, however, Will wanted my assistance with a letter to his lawyer in America. He had parted from Maureen O'Hara on far from amicable terms and was worried that he would be prevented from having access to their daughter, Bronwen, then aged about eight. He was devoted to his daughter and the thought that he might be prevented from seeing her was more than he could bear.

Progress with the play was intermittent because Will periodically disappeared for hours or even days without prior warning. I believe that he took himself off to the red-light district of Palma and Robert would worry about him until he returned. Sometimes we worked in the mornings, sometimes in the evenings, but I did not mind because I was happy to be there enjoying the experience of living in the community and meeting the residents and other visitors who had come to Deià for the summer.

Will was staying at the Hotel Costa D'Or at Lluc-Alcari, a hamlet comprising little more than a cluster of houses, the hotel and a narrow walkway down to a sandy beach, one of the few on the north side of the island, about four kilometres from Deià. By then Will and I had established a reasonable working relationship and he had nicknamed me 'deep-dish,' I could never fathom why. To avoid leaving him alone with his thoughts and drinking away his sorrows, we sometimes collected Beryl when work was finished for the day and the four of us walked down to his hotel for dinner which we ate looking out to sea from the open terrace that ran the length of the hotel.

Will enjoyed company and soon forgot his troubles when engaged in conversation, particularly when others joined our group and made it a party. It was a beautiful setting and the restaurant specialised in shellfish so cheap and abundant that you could eat as much as you wanted. It was during one of these evenings that I met an American who was attached to the American Embassy in Grosvenor Square. He and his wife were staying at the hotel until the following week when they were due to return by train to London and they asked me whether I would like to travel back to England with them.

I felt deeply indebted to Robert and Beryl for their many kindnesses and I would gladly have stayed much longer, but it seemed sensible to take the opportunity to travel with my new American friends. Robert agreed that this was probably the best arrangement since work on Susanna had temporarily halted.

3. Letters from Majorca

The chill autumn air and morning mist in London was an unpleasant change from the warmth and sharp light of Majorca; I kept thinking about the friends I had made on the island and imagined them taking breakfast outside in the morning sunshine while I tried to coax a little more warmth from the gas fire in my room. Nevertheless, after my stay of six weeks on the island I was mentally refreshed and ready to start looking for work.

I had written to Beryl and Robert to express my thanks for their hospitality and the help and encouragement they had given me. The following is an extract from Robert's letter in reply, which is dated October 1952.

My Dear Pamela:

Glad you got home safely. Not much news here; just packing up for the school-term at Palma. Our flat there is "Guillermo Massot 73". We hope Will reached England safely too. He was to have sent us a cable on arrival. (Dear Will, we got so worried about him; wouldn't harm a fly, only himself!).

Everyone is leaving Deyá now. The hotels are nearly empty. Rain falls.

X has shaved off his beard. Underneath was a good chin but a mean mouth.

I am back at my Mythology book again. When that is done, I shall resume Susanna; say Jan or Feb. If the new baby permits.

No money from Judd! I had to import £250 from England to pay the Costa D'Or bill for Will! He'll pay me back in London.

Thank you for behaving so nicely and discreetly while you were here; you were a great help one way and another and never let us down. Hope you get a decent job among people you like and trust; there must be such.

Yes, your visit here was very unforeseen and queer at first and sometimes you must have wondered where in the world you were; but it seems natural and right in retrospect, and you probably learned a lot and achieved the calmness which you came to find.

Love from us all
Robert
Kindest regards to your parents.
Sometime this month there will be a 'canned' broadcast of mine on the 3rd Programme; or even two. Watch Radio Times if you want to hear my voice again.

The reference to X relates to an English hotel keeper who shocked Deià by making a rapid departure leaving a string of unpaid bills behind. I believe that he shaved off his beard to avoid recognition. At that time such action was unheard of and the scandal is still remembered in Deià, but during a recent recession in Majorca several British traders also 'did a runner' much to the discredit of the British community.

The next letter I received from Robert was written from the new apartment in Palma the following month. It is in his easily recognisable style with a wide left hand margin in which he wrote after reaching the end of the page.

Dearest Pamela:

'Caravan' money not yet arrived: three months late. Will is in London at White's Hotel, Lancaster Gate, and has seen the enigmatic Forrest Judd, the producer, who has it seems no ready

money because Monsoon, the film on which he pinned his hopes, has been banned in U.S.A. and not included in the British quota. So Will, who is well and sober on quarts of coca-cola, and so on, may not after all go to India, or get a chance to direct World's Delight; which would be awful. As for us, there is still a hope of getting the promised 'blocked pesetas', and will know within the week; but it's a bad business, anyway you look at it. For immediate cash, I'm doing a sensational series for Picture Post Christmas numbers on the Nativity.

My dull talk on the Golden Fleece will be on Third Programme the last week in Nov. and a repeat first week in Dec. 28th Nov 8.55-9.20. Dec 1. 10.50-11.15.

The Posada has some beautiful glass doors to go outside the front door and let in light on cold or windy days.

Beryl sends love and thanks you so much for the letter and the photos. She has an awful cold, first for over a year, and neuralgia. Lucia and Juan have new schools and their character is greatly improved: except at home.

We go to Deyá weekends, it hasn't yet rained properly and I still bathe there.

Love

Robert

Also Personal Anthology by R.G. Tues. 23rd Dec. 3rd Pr 7.15-7.45 pm.

Robert and Beryl had taken the apartment in Palma to enable their daughter Lucia and younger son Juan to attend school there. Their elder son, William, was being prepared for his entrance examination to Oundle by Martin Seymour-Smith whose wedding I had attended earlier that year.

I was eventually offered a secretarial position with The Economist and was sharing a flat with a girl friend at Dolphin Square when in 1953 the news of the birth of Beryl's fourth and last child arrived. Robert's letter was written from their apartment in Palma, where the baby was born.

My dear Pamela:

The baby got born about four hours ago 4am Jan 27. Name Tomás (no h). All well. Thanks so much for your letter and as we take The Economist we feel in touch with you.

The film story gets more complicated: and is entering its grotesque law-suit stage. (Will is suing).

Will has had out 4 impacted infected wisdom teeth and very sorry for himself.

I'm still on my myth book, and passing proofs of my shattering Nazarene Gospel Restored 1247 pp royal oct.

Everyone sends love

Robert

It was while I was working at The Economist that I met my future husband. The following year, after writing to tell Robert and Beryl that I was to be married at St Michaels, Chester Square on 5th June 1954 and expressing my hope that they would be able to come, I received a reply dated April 27th which reads:-

Dearest Pamela:

We are so pleased that you are getting married to someone with an agreeably sounding name and at a reputable church. Is he an Economist?

Can't think of a suitable wedding present, unless you would like to have the Posada (with Antonia to cook for you) as your honeymoon residence for a fortnight or so. If so you'll have to indent for it at once, giving dates. It will be occupied from June 24th onwards.

We heard last week from dear Will, "gloriously sober and beaverish", who has done a technical course in television at Federal Expense (as an ex-naval hero) in New York and is now living at 25 Fifth Avenue in a bachelor's apartment and selling his bright programs on various bright subjects to the TV companies. We feared he had gone down the drain for good.

We have gone up in the world: bought an old but solid car, which Beryl drives, a sailboat, and a boathouse at Lluchalcari.

Guillermo Massot, 73-pral. 2.ª
Palma de Mallorca
SPAIN
Tel. 5051

Ap 27th I guess
1954

Dearest Pamela:

We are so pleased that you are getting married to someone with an agreeably sounding name & at a reputable church. Is he an Economist?

Can't think of a suitable wedding present, unless you would like to have the Posada (with Antonia to cook for you) as your honeymoon residence for a fortnight or so. If so, you'll have to indent for it at once, giving dates. It will be occupied from June 24th onwards.

We heard last week from dear Will, "gloriously sober & heavenist", who has done a technical course in television at Federal Expense (as an ex-naval hero) in New York and is now living at 25 Fifth Avenue in a gay bachelor's apartment and selling his bright programs on various bright subjects to the T.V. companies. We feared he had gone down the drain for good.

We have gone up in the world: bought an old but solid car, which Beryl drives, & a sailboat, & a boathouse at Cala Deya [illegible]. Wm. passed his exams into Oundle, & will go there in Sept. Martin & Tom have thereafter returned to England. I wrote lots of books as usual + & recently have been patronizing Punch, which pays widely well; & I find it very easy to write for them. The children are fine: you didn't know Tomás yet; he's 16 months & a very sweet child.

We won't be able to come to your wedding; not coming to England until Oct. when I have to give the Clark Lectures at Trinity, Cambridge (on English Lit.). But think of us & kissing you or lots of checks and (nipping the hickory) [illegible] [illegible] [illegible] in England [illegible] [illegible]? [illegible] [illegible] kissed you. Do you remember [illegible] this Spring [illegible] [illegible] [illegible] [illegible].

Love
Robert & Beryl.

+ I have seen new [illegible] out in the west [illegible] for Punch! [illegible] [illegible]

William passed his exams into Oundle, and will go there in Sept. Martin & Jan have therefore returned to England. I write lots of books as usual, and recently have been patronising <u>*Punch*</u>*, which pays wickedly well; and I find it very easy to write for them. The children are fine. You don't know Tomás yet; he's 16 months and a very smart child.*

We wont be able to dance at your wedding; not coming to England until Oct. when I have to give the Clark Lectures at Trinity, Cambridge (on English Lit.). But think of us as kissing you on both cheeks and gripping the bridegroom's hands; in England he hasn't to be kissed too.
Love
Robert & Beryl

I have seven new titles out in the next 12 months, and four Penguin old ones.

I replied at once, accepting his generous and unexpected present with enthusiasm. British European Airways had just started to fly their new Viscount turbo-prop aircraft direct to Palma and we booked our flight for June 6th.

We also wrote to the Hotel Formentor to reserve a few days in luxury at the end of our honeymoon: they quoted us 468 pesetas for full pension in a double room with private bath, subject to a service charge of 15%. and suggested that we make use of their private bus which ran once a day from Palma to Formentor and would only cost 50 pesetas per person for a distance of over 70 kilometres. A taxi to take us to the airport when we left would cost 425 pesetas.

When Robert received my reply gratefully accepting his kind offer, he sent a letter which indicates how little some things have changed in forty years. This is particularly the case with food where certain items are still almost unobtainable in Majorca while others can be purchased in Britain for only a fraction of the price. He enclosed a cutting of an advertisement for a paddling pool and wrote:-

Dearest Pamela:

Attached is what we want most for keeping Tomás cool and amused this summer. It weighs 32 oz which means 2 lb if you can spare the weight. Will repay in pesetas.

£1 a day for two is the maximum expendable, unless you go throwing parties or bull-fighting. Lucia saw her first bullfight on Sunday, which happened to be a good one, and loved every moment of it, and gave us accurate accounts of each bull. If either of you can manage a sailboat, there's fun for you. Ours is now in a Lluchalcari boat house, newly painted and all complete. I expect you'll have most of your lunches at the Cala.

For promised gift, please bring a large tin of Nescafé. It is just possible that the page proofs of my Greek Myths (Penguin Classics) will be ready by then; if so, I'll ask them to send you same to avoid customs delay.

Love

Robert

As was his custom, Robert then added a postscript:-
The Economist is having a gay smack at Washington. I like to see that spirit. Beryl then added another postscript:-
You can get these (paddling pools) *at Hamleys I think.*
We would also like a small pot of Marmite.

I could not believe my good fortune in having this totally unexpected opportunity to revisit Majorca and looked forward to introducing my new husband to my friends in Deià.

The following week I happily set out on a shopping expedition to locate the paddling pool. (It survived for many years and when it was eventually punctured beyond repair it continued to serve a useful purpose as a cover for the Graves's compost heap). In my reply I asked whether he had any recent news of Tommy. His answer again came from Palma and is dated May 3 1954.

My Dear Pamela:

There is a Sunday evening bus at 7.30 from Café Monumental, Calle 31 Diciembre about 100 yards W. along the Avenida from the new Iberia-B.E.A terminus.

Usually we go to Deyá for the day on Sunday but could be back in time to meet you at the Terminus and put you on the bus, having laid on everything at the Deyá end. Antonia will cook for you, and buy the food and make the bed and sweep; shouldn't cost you much - perhaps £1 a day for the 2.

Tommy Matthews: no! The father Tom Matthews has just married Martha Gelhorn, Hemingway's ex. I think I got confused – you were with the other party that Tommy brought – not a very good lot – o yes that's right – Mrs Thing came into the story.

Remind us nearer the time of your arrival.

Love,
Robert

Looking back it seems incredible that Robert could have found the time to attend to such matters of detail while writing books, poems and articles for magazines as well as preparing and presenting broadcasts and lectures. He had none of the office aids without which most modern authors would be paralysed and everything was given to his secretary in manuscript form. In addition he had a busy domestic life with his wife and four young children and also took responsibility for many friends, like Will, who could always rely on his assistance.

4. From One Posada to Another

It deluged during our wedding and it was raining again when we arrived at London Airport at the start of our honeymoon. In 1954 the European departure building was little more than a large hut alongside the Bath Road and we felt like VIPs because all passengers were then treated as valued customers rather than units to be processed. It took four hours for our Viscount to reach Palma, but it departed on time and there was no queue at the check-in. Today the actual flight often takes less than two hours, but this improvement is sometimes negated by various hold-ups such as those caused by the French air traffic controllers during disputes over pay and conditions. Such is progress!

The plane landed at Son Bonet which was then the international airport. We passed through Customs and were soon on the BEA coach, which had been waiting to take us from the airport to Palma.

There had been a slight change of plan. The Graves family were staying on in Deià for a few days and there was no need for Robert to dash back to Palma as we were quite capable of catching the bus for Deià unaided. Because it was not due to leave until seven-thirty that evening, the manager of the Café Monumental kindly agreed to take care of our luggage until it departed and we were free to wander around Palma and enjoy the tranquil atmosphere of the warm Sunday afternoon.

As we relaxed at a pavement café on the Avenidas, where the proprietor had charged us only four pesetas for two coñacs, we thought about the rain in England and watched the Majorcans parading in their best Sunday clothes. The traffic was an unusual sight because nearly every vehicle was vintage and some were almost veteran. The import of new vehicles into Spain was strictly prohibited so anything with four wheels and an engine was carefully preserved.

Many cars looked most extraordinary to us as the boot lid had been removed to enable a charcoal-burner to be installed in the back; others towed similar burners on small two-wheeled trailers with flexible hoses connecting them to the engine. Anything that would burn was used as the basic fuel, including the outer shells of the almonds which grow in most parts of Majorca, but water was also needed to produce a gas. Beryl Graves later told us that this generated about two thirds of the power of petrol, making it necessary to select one gear lower than normal.

The bus had not altered since my previous visit but, because it was Sunday, the Majorcan passengers were more formally dressed as they were returning from visiting relatives in Palma. Just as he had two years earlier, Robert Graves met the bus at Deià and it occurred to me then that he devoted a good deal of his time waiting for friends arriving from Palma. He was just as I remembered him and, after introducing my new husband, I listened eagerly as he brought me up to date with the local news.

We gave Robert a parcel containing a large wedge of our wedding cake which we had brought for the Graves family to share, but he was so engrossed in conversation that he absent-mindedly opened it and had munched his way through the entire piece by the time we reached the *Posada* where we were to spend the first part of our honeymoon. The thick-walled stone house adjoined the church and the door opened directly from the street into a large square room that still contained the table on which I had typed the film script two years before. I was unfamiliar with the rest of the house which was simply furnished and painted white throughout.

A lobby at the back provided access to a tiny kitchen where cooking was performed on a Majorcan charcoal-fired stove consisting of a stone 'hob' with a hole in its centre; an L shaped tube ran down from the hole and charcoal was lit in the base of the vertical section. To turn up the heat it was fanned through the horizontal tube by the cook, who needed one hand for this task while the other was used for culinary operations.

There was a delightful 'snug' featuring a brick and stone fireplace with a stone seat built into the wall to its right and extending a little way along the return wall. A door provided access to a small garden. A long stable ran along one side of the garden that featured the well which was the only source of water.

A staircase led from the *salón* up to the bedrooms. The largest of these had been prepared for us and was furnished with a comfortable wooden bed painted bright green. In one corner there was a washstand with a jug and bowl and a bucket for disposing of dirty water. The window was protected by *persianas* which, when opened, revealed an unforgettable view to the towering mountains behind. Ahead we looked down over the village and the road to Soller beside which were two *fincas* that Richard Branson would convert thirty years later into his magnificent Hotel Residencia. To the left the terraced hills extended down to a perfect blue sea. The sound of sheep and goat bells, which would provide us with a lullaby every night, floated across from the distant hills.

Robert asked us to call in on our way down to the beach in the morning and, wishing us goodnight, walked home to join his family at *Canelluñ*. I went to the stable in the garden; in those days it contained a small cupboard-like room quite a way from the main door which featured a hole in the floor over which a plank had been fixed to provide a seat. Shortly after I had shut myself into this very confined space I heard considerable movement outside, followed by the closing and barring of the outer door and then some heavy breathing just outside what had become my prison. I peeped out and came face to face with a very irate donkey who deeply resented any stranger in her quarters. My cries for help did not reach the house and it was some time before my husband came to investigate and eventually was able to rescue me by fending off the donkey with an old broom while I made my escape. Thereafter, we timed all visits to the stable to coincide with the working hours of the donkey who was called Isabella.

The electricity supply in Deià was unusual because it was provided by a water-driven turbine. A small head of water accumulated in a little reservoir during the day and this was used each evening to provide electric lighting for a few hours only. The current was briefly cut so that the lights flashed to provide a warning that the service would soon terminate for the night. The supply was distributed around the village on wires supported by cotton reels fastened by a nail to any convenient surface. Inside the house the switches had a T shaped turn button which one twisted to connect the light, quite often receiving a small electrical shock in the process.

The following morning my husband set off for the *panadería* to buy *ensaimadas* for breakfast. Although unfamiliar with the layout of the village, he had only to follow his nose and the delicious smell of freshly-baked bread led him to the little shop. Few things vary as much in quality as *ensaimadas*. When cooked by skilled hands and eaten while still warm they are light and fluffy and a worthy feast for the Gods. Sometimes however, they are cold and lifeless; their high lard content turning them into heavy greasy lumps of unappetising pastry. Time enhances memories, but those *ensaimadas* in Deià set a standard that we have never matched with ones bought elsewhere.

As arranged, we stopped off at *Canelluñ* on our way down to the beach and I was able to renew my acquaintance with Beryl and introduce my husband to her. She had fully regained her slim figure after the birth of Tomás who was already enjoying his new paddling pool and she decided to remain with him in the relative cool of the garden. Robert elected to come with us and we were soon joined by his secretary, Karl Gay, and his wife Renée, who lived in a small house in the grounds of *Canelluñ*. Karl had worked with Robert since before the Spanish Civil War and accompanied him when he was forced to return to Britain during the war years.

The days soon assumed a simple pattern; an easy stroll down to the beach in the morning, a *paella* for lunch at the *cala* and at the end of the day the long hard pull back up the mountain track. Hot and tired, we were grateful for an invitation to take tea with Karl and Renée on our way back to the village. Looking back, we must have seemed selfish, never considering how much we were imposing on their hospitality when they probably had many other things to do, but we really appreciated those refreshing cups of tea.

Once we thought we might break away from the inevitable *paella* at the beach. We decided to order a whole grilled fish for lunch and my husband attempted to convey what we wanted in far from perfect Spanish. The congenial cook at the café looked doubtful when my husband repeated that we wanted a large *pescado entero,* but soon the smell of grilling fish confirmed that the message had been received and understood. Before long it was served, beautifully presented on a long platter and garnished with slices of lemon; mouths watering in anticipation, we started to divide it equally on to our plates only to discover that it was indeed *entero* and had been cooked straight from the sea, ungutted or cleaned in any way so that the flesh was terribly tainted. After that we stuck to *paella.*

At the *Posada*, dinner was also a problem because my husband hates garlic. We found it impossible to communicate the fact to Antonia who was a good Majorcan cook with a range of recipes in which garlic was a major ingredient. We had *tortillas* in French and Spanish versions, but either way they would contain as many as six whole cloves of garlic. My husband called them depth-charges and dissected each portion cautiously to remove them before taking a mouthful. Curiously enough, when extracted with care, they left behind relatively little flavour. We also had chops with garlic and chicken with garlic. At the end of the week we decided to take the bus to Palma to see the sights and enjoy a change of diet.

Palma offered us much more choice. Fish was particularly attractive and quite inexpensive as the Mediterranean was not then over-fished. Large prawns, *gambas*, were cheap enough to find their way into a peasant's *paella*; every product of the pig was available at modest cost, and even the humblest Majorcan restaurant offered legs and shoulders of lamb cooked in a manner which would have made a skilled French chef green with envy.

We sat enjoying a coffee at a pavement café in the Paseo Generalísimo Franco (now renamed Paseo Des Born but always known locally as the Borne); a tree-lined street with traffic flowing on either side of a wide pedestrian walkway. The Borne was constructed over the old course of the diverted Torrente La Riera which now runs down the centre of the Paseo Mallorca. For many years the Torrente was a major problem for Palma as it periodically flooded the city; the most serious incident early in the 15th century claimed over 5000 lives and destroyed 1700 houses.

Stone seats under the trees and a large fountain at the southern end make this a cool and pleasant spot on a hot day. At the northern end there is a large obelisk and close inspection reveals that each corner of its base is supported by a tortoise, hence its name of *Las Tortugas*.

While we sat enjoying the sunshine we watched the bootblacks at work and it surprised us that so many people had an apparent fetish for clean shoes. By observing carefully we were able to see that they had an ulterior motive in visiting the bootblacks. The box on which one rested one's foot was full of contraband Chanel No 5 and the most popular brands of French and American cigarettes. The police knew, of course, but the trade was tolerated because any visitor who happened to be a heavy smoker was unlikely to survive on the Spanish cigarettes which were the only ones legally on sale at the *estancos*.

Our return journey on the bus on a weekday evening differed greatly from our experience when we arrived on a Sunday. This time the passengers brought with them evidence of a hard day's bargaining at the markets in Palma. Boxes of fruit and vegetables, crates of live chickens, sacks of flour, bicycles and two large mail bags were now packed into the galleried luggage rack. Instead of their fine Sunday visiting clothes, the passengers wore weekday attire, usually in various shades of black, but their animated chatter was even more lively than before as the finer points of dealing were discussed and prices were compared.

The weather was perfect and day followed day with clear cobalt skies stretching up from calm seas of an even deeper blue. We hired Pedro and his fishing boat to take us from the *cala* in Deià to Puerto de Soller. Pedro was the grandson of the fisherman who owned the little café at the *cala*; very handsome, unattached, and adored by every girl in the locality. His boat was completely open with one short mast and an inboard engine of considerable age but with a reassuring slow and steady throb. It had been made more comfortable for us by the addition of some cushions, which were obviously not part of its normal fittings, and a thorough washing had almost eliminated the smell of fish.

We greatly enjoyed seeing the north coast from the sea, the cliffs seemed even taller from such a low perspective and there were very few coves where a boat could come ashore. We realised that, while we could admire them for their strength and beauty on such a calm day, those cliffs must have been very menacing in stormy weather to a sailor in trouble. We sailed by Lluc-Alcari and rounded a point to enter the harbour at Puerto de

Soller, an attractive sandy palm-edged bay surrounded by mountains.

After the boat had been safely tied up, we strolled around the bay and then turned inland to walk the few kilometres up to the town of Soller. It is on a plateau covered by orange and lemon groves which provided most of its revenue prior to tourism.

The pattern of an inland town only a few kilometres from a port of the same name is repeated all over Majorca. It dates from the years when pirates frequently raided the island. By living inland, the inhabitants had greater advance warning of an attack and more time in which to organise their defence.

As the three of us walked up to the town, nearly every *señorita* we encountered fluttered her eyelashes and whispered '*Hola Pedro*' but Pedro looked innocent and resisted all of their advances. He had business in the town, so we arranged to part and to meet him again after lunch.

The main square in Soller is dominated by an impressive church with a fine rose window. Narrow gauge tram tracks run through the square, curving to avoid the central fountain, and several cafés vie to refresh the visiting crowds, their chairs and tables overflowing on to the broad pavements. Higher up, some of the houses on the south side feature fine casements projecting out from their façades while a bank on the corner facing the church boasts a beautifully worked grill over its large window. Fifteen large plane trees provide shade and make this a perfect spot for a leisurely coffee on a sunny day.

Access to Soller and its port used to be very difficult except from the sea. The route from Palma in the south climbs over the Sierra de Alfabia and a long succession of hairpin bends are required to take the road to almost 500 metres above sea level at the Coll de Soller and then down to the town. From both the east and west the roads are tortuous and difficult and because access was so much easier by sea the town traded largely with the French. Many Majorcans became wealthy by settling in France and dominating the trade in exotic fruit as far north as Paris. When they returned they brought their wealth with them and built the large houses that can still be seen in Soller. There is a story that one of these traders would travel into France and show a banana to the local people whenever he came to a new town. As soon as someone asked what it was, he knew that he had found a suitable site for his next shop.

After an excellent lunch we were too tired to walk back to the *Puerto* and took advantage of the little tram that connects the town to its port. Pedro rejoined us and we boarded the tram which was really a small train since the main unit, reputed to have been imported early this century from San Francisco, pulled two open-sided coaches. The body work was predominantly of varnished wood, fronted by an orange metal apron incorporating a single headlamp. It tooted as it rattled through the centre of the main square and then ran on down through the back gardens of the houses as it made its way down to the port. A woman quickly moved her basket of washing to prevent it being brushed by the little set of carriages as the tram hurtled by. Eventually the line followed the edge of the beach and terminated at the main quay where we had come ashore.

On the return journey in the boat, Pedro filled the gaps in our knowledge of the smuggling trade. Fishing boats, not his of course, would meet the smugglers well out to sea and bring the contraband ashore which would then travel with their catch to Palma without attracting unwelcome attention. At that time the trade was concerned with articles bearing heavy import duty such as perfumes and tobacco; the smuggling of drugs, now the same serious problem in Majorca as it is elsewhere in Europe, is a much more recent development.

The Graves family spent the week at their apartment in Palma because the children were at school there, but they returned to Deià at the weekend and we were able to be with them. Dinners at *Canelluñ* were informal affairs often attracting a small group of friends who came to enjoy the relaxed atmosphere and stimulating conversation. Both Robert and Beryl had a ready wit and Robert possessed an ability to make even complex explanations of Greek and Roman mythology interesting and understandable.

It was at one of these sociable evenings that we happened to mention that we had been given a Siamese kitten for a wedding present; he awaited our return from Majorca and had not yet been named. Robert asked whether it was a eunuch and we assured him that it very soon would be. 'Very well then', he said, 'he shall be named after the greatest eunuch of all time, you must call him Narises.'

We were sad when the time came to leave Deià because we had fallen in love with a way of life that we had never previously experienced. We were also sorry to be leaving the friends who had so generously welcomed us into their community, so it was with considerable regret that we climbed aboard the bus and waved farewell. As we left the village we saw Isabella the donkey picking her way daintily along the verge of the road being led back to her stable after completing her day's work pulling a small plough in the fields. Was I dreaming or did she really wink at us as we passed by!

The last few days of our honeymoon were spent in delightful luxury at Hotel Formentor more than 70 kilometres east of Palma. The trim little bus belonging to the hotel took us through the flat agricultural land known as the *Pla* which stretches east of Palma and occupies most of the space between the northern mountains and the southern coast. It is dotted with windmills in various states of repair; some of which are quite dilapidated, others have the remnants of a sail or two, while some are in good condition. (A society has since been formed to restore them and several are now in full working order).

The road runs virtually straight across the plain from Palma to Alcudia, but to reach Formentor it is necessary to turn off towards the mountains after passing Campanet and its caves. Soon the scenery changes as the road climbs into pine covered hills and then drops down to Pollença and its related port. To the east of Pollença a mountain range, topped by Puig Tomir at over 1,100 metres dominates the view.

We drove through Pollença and on to the coast at Puerto Pollença which was then just a small fishing port with some good hotels and some impressive villas overlooking a long curving bay with a fine sandy beach sloping gently into the water.

After leaving the port, the bus started a steep climb, passing a military seaplane base plastered with notices forbidding photography. Leaving the pine woods behind us, we wound upwards into a bare rock landscape to the Punta la Nao from where we had an outstanding view of the 300 metre cliffs of the northern coast before descending, through more pines, to the long white Hotel Formentor with its distinctive pink roof and blaze of crimson bougainvillaea.

The hotel was constructed by Adán Dielh, a millionaire whose refined taste was reflected in the layout and design. Situated beside a cove known, by a curious coincidence, as the *Pi de la Posada,* it advertised itself without false modesty as 'The most beautiful spot in the world.'

Not far distant, Cabo Formentor marks the most northerly point of the island. The entire peninsular; once owned by the family of the Majorcan Poet, Costa y Llobera, is rich in birdlife including the Peregrine falcon, rock dove, kite, wryneck and flycatcher; even an Eleanora falcon and a giant black vulture, with a wingspan of almost three metres, have been observed by ornithologists staying at the hotel.

We had a lovely room overlooking the bay. At that time even in a hotel of this rating not all of the rooms had their own private bathroom and the sight of ours, with unlimited running water, was too much for me to resist. I was enjoying the luxury of my first proper bath for two weeks almost before the porter had time to bring up our bags.

That evening the P & O cruise liner, *Arcadia*, anchored in the bay and the passengers came ashore to dance in the hotel gardens. The scene of the large white ship, its lights reflected in the water, with its passengers and the hotel guests mostly in evening dress, dancing in the illuminated gardens, created a scene which Noel Coward could certainly have exploited.

Later that evening we shared a table in the garden with an American couple who had the room next to ours. They were 'doing' Europe for the third or fourth time and evidently judged each country by the quality of its hotels. The following week they would be in England and would be staying at the Dorchester. They asked where we lived and, when we told them that we were renting a flat nearly two hundred miles north of London, the husband said: 'Fine, join us for dinner if you are that close.' He was short and big bellied, chewed cigars and wore a large gold wrist-watch and huge gold cuff-links, while his wife rivalled him with gold earrings, a gold necklace and a gold watch only a fraction smaller than that of her husband. She was an amusing character and told us about her genuine leopard skin sun-top and pants which she could not wear for long as they tickled too much. They liked Majorca because the hotel served generous baskets of fruit with every meal. Rome had not taken their fancy because there had been trouble with poor plumbing in their hotel. We realised that the Dorchester would have to bear heavy responsibility for their future opinion of Britain.

My husband ordered a round of drinks and we settled back to watch an exhibition of Majorcan dancing. Almost every town and village in Majorca has its group of dancers who perform at festivals and fiestas. The costumes vary, but the women typically wear a tight-fitting black bodice with three-quarter length sleeves, a long, full skirt in soft brocade-like material, a white embroidered petticoat, long white pantalets, white socks and black pumps and cover their heads with a white lace wimple. The men wear white shirts, unusual pantaloons, made of brocade or coloured cloth, often with a striped pattern, which fit tightly just below the calf, a wide cummerbund, frequently with a matching scarf, a fancy waistcoat, white socks and black plimsolls and sometimes a black hat or coloured handkerchief on their heads.

The Majorcans have carefully preserved many traditional dances, common ones being the *jotas, boleros, copeos, parados* and *mateixes*. These are performed in pairs, fours, sixes or larger groups to music played on guitars and occasionally other instruments including the violin and a version of the bagpipe known as the *xeremie*. Arm movements are as important as footwork and for many dances the arms are held high while the dancers may accompany the music with castanets.

It was a lengthy display and our glasses soon emptied, but our gold-encrusted friends showed no sign of buying their round until the husband caught the eye of a waiter and, without asking us what we would like, calmly ordered a jug of water and four glasses. Turning to us, he explained that he thought the bar prices were too high. When the waiter returned with the water there was no ice, so he was promptly sent back to fetch some.

We spent idle days swimming in the warm clear water and relaxing on the long sandy beach where thatched umbrellas provided some welcome shade from the strong sun. At sunset we enjoyed the large grounds which offered fine views over the huge bay of Pollença with the little island of Formentor in the foreground. White yachts dotted the bay and dark green pine trees covered the slopes of the hills behind.

The hotel has since been extended, but it has not changed greatly. It is perhaps a little more formal today and now boasts two swimming pools; the grounds are even more beautiful and a bar/restaurant has been opened on the beach.

Our flight home departed early and, because it is a long drive from Formentor to the airport, we had to leave before dawn. Our taxi arrived promptly at four in the morning and the early start provided us with one of the highlights of our honeymoon. Anyone who has not witnessed dawn breaking on the Majorcan mountains has missed an unforgettable experience. An artist could use almost any colour to portray the scene, because virtually the whole spectrum is deployed as the day slowly breaks.

It was still barely light as we stood near the dirt runway at Son Bonet and watched the Viscount gleaming gold in the light of the rising sun as it came in to land; its wheels sending up a cloud of red dust as they touched down. The time had come for us to leave our enchanted island and we were very reluctant to depart.

5. Majorca Revisited

We never forgot Majorca and followed developments there with interest. In 1956 Cassell & Co published an English language edition of *Winter in Majorca* translated and annotated by Robert Graves. The footnotes are extensive and the numerous corrections to George Sand's original text testify to Robert's extensive knowledge of the history and customs of Majorca.

Robert Graves was elected Professor of Poetry at Oxford in 1961, bringing him the wider recognition that he richly deserved. In Majorca, in 1965, he received the *Premio de los Premios* which is awarded to the person who has done most for Palma and in 1968 he was made the first ever adoptive son of Deià, which pleased him greatly as he genuinely loved the town and its people.

In 1976, *I Claudius,* the book for which Robert is probably best known, was transmitted as a television serial by the BBC. In the company of millions of other viewers in Britain, we watched every episode. It was a highly successful series with brilliant casting and held one spellbound from the moment a snake slithered across a mosaic floor during the introduction to the final frame.

Karl Gay, who had been Robert's secretary and right-hand man for over thirty years, left Deià in 1965 to take up the post of Curator of the Poetry Collection at the Lockwood Memorial

Library of the University of Buffalo which has a large collection of Robert's manuscripts. He worked there until he retired in 1978, when he and his wife Renée returned to Majorca to live in Palma.

Will Price genuinely tried to interest the film world in Robert's work throughout the middle and late 1950's. Unfortunately his reputation was against him, especially in America. He came close to success in 1957 with a project that would have resulted in Alec Guinness playing Claudius with a cast that was to include Ava Gardner but the film was never produced. Although Will tried to control his alcoholism, his health deteriorated and he died about five years later. I believe that he was never able to repay the money he owed for the debts Robert had paid on his behalf, including Kitten's bill at Lluc-Alcari.

Our house in Surrey, only a stone's throw from Charterhouse where Robert Graves had spent his unhappy schooldays, became too large for us when our two daughters graduated from university and left home to live and work in London. It took an entire day for my husband, bumping around on a ride-on mower, to cut and edge the lawns. Although we loved the place, we knew that it was time for us to leave it but the problem was to find somewhere offering similar peace and seclusion with which to replace it.

It was when we first started thinking about a move that we had a visit from Tomás Graves whom we had not seen since he was a baby of 16 months. He had come from Majorca to Surrey to look up an old friend from his schooldays at Bedales and when we heard that he would be in the neighbourhood we invited him to come and see us. As he talked, he vividly reminded us of the relaxed atmosphere of Majorca and the happy days we had spent there. A generally unfavourable press and television coverage had left us with the impression that the island had totally changed and become one large holiday camp, with lager louts rioting every night. It was obvious from what Tomás told us that this image was greatly distorted. It was then that we resolved to return as soon as we could.

We knew that there had been substantial development on the south west and east coasts with the construction of many new hotels and apartments. Work started on the widening of the Paseo Maritimo in 1963, partly on land reclaimed from the sea, which left the swimming pool of the Hotel Mediterraneo stranded between two lanes of traffic. The Hotel Villamil at Paguera stood almost alone on an empty beach and in 1965 it was calculated that a new hotel opened in the Balearics every two days, one hour and 42 minutes.

In 1967 the motorway from the airport to Palma was completed and 340,000 British tourists visited the island; the figure increased by 100,000 the following year and by 1968 the new international airport at Son San Juan was the busiest in Spain.

A most important event affecting the whole of Spain was the death of Generalísimo Franco on 20th November 1975. The country changed from a dictatorship to a democracy and the monarchy was restored when Prince Juan Carlos was sworn in as King the following day. A large house at Marivent which was built in 1923 by Juan de Saridakis, a Greek chauffeur who married a wealthy widow in Chile, was donated to the Royal Family for use as their summer palace; the suggestion being that it might be open as a museum when they were not in residence. This later proved impractical so the valuable contents were returned to the original owner and it is now closed to the public. The King and Queen and their family spend several weeks at Marivent every summer and participate in local events such as the sailing regattas.

The first elections for 41 years took place in 1977 and Adolfo Suarez became Prime Minister of a right of centre government. A Communist Party rally at the Palma Bullring that May attracted 17,000 people and 25,000 crowded into the same venue in June to hear Felipe Gonzalez address a meeting of the Socialist Workers Party.

A referendum was held in 1978 and a new Constitution was adopted; in Majorca 89% of those who responded were in favour. In 1979 the first general election under the new constitution again returned Adolfo Suarez and his party but in 1982 there was a landslide victory for the Socialists in another election and Felipe Gonzalez became Prime Minister.

In 1983 the first Autonomous Balearic Government was elected with 54 members and Gabriel Cañellas was invested as First President of the Balearic Autonomous Community. A new flag was created for the Community with four red stripes on a yellow ground, in one corner a purple square contains a white castle capped with five towers.

It was not until 1984, almost exactly thirty years after we had honeymooned at Deià, that we booked a flight to return to Majorca. By then over four million tourists visited the island every year, compared with about 200,000 when we were there previously. Booking was simplicity itself; instead of our having to write to the hotel and contact the airline, a tour company offered us a complete package including the provision of a car. We chose an hotel in the south west of the island – a part that we had not yet explored.

The moment that we arrived at the airport in Palma it was evident that Majorca was no longer controlled by a Dictator. Friendly officials merely glanced at our documents and our cases were not even opened.

We stayed at the four-star Hotel Coronado at Cala Fornells, which was then experimenting with modern tourism by being listed in the brochures of a few tour operators, but its main revenue still came from clients who returned year after year to enjoy its spacious rooms, indoor and outdoor pools and ideal location.

Cala Fornells is reached by a road leading south from Paguera. The attractive terracotta coloured apartments that cover the hillside were still being constructed during our visit but we realised how attractive it would be when the work was finished.

The Hotel Coronado is a long white building overlooking the bay of Paguera with a terrace virtually on the waterfront. It was comfortable and friendly and the food was always beautifully presented and served by efficient waiters, unlike the self-service buffet favoured by many other establishments.

The restaurant was managed with an iron hand by Miguel; a bustling, balding man, always dressed in black coat and pinstripe trousers, who came from the old school of hoteliers. He was able to communicate in several languages and could usually anticipate which one to use for each new guest, greeting him or her appropriately. He addressed me as 'lady' which he considered to be synonymous with 'madam' and professed a high regard for the English whom he treated as if they were still in the age of the grand tour.

At breakfast one of the waiters would sometimes push a trolley bearing an exceptional salmon or suckling pig from table to table inviting anyone interested to order a portion for lunch at a small extra charge. Miguel would extol its virtues and it was usually all reserved by the time breakfast was finished.

We loved the Coronado, especially in the evening when the lights around the bay were reflected in the still, dark water. Boats bobbed at anchor just below the terrace and large pine trees scented the air. A band came to play twice a week and we danced until midnight in the cool night air with a jug of *sangria* on our table to refresh us. We enjoyed every minute of the dancing, but the classes we had taken in England to improve our ballroom steps were of little use because they did not cover the latin rhythms that predominate in Majorca. To this day my husband still sambas with only a little more grace than a shunting engine!

The small beach at Cala Fornells can be rather crowded as it is shared by two hotels and a considerable portion has been concreted over to provide platforms for sunbeds but it has been made very attractive and offers shade cast by straw umbrellas and pine trees.

Two days after our arrival we were invited to tea at *Canelluñ* and, in order to see an area that was new to us, we left early and drove to Paguera which is a long narrow town bordering the sea. At that time it suffered from serious traffic congestion because the main road ran through it, but a new by-pass involving two tunnels has now greatly improved the situation. It is essentially a holiday resort, with good sandy beaches (including the first artificial beach to be constructed on the island) and offers a wide choice of hotels, restaurants, bars and many shops but nothing of architectural or historical interest.

From Paguera we headed north to Capdella along a road lined with blackberry hedges. Thereafter the drive demanded a cool head and a steady nerve because the road took us right into the mountains, sometimes following a valley but often winding in a series of hairpin bends, with a steep rise on one side and a sheer drop on the other, up and over the crest. Pine-covered lower slopes were surmounted by bare rock which changed colour according to the light, from pink to a gentle mauve.

The highest peak in this region is Galatzo at 1,025 metres. Its distinctive pyramidal shape can be seen for many miles and its smaller sister Mola de Planicie at 932 metres is part of the same northern ridge. Almost exactly in the centre of the area a very distinctive pine-clad mountain resembling an inverted pudding basin is called Bauza. It can claim only 614 metres but its location makes it almost as prominent a feature as Galatzo.

We followed the road as it writhed its way to Galilea; one of the highest villages on the island at 505 metres. It is a pretty place with a small square containing the church, a café and a restaurant from which there are magnificent views of the countryside to the south. The town has a biblical connection being named after Galilee, reflecting the deep religious beliefs of the earlier inhabitants of Majorca who frequently named their towns and villages after saints or places in the Holy Land.

Leaving Galilea we took the road which wound its way to Puigpuñent. Today, on the outskirts of the town, a 200,000 square metre nature reserve called La Reserva with 30 waterfalls and 3 kilometres of mountain paths, lies in a wooded valley on the slopes of Galatzo.

There is a small restaurant in the centre of the village called the English Rose at which we have recently had some truly memorable meals. It has but two small dining rooms but the food is prepared with loving care by the English proprietors. For Sunday lunch they serve a good roast of pork or beef and we like their mushroom pot as a starter with a bottle of Estola to accompany the meat. The smaller dining room downstairs has one large table suitable for a party of six or eight and in the winter, with a log fire burning in the corner, it is the ideal place for a relaxed dinner.

After passing through Esporlas we drove north to reach the coast road running between Banyalbufar and Valldemossa and soon found an excellent restaurant in an old manor house called the Vistamar. It is at the end of a long drive on the left of the road and we enjoyed our lunch on its spacious terrace. Afterwards we walked through the extensive grounds to a little gazebo from which there is a superb view down to the sea. Many years later we recommended this excellent hotel and restaurant to Don and Laura, some friends who spoke little Spanish. They decided to have lunch there and, after looking at the menu, Laura asked Don to order while she went to tidy up. She wanted suckling pig and he did his best to interpret the menu by identifying what he recognised as pig and leg but when the meal arrived Laura was astonished to find that she was being served with a large dish of pig's trotters!

After lunch we made a detour to the Port de Valldemossa where the road ends at a small harbour of no great beauty, but the drive down to it is really dramatic, offering fine views and requiring good brakes. Michael Douglas and his wife Diandra recently purchased a fine old estate nearby called S'Estaca which at one time belonged to the Archduke Luis Salvador.

We arrived in Deià in good time for tea with Beryl Graves. I had not realised how ill Robert had become; he was then 89 and although we saw him, sitting in his wheelchair, he was unable to communicate and did not recognise us. It seemed probable that this would be the last time we would see the literary giant and friend who had been so generous to us thirty years before and I was relieved to know that Beryl had her four children living on the island to comfort her when the end inevitably came.

After leaving *Canelluñ* we couldn't resist having a look at the *cala* and were surprised to find that we were able to drive down there. To our dismay we found that all of the sand had been washed away many years before in a severe storm and that the beautiful beach was now rocky.

Before leaving Deià we called on Tomás Graves who runs The New Seizin Press. He showed us his hand-operated French cylinder press called 'La Pédalette' which was brought to the island in 1911. The press had been carefully restored and is now used for high quality short-run publications, usually printed on hand-made paper. This took my husband back to his early days in publishing as it was many years since he had seen hand-set type. Tomás had been assisting with the production of a brochure for

La Residencia, the luxury hotel in Deià which was about to open. He took us round the hotel and showed us the newly decorated rooms, furnished with antiques and original oil paintings. Many of the bedrooms had four-poster beds and I could well imagine sleeping snugly in one while the wind whistled outside the window. We toured the immaculate gardens which included lawns, terraces and a swimming pool filled with water from a spring. It was obvious that this would soon become one of the leading hotels on the island.

Before leaving Deià we called in at Es Moli, a hotel on the hill which overlooks the village, and it was there that we met our old friend Pedro, who had married a girl from Soller and was then head barman at the hotel. Although it was thirty years since he had last seen us, he recognised me at once and with typical Spanish flattery he explained that this was because I reminded him of a famous film star, so much so that, at the beach café, I had secretly been nicknamed after her. My husband gave him top marks for charm, but doubted his honesty as he could not see the slightest resemblance!

We returned to Cala Fornells by the coastal route, skirted Valldemossa and turned down a narrow road on the right leading to Puerto de Canonge where we were disappointed to find the little beach spoiled by rather ugly boat houses. This is one of the many small roads in Majorca that end at the sea, so that it is necessary to return the same way to rejoin the main road. Having done so we headed west to Banyalbufar where there is very extensive use of terracing to make use of every scrap of land. A waiter in the Café Bellavista who served us a refreshingly cool *cerveza* told us that, in many parts of the island, each generation had the responsibility of constructing at least one new terrace.

The terracing of the island was commenced by Arab settlers who also arranged an elaborate watering system. Until the last century grapes were grown in the area and vineyards were re-planted six years ago but the vines are only just reaching maturity.

A consortium led by Richard Branson has recently acquired three large adjoining estates in this area called *Son Creus*, *Son Valenti* and *Ca'n Bunyola,* the last of which contains a fine manor house with its own beach. The consortium is reported to be planning a luxury-class hotel on the lines of the successful La Residencia. Access to this part of the island will be much easier once the partly completed tunnel on the road between Palma and Soller is opened.

We soon came to the Mirador de Ses Animes which demanded another stop to admire the exceptional coastal views. The next town was Estallencs with fascinating narrow side streets waiting for a sketch or photograph at every turn, with a tiny gravel beach and port about a kilometre from the town down a very steep and narrow road. Estallencs boasts the two star Hotel Maristel that gave us its brochure claiming that '*all room are running and telephone*'. The little shops in the town were obviously catering for tourists, but they offered an interesting selection of ceramics and other local handicrafts. We bought an oval dish with a typical Majorcan pattern of pink flowers, green leaves and alternate ochre and white stripes around the edge which we still use today.

The northern edge of the island features tall cliffs and some of the views along this length of the coastline are truly breathtaking. A few kilometres further on we came to Es Grau where, to the left of a short tunnel, the old Mirador de Ricardo Roca provided a splendid view of the coastline. We admired the work of the embroiderers who sat on the steps leading up to an old observation tower which had been part of the early warning system to counter raids by pirates. Soon after Es Grau we headed south through the attractive Coll de Sa Gremola with its hillsides covered with olive, pine, carob, lentisk and some fig trees, finally descending into Andratx from where we had only a short drive to reach our hotel in time for dinner.

The following day we drove a little way along the coast to Camp de Mar where we spent a quiet morning swimming and sunbathing on the perfect sandy beach bordered by pines and enjoyed an excellent *tortilla española*, an omelette containing potato and onions, followed by *gambas*, large prawns which were cooked on a charcoal grill at the little café in the bay which is reached by a wooden causeway from the beach.

There is a pleasant walk up the headland which separates Camp de Mar from Cala Fornells and we strolled up there after lunch following a path which led to an old observation tower dominating the point. It is one of a chain which ringed the coast and fires lit at these points gave advance warning of pirate attacks. As it was a little early to return to the hotel we took the car along the pretty coast road to Puerto de Andratx; another of the many examples in Majorca of a port backed by an inland town of the same name.

On the hill just before one enters the Puerto there is a small *hostal* called the Moderno which is owned and run by Guido, an Italian, and his Majorcan wife, Maria. This is where we often go for a traditional British Sunday lunch of roast beef, Yorkshire pudding, roast potatoes and fresh vegetables. Unfortunately, even in some British run restaurants on the island, the meat is cooked early in the day, sliced mechanically when cold, and reheated just before serving; the result, swimming in a watery gravy, is not unlike wet shoe-leather. The Moderno, although essentially an Italian restaurant, is curiously one of the relatively few places where the beef is carved fresh from a large joint and one can have it rare, medium or well done according to one's preference.

Puerto de Andratx is almost landlocked and steep hillsides, originally tree-clad but gradually being covered by villas and apartment blocks, surround the water in a horseshoe shape with a point – La Mola – extending from one side; inland higher mountains dominate the skyline. Although it is still a fishing port, much of the harbour is now dedicated to the needs of the yachting fraternity and in the Puerto every other building seems to be a bar or restaurant. For much of its length the road has the water on one side and shops, bars, restaurants and an occasional small hotel on the other.

Chairs and tables were set out on the coast side of the road and the waiters had to dodge the traffic to serve the customers eating and drinking in the open air. We saw one heavily laden waiter emerge from the doorway of a restaurant just as a car pulled away from the pavement; the driver was not expecting anyone to walk out in front of him and the waiter was concentrating on picking out the customers who had ordered the dishes he was carrying. There was a screech of brakes and the startled waiter literally went into a spin, holding his tray aloft as he pirouetted and attempted to regain his balance. He spiralled to the safety of the opposite kerb and collapsed onto a chair to recover for a few moments before serving the meal as if nothing had happened.

Later that week we drove to the town of Andratx, almost four kilometres inland from the port, nestling in a hollow in the hills. It has an impressive church, typical of many of the older towns in Majorca where the church seems to be a little oversize.

The main feature of Andratx is its large market which is held every Wednesday when most of the streets on the east side of the town are lined with stalls selling hand crafted items, artificial flowers and garden plants, wool, cushions, table linen, carpets, nuts, sweets, dried and crystallised fruit, spices, herbs, cakes, sausages, hams, cheese, wine, hens in crates, petfood, fertiliser, seeds, ladies underwear, stockings and all types of clothing including beautifully decorated baby clothes, knives, cooking pots, pans and other kitchen equipment, toy cars and dolls, games, picture frames, leatherware of all kinds such as handbags, wallets, purses and shoes, jewellery, watches and wooden items, including beautiful bowls made from olive wood and some peculiar devices with no obvious purpose.

We puzzled over an object made of wood and shaped like a roller skate with a handle; eventually our curiosity got the better of us and we asked its purpose. The jolly lady at the stall rolled it over her ample frame and explained that it was for reducing cellulite and was best used immediately after a bath. Another odd item consisted of little more than a piece of wire with a loop attached. It was being demonstrated by a girl who first peeled a potato and then screwed the device into it to produce what looked like a coiled spring; this left a hole right through the potato which she then cut into slices, producing rings; the suggestion was that when fried the spring-like core and the rings provided an interesting alternative to conventional chips. She was having only limited success and by the end of the morning was barely visible behind a pile of potato rings and springs.

We shuffled along with the crowd, looking at the stalls as we passed and making a mental note of any that looked interesting enough for a stop as we returned to our car. Locals mixed with tourists; the former mainly interested in food and other domestic requirements, while the latter were attracted to the leather goods, linen and casual clothing. Vendors of records and tapes played popular music while the mouth-watering smell of frying onions from a mobile café reminded us that we would soon have to think about lunch.

In most shops and markets prices are firm unless one is buying in bulk or business is very slow, but the absence of any marked price on an elaborate hand-embroidered tablecloth, complete with matching napkins was a clue to the fact that it just might be negotiable so, when we were quoted a figure that was rather higher than we anticipated, we did not immediately accept it. The vendor did not seem very surprised when we shook our heads sadly, expressed regret that it was more than we could afford and started to take our leave. He had no intention of missing the sale and we were soon involved in a brisk session of bargaining which eventually resulted in our paying substantially less than had originally been asked.

Due west of Andratx, a road took us through the little village of S'Arraco and on to the coast at Sant Elm (marked on some maps as San Telmo). It has an excellent wide sandy beach, a car park under some trees on the landward side of the road, an abundance of restaurants and bars and a small harbour from which a short boat trip takes one to the island of Dragonera. The area is a paradise for bird watchers with a wide range of gulls and a colony of ospreys as well as owls, warblers and red kites.

Dragonera narrowly escaped development but it was saved by a local preservation group and is now well protected. Five years later we joined a party of about thirty members of the English Speaking Residents' Association who hired a boat and spent several hours exploring Dragonera. It gets its name either because it has a ridged spine like the back of a dragon or because of the myriad of *geckos*, small lizards, which live on its corrugated surface. Its main feature is a lighthouse on its highest point which is over 300 metres above sea level and was badly damaged by lightning. This has never been repaired because frequent mists rendered it ineffective.

A serpentine road leads from the little port up to the summit and it is a steady pull all of the way. It was a little too much for me, but my husband joined an athletic friend of about 60 and they maintained a steady pace until, puffing slightly, they circled a wall at the top and reached the old lighthouse building. To their amazement they were greeted by a lady many years their senior, a perfect example of those who seem to have found the secret of eternal youth in the warmth of Majorca. She had started the climb with them but had gone on ahead and had already finished her sandwiches by the time they arrived.

We were enchanted by the beautiful scenery of the western half of the island with its narrow winding roads, pine forests, mountains and occasional views down the valleys to the sea. Later in the week we explored the remainder of the area by driving through Establiments to Esporles; a very pleasant town with a long tree-lined main street where Chopin and George Sand spent several weeks at a house called Son Vent. Unlike Valldemossa, Esporles has never capitalised on their stay.

A few kilometres to the west of Esporles lies La Granja which is the Spanish name for a farmhouse or country house. It exactly describes this old building, once owned by Cistercian monks, which has been restored and partly converted into an exhibition of rural activities. There are performances by folk dancers, blacksmiths, weavers and potters, a display of wine-making equipment and live demonstrations of the manufacture of butter, cheese and cream, all by staff wearing traditional dress. Other exhibits include a large collection of old farm equipment, tools and kitchen utensils, a working farm and even a torture chamber complete with its horrible instruments. The water that comes in abundance from a spring on the site is used to good effect in the extensive gardens and there is an inexpensive restaurant where traditional Majorcan food is served.

After Esporles we headed for Esglaieta where, on the road between Palma and Valldemossa, we stopped to watch glass being blown at the Lafiore factory. Articles made on the site can be purchased in their large showroom which also displays a wide selection of Majorcan pottery and other souvenirs including large glass goblets, too big to use for wine but ideal for holding candles when entertaining in the garden.

Skirting around the west side of Palma, we soon found ourselves in Genova (pronounced Henova) a popular residential area, high enough to offer good views over the Bay of Palma. In the Calle Barranco we had dinner at Casa Jacinto which is very popular with the Majorcans; its specialities include snails in garlic sauce and a wide range of fish and meat cooked on a charcoal grill. Genova abounds in excellent restaurants and one of our favourites is Ca'n Pedro which recently moved to large new premises on the road leading to Na Burguesa.

After our meal we took the road that wriggles up to the tall monument which is a landmark in the area as it can be seen for many miles. It commemorates the fallen in the Spanish Civil War and is surmounted by a statue of the Virgin (somewhat incongruously under a red light which is a necessary warning to aircraft). From the car park we enjoyed a panoramic view of the entire Bay of Palma, with Bellver Castle and its woods in the foreground, the port area, the Maritimo, the marina still displaying some activity as crews made yachts ready for the night and the Cathedral in the middle distance, beyond which the bay extended from Palma right round to Cabo Blanco. The view was so dramatic that we lingered there until it grew dark, watching the lights appear one by one until they turned the scene into a film set with the glowing curve of the bay twinkling with street lamps. Bellver Castle and the Cathedral were bathed in floodlight and the sea reflected a moon path to a dimly visible horizon.

At the airport the next morning we felt a little depressed at having to leave Majorca and return to the UK. We realised how little we knew about the island, there were still large areas that we had not visited and we had barely scratched the surface of those parts we had seen.

It was not just the beauty of fragrant green pines against the clear blue sky with a sparkling sea beyond or mellow stone buildings relieved by green or brown shutters that we found hard to leave, it was a way of life that exactly matched our temperament. The enjoyment of a coffee at a pavement table with no pressure to hurry; meals eaten in the clear warm evening air, served by waiters who seemed happy in their work even though it would keep them up until two in the morning; food carefully prepared and attractively presented in the knowledge that the majority of those who had ordered it would appreciate the skill of the chef; and *rioja* and other wines, still inexpensive but tremendously improved in quality during the years since our previous visit.

As our aircraft took off for Gatwick my eyes were pricked with tears as I looked down on the island I had come to love. My husband must have felt much the same because he asked: ‘How soon can we come back?’ We spent most of the flight planning our return.

6. A New Home

We soon dropped back into the weekly routine at our home in Surrey, but we started to question why we continued to live in a large house with three acres of garden that was difficult for us to maintain and left us no time to relax. It was not essential for us to stay in England; my husband is a writer and all he needs is a study where he can plug in his computer and have some peace and calm. Our daughters were well launched on their careers and could more easily spare time for a short holiday abroad than numerous week-end and evening visits.

We considered the possibility of two homes, one in England and the other – possibly an apartment – in Majorca but that was rejected outright because of Tia Maria and Caligula (known as Ziggy) our two Siamese cats who would not tolerate going to a cattery every time we went abroad. The word cattery was actually unmentionable in their presence and we dreaded taking them to one as they screamed at the top of their considerable voices all the way there, so that by the time we arrived I was a nervous wreck. In contrast, when collected they sat silent and smiling on the back seat throughout the return journey and then expressed their displeasure by totally ignoring us for two days. They would come with us if we decided to live overseas, but would never accept repeated visits to the cattery while we enjoyed ourselves in a holiday home.

We booked another visit to Majorca for October 1984 and wrote to several estate agents there asking if they would come to our hotel and show us what they had to offer. Our needs were simple, but Tia and Ziggy were more particular, demanding plenty of safe open country, no busy roads and a reasonably large garden to defend against anything that walked, hopped or flew. We thought that it would be easy to find a suitable house on Majorca. All of the agents we contacted assured us that they had plenty of properties to show us, and one by one they called at our hotel and took us to see them.

We rather liked the description of a house situated between Andratx and Puerto de Andratx so we arranged to see around it. It was newly-constructed in the centre of a large square plot which was still bare ground baked solid by the sun and no attempt had been made to create a garden. When we arrived we were greeted by two St Bernard dogs which were beautiful animals, but the plot was littered with their droppings that looked like small piles of horse manure. We dismissed this as a temporary problem and entered the house which had been designed by the couple who owned it.

The main rooms were well proportioned; most of the bedrooms were on the ground floor but there was a staircase leading up to the main bedroom and bathroom above. My husband started to climb the stairs and nearly knocked himself out because, due to some miscalculation in the design, there was less than five and a half feet between the stairs and a large concrete beam which would be difficult, if not impossible, to remove as it was obviously there for a reason. This was definitely a detraction but we pressed on with the tour and were shown the master suite complete with a large bathroom; one wall of which consisted entirely of clear glass rather like a shop window. There was no curtain or blind and little room to fix one, so anyone using it was in full view from the road and garden; we registered this as an additional negative point. On leaving we were surprised to see that the ceiling of the porch seemed to have been painted black but closer examination showed that it was black with flies, not paint. Just behind the house there was a chicken farm and in the heat of the day the flies gathered in their thousands to settle on that particular spot which was obviously especially to their liking. We explained as tactfully as possible that the house was not quite what we were seeking.

We were shown a house with a cracked pool; a house with walls bulging and leaning at alarming angles; a house owned by several families who had acquired it by inheritance many years before and were still arguing over the exact share due to each member; and a pleasant house with a pool outside the lounge, unfortunately it was only just outside and anyone walking out of the room was in danger of taking an involuntary bathe.

There was a house next door to a cement block factory; we did not disbelieve the owner's assurance that it was only noisy and dusty on Thursdays when the cement was mixed, but we explained that we wanted a house that was quiet for seven days a week. A house on the north coast had possibilities until we inspected the kitchen. A curious structure in the centre of the room proved to be a well complete with bucket and chain; this was the only source of water and muttering 'ding dong bell, pussy's in the well' I fled from the house leaving the agent open-mouthed in bewilderment.

Through a friend we heard of a house that was for sale on the edge of Valldemossa which had not yet been placed in the hands of an agent. It sounded possible so we went off by ourselves in high hopes, but it was totally unsuitable. To console ourselves after another fruitless journey we decided to have lunch and found a pleasant little restaurant called Sa Costa close to the Cartuja.

We ordered the *menú del dia* and were soon enjoying *sopas mallorquinas* and some excellent *vino de la casa*. With our spirits fully recovered we began to take more interest in what was going on around us and became aware of an English conversation at a neighbouring table. I was fascinated because although the English was perfect, there was a trace of an accent and the owner of the voice, who was obviously a local resident, was far too flamboyantly dressed to be an Englishwoman. She was wearing a colourful kaftan which resembled a tent, because she was of considerable size, and her dark hair hung loose to her shoulders. As she talked to a teenage boy, she waved her arms in all directions to illustrate particular points she wished to stress. At a break in the conversation, I leaned across and asked: 'Where did you learn to speak English so well?' With a broad smile, she replied: 'In England, I lived there for some years but I am actually a white Russian.'

We all introduced ourselves and she joined us at our table with the young man, who was her elder son. She told us that she also had a daughter and a younger son and that her husband was away on business in Berlin; her name was Marina Burwitz and her home was in Valldemossa. She invited us to lunch the following week by which time her husband would have returned. She knew that he would be delighted to meet us and was sure that we would like him.

We did indeed like Nils Burwitz, it would be impossible not to feel affection for this modest and talented artist. He was tall and very slim with brown hair, beard and moustache and cobalt blue eyes behind large spectacles. Born in 1940 in the Baltic within a stone's throw of the iron curtain; his parents fled to West Germany in 1945 but found it difficult to settle there and in 1958 they moved with Nils to South Africa where he obtained a Bachelor of Arts degree and later became famous for his powerful drawings and paintings, many of which had a strong political influence. He settled with his wife and young family in Majorca in 1976.

Nils was working on an unusual project with Tomás Graves. This was a combination of nine engravings by Nils, plus text beautifully printed by Tomás on hand-made paper. The engravings illustrate events described in the definitive translation by Robert Graves of George Sand's *Un Hiver à Majorque*. The text reproduces the Foreword and Historical Summary in English, French and Catalan and the whole collection is beautifully presented in a box covered with hand-woven

Majorcan cloth. Only seventy five prints were made from each plate and we ordered set number two – I believe that a museum just beat us to set number one.

We inspected old houses, new houses, houses requiring renovation and houses that had been restored. We exhausted several agents who found us easy enough to please but could not satisfy the demands of our cats. Only one showed a tireless determination to find us exactly what we wanted. His name was David Russell and he fully understood our absolute resolve that our home in Majorca would be acceptable to Tia and Ziggy. Where other agents enthused over a new kitchen or attractive pool, David concentrated on the quietness of the area, lack of traffic and abundant open countryside in which a cat could roam in safety.

We had only booked for a fortnight in Majorca and were already well into the second week and feeling somewhat despondent when David came up with a new suggestion. 'What about a site?' he asked. 'I know of one which may be the answer.' He took us the same day to meet the owner, a Majorcan called Carlos, who had inherited several thousand acres on a mountainside. He lived in a large *finca* which had once been the farmhouse for the area and was developing the surrounding land with great care to ensure that the environment was preserved. The plot size was 4000 square metres or about one acre which was all that the Spanish authorities then allowed a foreign couple to purchase.

Carlos was short and swarthy with black crinkly hair, eyes like gimlets and an abundance of charm. My husband realised that he would be a tough man to bargain with, but soon found him to be totally honest and genuinely concerned that we should have the home we desired. He spoke a little English and was something of an Anglophile as was his Swedish wife.

The site was at the top of the mountain with incredible views all round. It was protected at the back and on one side by *zona verde,* the Spanish equivalent of green belt; on the other a house had been built well away from the boundary behind a belt of trees; in front the road terminated at the neighbouring house so it was little used. To the south we could see several miles of coastline with the Coronado Hotel clearly visible; to the north Galatzo and Bauza rose above the little village of Galilea; while to the east the view extended over open country as far as the hills of Na Burguesa.

The ground was rocky but it featured numerous large pine and olive trees and a scattering of holm oak with its curiously assorted mixture of leaves, some as spiny as holly, others round or elongated, but always dark shiny green on the upper surface and greyer beneath. Filling the spaces between the trees, *lentisks,* mastic trees, abounded with their resinous scent and shrubby growth competing with *cistus,* rock roses, for any drift of earth between the rocks. There was even some wild lavender, honeysuckle and asparagus. As we stood in the clear air of the mountain top with its breathtaking views we both knew that our search had ended.

Carlos had an arrangement with a local builder and undertook to construct a house to our design at a fixed price which would include the land. He supplied us with the drawings of some houses that he had already built within our price range and we took them back to England to use as the basis for our design. My husband sketched out the plan and elevations of the home we wanted and we returned to Majorca to finalise the details.

It was then essential for us to appoint a Spanish lawyer to advise us and we obtained a list of English-speaking *abogados* from the British Consulate. We selected one whose name had already been mentioned to us as honest and reliable and asked him to draw up a contract and institute searches to ensure that we would have a good title and that there were no charges outstanding on the land. In Spain debts go with the property, so if one buys a house or land on which there is a mortgage one automatically becomes liable for the loan, even if its existence was not revealed.

In one tragic case an Englishwoman purchased a house in Majorca from a British couple who took out a mortgage on it just before the contract was signed. They then fled to England taking with them the mortgage money and the full price from the purchaser. It was several years before the innocent owner received a notice from the bank that had loaned the money informing her that her property would be sequestered to repay the capital and accrued interest on a mortgage that she did not even know existed. Despite attempts to have the cheats arrested and brought to justice, she eventually had to sell her home to repay the bank.

There are many other matters that an efficient lawyer must investigate such as any proposed development in the area, rights of way, availability of services including electricity and telephone, planning permission and site boundaries. The golden rule is to sign nothing and pay nothing without the knowledge and approval of one's legal advisor because deposits may not be returnable and the English translation of a Spanish document may not be completely accurate.

We appointed an architect to convert my husband's sketch plans into working drawings from which Carlos and his builder were able to produce firm cost estimates. Within a few months the final design and price had been agreed and we were ready to sign a contract. At this point it was necessary for both of us to make Spanish wills because any assets we possessed in Spain would be subject to Spanish law.

With all of the formalities completed, work commenced in April 1985. David Russell kept us informed on progress with the house by visiting the site and taking photographs and by August it was time for us to return to Majorca to see the shell of our future home. We only booked for a week and were quite unprepared for how much there was for us to do. Our first appointment was with the electrician who wanted to know the position of every switch, light point and socket, which he duly marked directly on to the walls in blue paint.

Our only problem was how to explain that we wanted two tubes under the floor to carry cables for the hi-fi speakers – I hate trailing wires and the logical layout for the *salón* was to place the amplifier, cassette decks and turntable in a wine cabinet on one side of the room with a speaker on each side of the fireplace on the opposite wall. The electrician could not see why this was necessary or why we wanted special wires in the tubes. Fortunately, Carlos appeared at this point and in a stream of Majorcan, in which the word *música* featured prominently, he soon had matters sorted out.

We noticed a blue line running horizontally along every wall in the house and asked Carlos its purpose. He explained that it was called the metre line and it had been carefully marked out with a theodolite. Any flooring, no matter what its thickness, would be laid so that the surface was exactly one metre below the line and all the floors would thus be perfectly level.

We saw the plumber and went through a similar routine, marking where each radiator and sanitary appliance was to be fitted. Carlos took us to a large builders' merchant and, within the space of a few hours, we had chosen the bathroom fittings, the wall tiles for the bathrooms and kitchen and floor tiles for those rooms where we did not intend to have marble flooring.

The kitchen would be completely tiled by the builder but it was up to us to arrange for a contractor to design and fit the units. This involved another trip to Palma where we visited several kitchen showrooms. It was a time for making instant decisions since we had to select the oven, hob unit, refrigerator, dishwasher and sink and decide where to place them. Within a few hours one company produced floor plans for the kitchen and even a three-dimensional coloured sketch of the final effect. All of this was accomplished within our limited range of Spanish since the showroom staff were unable to speak English. We were so impressed with their efficiency that we placed the order with them and they promised to liaise with the builder and ensure that the kitchen would be installed as scheduled.

Fate then intervened to prevent us spending Christmas 1985 in our new home. I had been feeling a little tired but was quite unprepared for the results of tests in October which indicated that I needed a coronary by-pass. In November I underwent surgery in the Harley Street Clinic and plans for our move to Majorca had to be postponed until I was fit enough to travel.

By May I had recovered sufficiently for us to start making plans again and we were just completing the final arrangements for our removal when it was my husband's turn for a medical shock. A small lump proved to be malignant and he had to have surgery followed by radiotherapy on an elaborate machine at a hospital in Guildford. His specialist did everything possible to keep the course of treatment as short as possible and it was decided that it would be safe for us to reschedule our move for 30th June 1986.

While I was convalescing we received the sad news that Robert Graves had died on 7th December. Although this was not unexpected, we were especially sorry that we had not been able to see him one more time and that it would be impossible for us to attend his funeral. He was buried in the little cemetery of the church in Deià and his gravestone is simply marked Robert Graves, Poeta, 24.7.1895 – 7.12.1985.

Another blow came while my husband was in hospital recovering from his operation. I returned home from visiting him and found that Ziggy had been hit by a car when crossing the road. Unfortunately he had a wanderlust, in spite of the fact that we had a large garden, and we were unable to prevent him from hunting the rabbits which abounded in the fields the other side of the road. The vet could not save him and he died on the operating table. That night I went to see my husband and decided not to tell him the sad news. This was a mistake because he could see that I was dreadfully upset and assumed that I knew something about his condition that he had not been told. Eventually one of our daughters thought it best to explain what had actually happened.

With our medical problems behind us we started to prepare for the removal. Spain was not then part of the EEC and we had already experienced a few difficulties with its many rules and regulations affecting financial transfers and bank accounts for foreigners. To import furniture and effects at that time it was necessary to prepare a fully detailed inventory, taking especial care to list every electrical and electronic item with its model number and age. Our remaining Siamese, Tia Maria, also required several documents, one of which had to be signed by a vet no earlier than 24 hours before she entered Spain.

We had a most helpful remover who knew the routine, and an invaluable contact in Majorca called Frank Short. His company, which is located in Avenida Antonio Maura, an extension of the Borne, has assisted thousands of British expatriates in matters affecting the Spanish authorities from customs documents to tax returns and *residencias* – the essential certificates entitling one to live in Spain which have to be obtained from the police station.

Frank Short's grandfather was active in assisting British residents to evacuate at the start of the Spanish Civil War and amongst those he helped were Robert Graves and his secretary Karl. After living for 30 years in Spain he was deported in 1941, being given just three days in which to settle his affairs. He was held with sixteen others in a 3 metre by 2 metre underground cell in Barcelona for 51 hours before the British Consul was able to arrange for his release and transfer to Lisbon.

I was determined that Tia would not travel to Majorca in the hold of the aircraft. After many enquiries I found that Iberia would allow one animal in the cabin on each flight, subject to the Captain's agreement, and I was told to purchase a regulation IATA travelling box for her although she could come out of it once the plane was airborne. Eventually reservations were made in Club class for two passengers and a cat - the cat being charged by weight.

Fate had one more trick in store. A week before we were due to leave, the machine on which my husband was being treated broke down. He was transferred to another unit at Midhurst, but this involved a delay of several days and he was unable to travel with me. We traded his Club class ticket for two seats in the economy class and two of our friends, Rita and Eric, kindly agreed to accompany me and help me with the move.

At the airport I reported to the check-in with Tia screaming vile Siamese oaths in her new travelling box which was a plastic affair, big enough for a medium-sized dog. The girl at the Iberia desk was at first doubtful whether Tia could travel in the cabin, but by then I knew the regulations by heart and recited them to her so completely that she decided to change her tactics. 'That box is far too big to take in the cabin,' she said. This was a powerful argument with which I was forced to agree. IATA in giving their approval to the box had obviously anticipated that it would be put in the hold, there was no way that it could have been stowed in the cabin. By this time I was starting to get a little upset and Rita intervened to warn the poor check-in clerk, who was only trying to perform her duty, that I was just recovering from open-heart surgery and should not be subjected to any stress. This produced an instant solution. 'The cat can go into the cabin if you put it in a smaller box; we do not have one but you can get one from Lufthansa,' said the clerk. Eric thanked her and agreed that this was indeed the answer with just one proviso – she should go and get the box.

The Lufthansa box was made of relatively thin cardboard, constructed so as to pack flat. It assembled into a little house with a peaked roof closed by two cardboard handles on the ridge. Tia flexed her muscles and eyed this with interest. Once inserted she went straight into her Houdini routine; first one paw and then the other forced its way out of the roof ridge and it was not long before her head was firmly trapped. My only means of keeping her captive was to hold the box closed with one hand, using the other to push back any parts that forced their way through the opening at the top.

Once aboard I found that I had two empty seats beside me. I waited until we were airborne and then allowed Tia to emerge. She had a great deal to say about her treatment and did so at the top of her powerful voice. I invited her to sit on the vacant seat beside me but that was not to her liking; instead she climbed up on to the rear of my seat and amused herself by making faces and showing her teeth to a nervous old lady in the seat behind.

I was unaware of what was going on until the stewardess came to me and asked me to remove the cat because it was frightening one of the passengers. Fortunately by then lunch was being served which included smoked salmon. Tia expressed interest in this and consented to come down only on condition that she could have my entire portion, which she consumed with remarkable speed. Thereafter she slept happily beside me looking serenely innocent.

I was prepared for difficulties with the authorities at Palma. All of Tia's documents were in order but I had been told that there might not be a vet at the airport; in which case Tia would have to stay there for the night and be examined by one in the morning. In the event nobody even wanted to glance at her documents and we passed through Customs with no delay whatsoever.

Carlos and his wife kindly loaned me an apartment until the furniture arrived four days later. I needed a little time because there were many formalities to complete to ensure that it would be allowed to proceed from Customs. These included the payment of quite a large deposit that would be returned to us after two years, providing we had not disposed of any item in the meantime. I also had to arrange to purchase a car and obtain my *residencia* and there were several matters to sort out with the bank, plus insurance to arrange for the house and car. My friends were wonderful, they hired a car and chauffeured me from office to office until all of my tasks were completed.

Our furniture arrived in Palma on 4th July. It was in a powerful Mercedes van which had also towed a trailer almost as big as itself from England. The trailer contained other furniture which belonged to one of those clever men who know a way round all regulations. He had not bothered about an inventory because he thought he had found a loop-hole in the law which made it unnecessary. The removers left him gesticulating wildly as his furniture was unloaded from the trailer by the Customs and transferred to a bonded warehouse where it was to remain for several weeks while his paperwork was sorted out.

I am an inveterate planner. Every item on the van had already been allocated its place in the new house and all of the boxes were marked for easy identification. I stood at the door calling out: 'dining room,' 'main bedroom' or 'kitchen' as appropriate. There were, however, thirty or so tea-chests that had to await unpacking which I allocated to the various terraces. These I indicated by calling 'north terrace, south terrace or east terrace' After a while I heard one of the men remark to his companions: 'Blimey, I wish I'd brought my bloody compass with me!'

By the evening everything was unloaded but I noticed that two old stone urns were missing. Because the van was completely full, the men had put them in the little kitchen which formed part of the cab and they removed them whenever it was used. Unfortunately the urns had been left on the quay in Palma. The men were most apologetic but promised to bring them the following day and next morning the huge van came all the way up the mountain loaded with just two urns.

During the next few days Rita and Eric helped me to unpack but we still used the apartment as a base and left Tia there while we worked. They stayed as long as they could and timed their departure to coincide with my husband's arrival. I was determined that we would spend the first night in our new home together and was relieved when I heard his taxi coming up the hill.

As I drifted off to sleep I was acutely conscious of the magnitude of the step we had taken. We were alone in a foreign country with only an elementary command of Spanish; our health demanded regular tests; we were many miles from our daughters and we faced the Herculean task of turning a building site into a garden. However, in the morning, when we threw open the *persianas* and looked down on the incredible view, with the sun starting to rise in a cloudless blue sky, we knew that we were going to enjoy our new life in Majorca.

7. *Early Days*

Shortly after we moved in we were invited to a party given by Carlos and his wife. This was held in the open courtyard of their *finca* with about a hundred guests seated for dinner at long trestle tables. There was a seating plan and I found myself between an Englishman and a Dutchman with my husband sitting opposite between their wives who were Belgian and Scottish respectively.

The atmosphere was almost feudal. The *Predio* is an old farm house and its land once extended over thousands of acres. Many of the guests were the owners of sites that Carlos had sold locally. In former days the courtyard would have been filled with estate workers, but the general scene would not have differed greatly because everyone was casually dressed. The food was simple but the wine was plentiful and the noise level of the conversation rose considerably as the evening progressed.

My English neighbour, who had been a wholesale butcher in the UK, had considerable experience of building on the island and was eager to help us if he could. When my husband mentioned that we needed someone to construct a pool for us he told us that he knew just the right man and would bring him to meet us. Although the house itself was finished, the pool was still just a hole in the ground that had been dug when the foundations for the house were being excavated.

We obtained quotations from several pool contractors, but the one recommended by the former butcher was the obvious choice. He radiated confidence and was able to show us many examples of work he had completed, including a large pool for the local Council. He explained that the law required that we should have an architect to draw up the plans and that the architect would insist on a quantity surveyor being paid, but neither would call at the site and, if they did, he would chase them off because no architect knew as much as he did about the mysteries of pool construction.

Quite a few people had told us terrible tales of pools slipping down mountainsides and pools which cracked and defied all attempts to repair them. One calamity happened only a kilometre or so down the road when a pool, designed and constructed by an architect who owned the house, lost its end wall and flooded the road one morning. We saw him scratching his head and surveying the damage when we drove down to buy a paper and collect our post.

In due course we found an architect who copied some plans that my husband had drawn and submitted them to the Council. His fee was enormous but it ensured that we had approval for the design from the College of Architects and our pool would be legal. That was the last we saw of him and we never even met his surveyor.

The pool contractor looked at our hole and then up at the house and suggested that there had been an error somewhere. The house had been set higher than originally planned and although this improved its superb view over the coast it was now several feet above the top of the hole that had been dug for the pool. There was no alternative but to fill in the expensive hole the builder had excavated and set the pool above the sloping ground so that its top would come closer to the level of the house.

Having paid for rubble to be delivered to fill up the hole, work commenced on the construction of the pool. Four men arrived early the next morning and the cement mixer started up promptly at eight, but at nine there was a curious silence, rather as if a strike had been called. We peeped out and could see no sign of movement although the smell of toasting bread and sardines wafted across from where the men had made a small camp. We soon became used to this custom of Majorcan building workers to have their breakfast on the site, usually making a small fire on which to heat coffee and warm up sardines. For months after they departed we were still finding discarded sardine cans under bushes.

Blocks were used to form an outer shell for the pool which was lined with an intricate basket of steel reinforcement carefully placed to cater for every line of stress. Then followed a terrible session, lasting for several days, during which a very noisy machine blew a fine mixture of cement, sand and water on to the steel mesh. I believe that it is possible to construct ships using a similar technique and, the pool, which is now eight years old, has never leaked. Most of the mixture went on to the mesh but some inevitably escaped and the terraces and window ledges were soon covered by a thick layer of grey dust. The machine had a curious habit of blowing a loud raspberry followed by a whistle as it was switched off and I was very glad when it was loaded back onto its lorry and driven off to another site.

A week or two later we were surprised to find that the pool had apparently been lined with brown paper. Closer examination showed that the backs of small glass tiles had been cemented on to the walls and bottom of the pool and the paper was stuck to their outer face, leaving them perfectly spaced with a small gap between each tile. After the paper was removed they were accurately positioned and ready for grouting to form a mosaic finish.

The pool was to have a Santanyi stone capping which had to be shaped to fit its Roman ends. Santanyi is the attractive smooth sandstone quarried in the south eastern corner of the island which was used for most of the major buildings in Majorca including the beautiful Cathedral in Palma. This was a job for another specialist who called and took numerous measurements, returning a few weeks later with the stones all cut and carefully numbered.

Before being cemented, the coping was laid in place around the edge of the pool and all went well until the builders came to the final stone which was much too large. For an hour or so the stones were tried in different positions, but every combination resulted in one being too big. Many theories were advanced, perhaps the pool was narrower at one end than the other, maybe the radius had been miscalculated or the gaps between the stones should be narrower. Eventually a telephone call to the specialist revealed that one stone had been deliberately left oversize so that it could be cut on site to make a perfect fit.

The contractor installed all of the filtration plant and the lights to illuminate the pool at night, but he could not connect the wiring to the mains. That was a job for an electrician who, we were told, would arrive in a day or so.

We had transported only the best of our furniture and effects to Spain, the remainder having been sent to a sale-room in Godalming. We were enjoying perfect weather and, as we had not brought much of our ageing garden furniture with us, we went shopping for some in Palma. Galerías Preciados, the big store in Avenida Rey Jaime III, had a special offer that we could not resist. We bought four very comfortable chairs, two footstools and two loungers on wheels all with thick cushions covered in a pretty blue and grey striped material with a matching sun umbrella and a large coffee table.

The following morning their van delivered all of these items in cardboard boxes and my husband started to unpack them and screw them together. During the afternoon a car arrived and a man carrying a toolbox came to the door. My husband abandoned his work and took him down to the pool room to show him the mass of wires that required connecting. The leads to the lights and the pump were identified and the positions of the switches and fuse box were quickly agreed but the man seemed very reluctant to start. After a flood of protests in rapid Spanish he eventually conveyed to us that he knew absolutely nothing about electrical wiring and had been sent to assemble the garden furniture.

In due course the real electrician arrived and connected up the circulating pump, enabling us to arrange for the pool to be filled. All of our water is delivered by a tractor pulling a water tank up the hill and it required fifteen loads to complete the task; the tractor grunting up the mountain towing its heavy load and bouncing down with the empty tank rattling behind it. We added the necessary chemicals, waited for the water to warm up in the sunshine and finally we were able to take our first bathe.

Raising the height of the pool had created a new problem; it sat above the surrounding ground like a ship awaiting its launch. A small ladder provided access on a temporary basis, but was obviously not the final solution. A broad terrace was needed to link the pool to the house; we considered filling the gap between the house and the pool with rubble and laying the terrace on top, but a little effort with a calculator showed that hundreds of tons of fill would be needed to make up the height. The house would hold it in place on one side, but walls would be needed on the other three sides to retain it.

My husband decided that it would be best to build walls and fit concrete beams between them and the pool sides, the beams could then be decked and the resulting terrace paved with tiles with a pool room under the terrace at its far end where the falling ground provided sufficient headroom.

This was a massive construction project and help would be needed, so we turned to Juan the local carrier. Juan had a fine new Renault lorry which had brought all of the materials for our house up the mountain. He was a small friendly man, tanned dark brown from spending much of the summer on building sites.

Despite his size Juan was able to deliver heavy beams, loads of blocks, roofing tiles, and bags of cement without any assistance. The secret lay in a small hydraulic crane fitted behind the cab of his lorry. Although it was quite compact, it could extend telescopically for an amazing distance to deposit the palleted materials wherever they were required. Bundles of pantiles, for example, would be set down on the gently sloping roof right by the side of the man who was fitting them and this avoided carrying the tiles up ladders. The crane was also used to set heavy reinforced concrete roof beams in place; they were simply unloaded from the lorry and lowered on top of the walls. If the lorry was unable to get close enough they were placed on the bucket of a tractor shovel which lifted them up to the top of the wall. The Majorcan workers are not lazy, but they do believe in mechanisation.

Juan warned us that we were undertaking a substantial task, but assured us that he knew just the man we needed to advise us and guide my husband in the use of unfamiliar materials. The following evening there was a knock at the door and Juan introduced us to Mateo who was short like Juan, but much more powerfully built. His face was creased with lines created by a permanent smile and his hands were like dry leather from handling the rough hollow blocks that are the prime component in most modern Majorcan buildings. We liked him instantly, he spoke no English but his Spanish was slow and clear and communication was never a problem.

My husband showed Mateo the drawings of what we proposed and he examined them at length; finally he turned to us and with a broad smile said: '*No Problema.*' It was agreed that he would call whenever he had a spare moment, to supervise the work and assist whenever four hands were better than two.

Mateo was quite unperturbed by any disaster. When the plaster that my husband had laboriously applied to a wall curled away to drop on to the earth, Mateo would quietly murmur '*tranquilo!*' to soothe his ruffled temper and show him how to throw the plaster from the trowel onto the wall so that it stuck. When his attempts to place mortar around the narrow edges of a hollow block resulted in it sliding off and into the hole in the middle Mateo took his trowel, which was quite unlike an English one because it had a long cranked handle, and drew it across the surface of the mortar to roll a sausage of mortar onto its face, a flick of the wrist then deposited it neatly on the edge of the block. It took a little while before my husband got the knack of it but soon the walls started to rise quite quickly.

Mateo was dark-haired and his face was covered by heavy stubble which never quite grew into a beard and we wondered when he shaved. He found it difficult to exist for longer than fifteen minutes without a cigarette and all our photographs of him show one dangling at an angle from the corner of his mouth. Periodically I would have to respond to a cry of '*agua!*' as the two men toiled in the blazing sun. We soon became very fond of our new helper, nothing was too much trouble and everything had to be perfect before it was approved by him smiling and saying '*bueno.*'

We were fortunate to have his advice and guidance because Majorcan building methods are very different from those used in England. When the walls reached the required height, reinforced concrete beams with an 'I' section were used to bridge the gap between them and the pool. *Bovedillas*, hollow cast objects with one curved and one flat face, were then slotted into the webs of the concrete beams with their curved side uppermost to form a rough deck. These had little strength and were really only formwork to support concrete which was poured over them to form a perfect arched bridge between the beams, strong enough to take any load.

The block walls were reinforced by metal rods inserted through the hollows at the corners and at intervals along the sides. Liquid concrete was then poured into the holes which acted as a mould to form reinforced concrete pillars, metal tie bars were then laid along the top of the walls and anchored to the end pillars to form a massively strong structure.

For privacy and safety the walls were continued above the new floor level and topped with a capping made from pantiles. These had to be cut to fit and Mateo produced the necessary machine with a disk which sliced through them like butter and never cracked the delicate pottery. Paving slabs were then laid over the concrete and Mateo worked out the levels so that all rainwater would drain into a large *aljibe* nearly as big as the pool in order to store it for use on the garden during the summer.

A stone balustrade was constructed to fill a gap deliberately left in the wall so as not to obscure our view to the coast, with a double flight of steps leading down to the ground on the side farthest from the house. An archway was made to permit access from the drive, a roof was built over part of the terrace to provide shade and finally the walls were plastered and painted.

Mateo guided my husband with every stage of the work, ensuring that tubes for the wiring for the lights were inserted as the walls were built; finding a carpenter to shape the roof beams for the covered part of the terrace and arranging for Juan to deliver the many tons of building materials that were required. It would certainly have been impossible without him. Eight years later the work he supervised has never displayed even the smallest crack.

We were delighted with the house and the high standard of the carpentry. Virtually no standard joinery was available on the island at that time so every door, window and shutter was made to measure in northern pine. When my husband was designing the room to house the pool filter and pump, he went to several builders' merchants asking for the dimensions of standard doors and windows so that he could allow for an appropriate hole, but he was always asked what size he wanted. This chicken and egg situation was resolved by the purchase of second-hand items salvaged from a demolition site which cost a small fraction of the price of purpose-made joinery.

We suspected that our builder might have been cutting his teeth when it came to central heating. The boiler was gigantic compared to the one that had efficiently heated our much bigger house in Surrey and large cast iron radiators were liberally scattered throughout the rooms. A substantial extension had been constructed to take the oil tank but when my husband entered it he found that the room, which had been built at considerable extra cost, held only a battered oil drum with a small puddle of oil at the bottom into which a copper pipe had been draped.

The builder explained that domestic oil tanks were not available in Majorca. We asked how we could have oil delivered by a tanker when we had so little storage capacity. The answer was simple; in those days, oil tankers visited large commercial premises but not private homes. We would find that fuel oil was obtainable at garages and we could take the car and collect some. Our much smaller boiler in England had used about four thousand litres of oil each year and we estimated that our consumption in Majorca would not be less than two thousand litres every winter. The car would be hard-pressed to transport so much fuel up the mountain.

Until this point we had not made any serious mistakes, but we were to regret our choice of a contractor to make us a fuel tank. In retrospect we realise that our butcher friend would have been able to warn us, but we foolishly put our trust in one of the British sharks who prey upon the expatriate community. Although we did not know it, he had left a trail of botched work throughout the area but he was plausible and assured us that one of his many companies specialised in metal work. As a favour he would have a tank specially made for us for only five hundred pounds!

We were probably fortunate that the tank ever did arrive, but we had at least been shrewd enough not to part with any money in advance. It came one morning in a very old Peugeot 504 estate which it completely filled. The car displayed British plates but was so dilapidated that it must have made the journey to Majorca a great many years before. It was driven by a tall, rough-looking Englishman who explained that he needed help to unload the tank. My husband went to assist and found that the interior of the car and most of the man's clothing were covered in orange primer. The tank was still wet as the painting had only been finished that morning after it had been loaded into the car and it was so slippery that it was impossible to grip. After several abortive efforts to dislodge it my husband, barely concealing his annoyance as he wiped his bright orange hands, told the man to go away and return when the paint was dry.

The following morning the old Peugeot again struggled up the hill and gasped to a halt in our drive, the tank still protruding through its open tailgate. The paint was by then touch-dry; it had hardened where it had been thinly applied but was still liquid where it had settled into fat runs. We decided that there could be no more delay as we needed to get the boiler working to supply our hot water, but it proved very difficult to prise the very heavy object from its cage. It was constructed from thick steel sheet which had been welded to form a container seven feet in length and three feet in each of its other two dimensions. Threaded pipes protruded at various points which served as hooks to anchor it firmly to the interior of the car. The language became bluer as hands and clothes turned orange. Eventually, with the aid of a crowbar used as a lever through an open rear door, the tank shot out of the car bringing with it assorted scraps of upholstery and head-lining.

A little plinth had been constructed to raise the tank about four inches from the floor of the room that had been built to accommodate it and with much grunting and heaving the tank was set on top of it. My husband was puzzled as he had imagined that it would be fitted with its greater length horizontal, but he was assured that it had been designed to stand upright in order to conserve floor space. After a few more hours work, it was connected to the boiler and filled with a few litres of oil. All went well, the boiler lit without difficulty and the fitter departed in his old Peugeot, now about six inches higher at the rear than when it had arrived.

We discovered a supplier willing to deliver oil and he promptly brought up a little lorry loaded with about ten large oil drums. It had a small electric pump but, as the motor was 220 volts, it had to be plugged into the house. Unfortunately the cable was too short to reach any socket and my husband had to drive down to the village for extension leads. Eventually there was the satisfying sound of 1000 litres of oil splashing into our new tank.

I heard the explosion shortly after tea. It was slightly muffled, but there was no possibility of doubt. The sound had come from the utility room where the boiler lived and when we opened the door a flood of oil rushed out and cascaded over the step.

The boiler had stopped working and a row of red lights indicated that something was very wrong. The immediate problem was obvious; a high pressure flexible hose leading from the supply pipe to the burner had burst and oil was pouring from the rupture. My husband ran to the oil tank, turned off all the stop cocks he could find, and the flow of oil eventually ceased.

By the time the old Peugeot arrived the following morning my husband had read the literature supplied with the boiler. It suggested two methods of siting an oil tank: it could be below the level of the boiler, in which case an integral pump would lift oil from the tank; or it could be mounted higher than the boiler with the pump disconnected, since the oil could flow by gravity. Our tank fitted neither category: when it was part-full its contents were below the boiler and needed pumping out; but above that point the oil level was higher than the boiler and no pump was needed. We now had about 600 litres of oil eager to flow to the boiler as soon as the valve was opened and about 400 litres that required pumping. Under the watchful eye of my husband, the fitter had to install an elaborate system of non-return valves and pressure control devices to enable the system to work and the old Peugeot and its driver were with us for over a week until it functioned correctly.

The boiler was now working well, but it was only connected to the chimney by a corrugated aluminium tube, so thin that it started to leak after less than a week. This was obviously a temporary measure and we were assured that the 'iron man' was making the required right-angled bend because no suitable component was available off the shelf.

The bend arrived a few days later, proudly carried by a workman who was the saddest looking man we had ever seen. Everything about him drooped; his shoulders, his mouth and especially his moustache. He held what appeared to be part of a suit of armour, elaborately constructed from about fifteen intricately shaped pieces of steel welded together. It was a minor work of art and might have been accepted by a London gallery.

This was no mere right-angled bend; it was delicately curved to permit the free flow of fumes and a little access trap had been incorporated which was closed by a tight fitting lid that could have been salvaged from an old iron kettle. He offered it to the boiler which promptly rejected it. It was not that it had been wrongly constructed, the problem was rather that it was a little too exact.

If a giant hand could have moved the boiler or the chimney, sufficient clearance would have been provided for the object to be fitted; but when it was attached to the chimney it could not be twisted to fit the boiler and if it was first joined to the boiler it could not be dropped enough to engage with the chimney. The dejected-looking fitter tried every possible method of making the connection and, when he realised that alterations would be required to his masterpiece, his moustache drooped even lower and an expression of utter disbelief flooded his face.

He returned a few days later triumphantly bearing a modified version which fitted without difficulty and it was rewarding to see his expression change from one of abject depression to the suspicion of a smile.

Our heating worked efficiently for several weeks, but one morning my husband descended the stairs and stepped into a pool of water. The entire marble floor in the *salon* was covered to a depth of nearly an inch and some carpets we had only just bought were soaked. After emergency mopping-up operations we telephoned the builder and a small army soon arrived, headed by Carlos's son.

It was obvious that a pipe under the floor had burst, but the problem was how to locate the source of the leak. Unfortunately there was no plan of the central heating layout; the pipes had simply been positioned on top of the concrete foundation as required to link up the radiators and covered with a layer of gravel which had been carefully levelled. The marble had then been laid in cement on top to form a sandwich that had filled with water. The leak could have been anywhere; water oozed from every skirting throughout the ground floor of the house.

Many suggestions were made as to how the leak could be traced. Perhaps, by placing an ear to the floor, the sound of gushing might be heard. In no time the ground floor, from which all of the furniture had by then been removed, was covered in prostrate forms getting first one and then the other ear wet in an attempt to put this idea into practice. The result was inconclusive so the next suggestion was implemented. This involved setting the boiler to maximum and then turning on the heating, the idea being that the source of the leak would heat up sooner than any other area and if we walked barefoot over it we could trace the leak.

The boiler worked until it was throbbing from its exertions and the near-boiling water was released into the central heating system which protested with loud clicks and bangs as pipes reacted to the sudden shock. We took off our shoes and walked over the floor to sense where it was hottest but there was only a general warming of the floor wherever a pipe ran underneath it, with no particular hot-spot. Although not the complete answer, this at least gave us an indication of how the pipes ran and we were able to estimate the possible position of joints.

We still shudder at the memory of the next stage of the repair work. The marble was my pride and joy and it shone like a mirror over approximately 150 square metres of flooring. The mournful labourer who had fitted the bend to the boiler took a chisel and proceeded to smash holes wherever a joint was suspected. By mid-day there were six large pits in the floor, each of which was full of water, making progress from the front door to the kitchen into a hazardous journey.

By day two, enough water had been bailed out to reveal the pipes at the bottom of the holes and, sure enough, one had split. Its function was to run the entire length of the house as the main feed pipe but a bend like a little hump-backed bridge had been inserted where it passed over another pipe running across the width of the floor. This prefabricated bend had taken the full force of the expansion and contraction of the very long run of copper pipe and had cracked with fatigue.

My husband caught the plumber just as he was soldering in an identical bend. He pointed out that a repetition of the problem would be inevitable unless the layout was changed, but the plumber thought otherwise; in his opinion the old bend had been faulty and the new one would effect the necessary repair. Our Spanish was not good enough to enable us to win this argument, especially as we were only amateurs contesting the expertise of professionals, so gravel was poured over the pipe, new marble was carefully set into the six holes and the furniture was replaced.

Thereafter we monitored the amount of water that was let into the system and it was not long before it was evident that far more than could be lost through evaporation was being used. Damp patches re-appeared on some walls and we knew that our problem had returned.

Our doleful friend again smashed his chisel into the polished marble, but this time he knew where to dig so the damaged area was reasonably small. We soon discovered that water was pouring out of the replacement bend and it was at this point that my husband took charge and insisted that the layout was altered to provide an expansion joint. That was six years ago and since then we have had no more trouble with the heating. We think that the plumber has now learned a little more about the coefficient of expansion of copper.

Our magnificent view to the south was marred by an ugly telephone pole which had been erected to enable a temporary line to be run to the site for use by the builder. At that time there was a shortage of lines and it was absolutely essential for us to have a telephone; so it was agreed that we would take over this crude installation and rent it from the builder; on the understanding that when our own line was allocated the pole would be removed and the wire would run underground from another pole which was well out of sight behind some trees.

The man who eventually came to install our own telephone was polite but firm. He was only authorised to work internally and could not interfere with the external line. We wanted one phone downstairs and an extension upstairs in our bedroom. He had no objection, but there was a problem. He was authorised to drill holes through walls but not in floors or ceilings. My husband asked if he could borrow his drill and make the hole for him; that was in order; so in a few moments that difficulty was overcome.

We were determined that the offending pole should go. In every photograph taken from the house it cut the view into two parts and we began to get quite paranoid about it. With the help of a Spanish-speaking friend we wrote to *Telefónica* asking them to remove the eyesore as soon as possible. My husband dug a trench along the new route of the line, buried a conduit to take the new wire and covered it with the required amount of concrete.

It was not long before a fleet of vans arrived at the gate, men swarmed up the pole, along the drive and around the new trench. My husband went out to explain how simple the task would be; they had merely to detach the existing wire from the top of the pole and thread it underground in the new tube he had constructed to lead it to the house. The work would take less than an hour, after which they could cut down the pole. However, there was another problem; they had not come to carry out the job merely to estimate for it and a letter would arrive in due course advising us of the cost.

When it arrived the quotation was for '*aproximado de 56,179 pesetas*' or about £280. We thought this rather high for an hour's work and delayed accepting the estimate until we had asked our friends for advice. Before we had a chance to do so help came from an unexpected quarter that night in the form of a terrible storm. Because the house is situated on top of the mountain we are so high that we were encircled by the lightning which flashed all around us and crashes of thunder shook the house. At the height of the storm there was a sizzling noise which was followed by a tremendous bang and all the lights went out.

In the morning we found that we had suffered considerable damage. The lightning had hit our main electricity supply box containing the meter which had been turned into a congealed mess of plastic and gear wheels. The pump for the swimming pool and the motor of the washing machine in the utility room were burned out. In addition, the lightning had struck the telephone wire, burned away its insulation and charred the offending pole. We contacted *Telefónica* and when their man arrived my husband told him not to worry about replacing the pole but to run the replacement wire from the pole hidden behind the trees and through the new conduit in order to reconnect the telephone. He did not argue and there was no charge.

A little while later our neighbour came with a power saw and cut down what remained of our *cosa antiestética*.

8. Friends and Neighbours

When we return to Britain to visit old friends we are frequently asked whether we feel homesick living abroad and how we fill in our time. We have never felt homesick because Majorca is now our home, so much so that when we are in Britain we sometimes find ourselves counting the days until we can return. As to keeping ourselves occupied, the problem is rather how to find enough time for our business interests, charity work, the house and garden, and an enjoyable social life.

In Surrey we lived in the heart of the commuter belt where husbands left home early to catch trains or drive to London, and returned exhausted about twelve hours later, ready for a meal, an hour or so of television and then bed. We loved entertaining, but our attempts to hold dinner parties during the week were likely to be sabotaged by one of the guests being detained at the office or by problems on the roads or railway, making it essential to invite them for no earlier than eight. By ten-thirty they were usually fighting to keep their eyes open and concerned about getting enough sleep to face the next day.

In Majorca many of the expatriates are retired or at least semi-retired so there is much more time for entertaining. We gradually widened our circle of friends until we were giving at least one dinner party a week and attending several others. Social life is also assisted by the hundreds of relatively inexpensive restaurants that make eating out affordable and enjoyable. After a few months we found that we could seldom go into Palma without meeting someone we knew and we began to encounter some of the characters that make life in Majorca so varied and interesting.

Most of our initial friends lived in local houses that had been built on land previously owned by Carlos. We discovered that many of them already knew all of the details of our new home because when a house is under construction everyone has a look round it to comment on the layout and speculate about their future neighbours.

Not long after we moved in an Englishman, looking rather like an eccentric professor, appeared unannounced on our terrace. He was elderly, little more than five feet tall and spoke in short sharp sentences, conveying the impression that he might lose his temper at any moment. His greying hair had not been cut for many months and fell well below his collar and his generally hairy appearance was emphasised by very bushy eyebrows and bunches of whiskers that sprouted from his nose and ears. A black cord connected a gold monocle, that he wore in his right eye, to the lapel of his jacket.

Within the space of a few minutes he had suggested that we had not provided enough storage space when we designed the house; told us that the hole for the pool was too deep; informed us that we would have great difficulty making a garden and added his opinion that we had arrived too late because Majorca was not what it was. He then stated that he had decided to sell his house, which was a little way below us on the hill, and return to England.

We still had about thirty almost new tea chests in which we had brought our books, china and kitchen utensils and, because of his impending removal, we thought that he might like them but he declined our offer saying that it could be some time before he found a buyer. He then painted a picture of gloom regarding the conduct of many of the British residents on the island and in particular warned us about another neighbour whom he suspected of being mixed up in drug smuggling.

His reasons were not entirely convincing. They centred on the fact that the man had a fierce Doberman guard dog and a high fence around his property. We suggested that the fence might be to keep the dog captive but he dismissed this with his second piece of evidence which concerned some lights. We had noticed these lights ourselves; one wall of the 'suspect's' home was sometimes floodlit in colour giving an unusual but quite attractive effect. The 'professor' explained that he had been observing these displays and had noticed that soon after the lights were switched on a large black car would often arrive. We ventured the opinion that they might be used to greet a regular guest, but he disagreed. He had calculated that they could be seen from the coast and were almost certainly a signal for drugs to be brought ashore from a boat and loaded into the car which would then bring them up to the house. We were more than a little relieved when he left abruptly and trotted off down the hill. At that time we never thought that we would eventually become very fond of our eccentric neighbour.

A week or two later we were driving home late at night after dining with some friends and were commencing the final ascent to our house when we were startled by a figure emerging from a bush by the side of the road. We soon realised that this apparition was the 'professor' so we stopped and asked him what he was doing out so late on such a dark night. 'Having a piddle,' he replied. There is abundant water where we live but it is not piped to the houses, instead they have large *cisternas* which are filled periodically from a tank drawn behind a tractor which fetches it from a local well. The system works efficiently and provides us with good quality water but we naturally have to pay for the service. The 'professor' was convinced that most of the water he bought was wasted by flushing his loo so he always used any convenient bush rather than add to his expenditure.

He was correct in his assumption that it would take him some time to sell his property. There were two reasons: the first was that the paperwork was not completely in order, a common situation with houses built some years ago but one which creates serious problems when one wishes to sell; the second was that his house had been built by the same doubtful character who had supplied our oil tank and several faults required rectification. One prospective purchaser suspected that something might be wrong and asked if he could roll back the lounge carpet, only to be subjected to a barrage of objections to such an unreasonable request. Other potential clients were given lectures on the rising cost of living on the island, the undesirable changes that were taking place and the eagerness with which the 'professor' was looking forward to leaving the island.

The situation was saved by his wife taking charge and insisting on him allowing her to sell the house; it was only after she persuaded him to go for a walk whenever a potential purchaser called that they eventually found a buyer.

They frequently came to dinner but only on the strict understanding that the 'professor' would use our bathroom rather than the garden as we were having quite enough problems with our plants. It was during one of these visits that they told us that they had definitely sold their house and would soon be leaving. As their car was only about three years old they wondered whether we would like to buy it because they did not want to take a left-hand drive model back to England.

The car was a Citroen estate with quite a large body but only a 1300 cc air-cooled engine. It found our hill a bit of a struggle and had such heavy steering that I could not manoeuvre it in car parks; its hand-brake lever looked like an umbrella that someone had rammed into the dashboard and it behaved like a camel when one started the engine, first lifting its front and then its rear as its hydraulic suspension pumped itself up with a series of clicks and flashing lights. A lever between the front seats enabled one to raise the body so high that it was quite difficult to get out and step down to the ground. It was, however, almost the perfect second car for us because when one raised the tail-gate there was a flat floor with not even the smallest lip at the rear. Bags of fertiliser and cement, bricks, tiles and chemicals for the pool could be loaded and unloaded with ease, the camel action of the suspension bringing them quite close to ground level once the engine was switched off.

We bought the Citroen and it proved to be very reliable apart from one fault which was intermittent but irritating. From time to time nothing happened when the key was turned to start it. The dashboard was ablaze with lights and we knew that the battery was in good condition, but there was not even the slightest click when this problem struck. Fortunately the car was one of the last models to be supplied with a starting handle so we were never stranded, but we decided that the fault must be attended to and went to our local garage which is run by a superb Majorcan mechanic called Toni.

It took several visits because the car was always cute enough to start perfectly every time Toni tried it, but eventually he tricked it into misbehaving and started delving into its wiring to trace the fault. He came back carrying a small hammer and a piece of chalk. 'You have a sticking brush in the starter' he explained. 'No problem, if this happens again all that is needed is that you hit the starter with a hammer here, not too hard, just enough to jerk the brush into contact'. He took the chalk and drew a cross to indicate the exact spot that should be tapped.

It was certainly an attractive solution cost-wise, but the car was due for its annual inspection which is quite rigorous in Spain. The idea of my husband taking out a little hammer, opening the bonnet and tapping the motor each time he was told to start the engine did not appeal to him, so he asked whether the brush could be replaced. '*Mucho trabajo,*' said Toni sadly. It seemed that the car had been assembled by laying the starter motor on the ground and then building the rest of the vehicle around it. Exhaust pipes, wires, tubes, a large cowl over the fan and possibly the radiator might have to be removed to gain access to the offending object, but my husband was adamant that the fault must be repaired.

We took the precaution of calling at the bank before going to collect the car the following day. When we arrived Toni was beaming, the car was ready and the bill was minimal. He explained that he had managed to extract the starter with difficulty but without taking the rest of the car apart. Once he had removed it he had inserted a new brush and we would have no more trouble. This was a typical instance of the fairness with which we have always been treated by local Majorcan traders; we were fully prepared for a large outlay and many garages would have replaced the entire starter rather than strip it down for repair.

It was only a month or so later that our other car developed an odd fault. It went very well until we tried to reverse it up a slope. On a flat road it was fine, but the slightest incline caused it to make very rude noises and then stall. It was remarkable how often we found that we had parked on a hill and needed to reverse when the noise was loud enough to attract quite a crowd. Our problem was to convey all of this in our elementary Spanish to Toni.

My husband drove the car to the garage and was met not by Toni but his very attractive young sister. We had taken the precaution of looking up 'fart' in our Spanish dictionary, but it was obvious that some other word would now have to be used to describe the very embarrassing noise. Eventually the conversation ended with her walking backwards up a ramp, blowing loud raspberries and finally collapsing into a fit of giggles. My husband said '*si*' and left the car at the garage, knowing that its fault would be correctly recorded.

A couple who had been living in Bermuda were renting a house next door to the 'professor' while they had a new home constructed on some land they had purchased nearby. One evening we heard loud howling, like a wolf or dingo and soon afterwards it was answered by a similar call. We discovered that whenever there was a new moon the 'professor' would start the howling when he went outside to visit his favourite bush before retiring for the night. His neighbour would then come out onto his terrace and reply in similar vein and the two of them would keep it up for several minutes.

Mr Bermuda was himself a colourful character. He had very definite ideas about the construction of his new home which was to include an unusual suspended spiral staircase. He appointed an architect but was unable to persuade him to depart from conventional techniques using available materials; so he sacked him and tried another with similar results. He had a little more success with the next until he discovered what he considered to be a serious error on the drawings. Architect number four died before he produced any proposals and at this point architect number three threatened legal action. Mr Bermuda left to buy a house in America before architect number five had submitted any suggestions and the site remains undeveloped.

Mr Bermuda's attempts at property development were followed very closely by another of our friends, the former butcher, who tended to have a single topic of conversation at any one time to which he would constantly return no matter how hard one tried to divert him. He would drop in occasionally to bring us some cuttings from his garden. While he enjoyed a beer, any discussion would inevitably turn to Mr Bermuda's latest attempts to build his dream house and the impracticality of departing from tried and tested local techniques. He considered himself to be an expert on building in Spain and he was indeed an invaluable source of advice on where materials could be obtained.

When Mr Bermuda left, the butcher switched his attention to our friendship with an elderly widow who had lived on the island for many years. He disliked her intensely but we enjoyed her company and ignored his continual warnings that we should not become too involved with her. I frequently found myself seated beside him at dinner parties and he would spend much of the evening cautioning me not to fall under her spell. With considerable effort, I could sometimes manage to get him off this topic and then found him quite amusing, but his habit of always returning to his favourite theme exhausted me.

Eventually he became obsessed with a new interest in the form of television. He installed TV in every room, including the kitchen and bedroom, and watched until late into the night. It was bad enough when he could only receive Spanish stations, but the day came when he installed a fully rotatable dish which could pick up satellite programmes from as far afield as Russia and China. At this point he virtually withdrew from local society and we have seen little of him since.

Several of our closest friends only spend part of the year on Majorca as they also have houses in Britain. Don and Laura have a holiday home quite near to us and we greatly look forward to their frequent visits. Don suffers from asthma and one summer he had an especially bad attack shortly after they arrived. We recommended Dr Michael Stoma, our own doctor, who immediately arranged for him to be transferred to hospital where he could receive proper care. After a few days he had almost recovered and was eager to return home and resume his holiday. He was discharged on condition that he had one final injection at home and left with a syringe and a phial containing the last dose. It was arranged that a male nurse would call at his house the next day to administer the injection.

The following morning a car drew up at the house and a smartly dressed man carrying a small case presented himself on the doorstep. Laura, who speaks little Spanish, mentioned the doctor's name, which the man obviously recognised, so she took him through to their bedroom where Don started to remove his trousers ready for his jab. They were astonished when the 'nurse' went off in a cloud of dust in a car piled high with carpets. They had accidentally discovered the perfect way of getting rid of a door-to-door salesman!

Only a little way down the road a Yorkshire couple with very broad accents purchased a bungalow. They were known locally as the 'Ee-by-gooms' and were what might be called accident prone. They had many minor misadventures but met with real trouble when they decided to build a swimming pool. Their site was unusual in that its magnificent view of the coast was ruined by a high voltage line which actually ran over their property. There was even a large pylon in their front garden which they were forced to make the centre-piece of a turning circle in their drive.

They had quotations from several suppliers of conventional pools but decided that the cost was prohibitive, so they elected to have a large prefabricated fibreglass pool. A firm price was agreed but problems started when the pool was delivered. 'Where is the hole?' asked the foreman of the gang that had come to undertake the installation. It transpired that the quotation they had been given was for the plastic part only and a hole would first have to be dug and a concrete base laid at extra cost.

At this point they made the mistake of engaging the doubtful contractor who was responsible for our oil tank and was always waiting in the wings to pounce on any unsuspecting victim in our area. At enormous expense he arranged for the digging of the hole and the essential concrete and the pool was then installed. Shortly after the work was completed a representative from the local Council visited them and pointed out that it was illegal and dangerous to have a pool underneath high voltage cables.

They approached GESA, the electricity company, to see if the pylon could be moved, but got nowhere. They examined the possibility of moving the pool to another location, but by then it had been firmly fixed and in any case there was not enough space to re-locate it. Finally, careful measurements established that only about one-third of it actually contravened the regulations, and the problem was solved by building a wall across it. The part under the power line was then filled with earth and planted with flowers and they were able to swim in what remained.

Some friends who live near the east coast of the island also had pool trouble; they built one without planning permission and were ordered to remove it. Being resourceful they lined it with polythene sheeting and filled most of it with sand before adding a thin layer of earth on top. Bushes were inserted without being removed from their pots and in next to no time there was no trace of the offending pool. A year or two later they applied for planning permission which was granted, so they simply disentombed the original pool which had survived its burial without damage.

Much of the local building activity is now supervised by a Majorcan called Raphael who used to drive the tractor that pulled the water cart. It took some time to discharge its load and on a hot day we would give him a cool drink and talk about the countryside which he knew like the back of his hand. One day he asked if he could continue to gather *setas* from our grounds and we gladly agreed. Raphael promptly disappeared into our woodland and returned carrying a handful of fungi which looked rather like open-gilled mushrooms but flatter and almost salmon-coloured. *Setas* are considered to be a great delicacy in Majorca and are sold in supermarkets for around £15 a kilo. Although we know approximately where he goes, we have never seen them growing and he seldom finds many, but only a few are needed to improve the flavour of a steak.

Gregoria is a jolly girl who had only recently been married when she came to help us six years ago. When we got to know her better, she brought us a videotape of her wedding and in the evening we settled down to watch it, anxious not to offend her by ignoring it, but fearing that it might be an amateur effort taken with a constantly moving hand-held camera. We could not have been more wrong and were treated to a professionally produced and edited insight into a Majorcan courtship and wedding. There were charming scenes of the couple before their marriage and then every detail of the ceremony was recorded, including a close up of the ring being slipped on to her finger, which seemed to have been filmed from behind the altar. After the church ceremony we were shown the reception where nearly all of the guests were related to the bride or groom. Majorcans tend to marry a partner from the same area so that many members of a family often live close to one another and this results in the large parties that are a common sight in local restaurants when an entire family gathers for a meal.

In autumn, after rain, our garden abounds with snails that are hungry and thirsty after the heat of the summer. Gregoria's family considers them a delicacy and we sometimes try to find some for her, but snail catching demands great knowledge of the habits of the snail. Fat snails emerge from under every pot and stone when we are gardening, but they have an early warning system which operates as soon as we commence a snail hunt and we can seldom find more than ten miserable specimens. Gregoria and her husband go into the woods near their home in the evening with a torch and soon collect several kilos. Majorcans even have a special vase-shaped clay pot in which to keep live snails called a *caragollera*. It is perforated with small holes and has a lid to retain the snails which can be kept in it for several weeks until required. Snails with garlic sauce are an almost universal item as a starter in any Majorcan restaurant.

Gregoria has had two daughters while she has been with us and I was concerned for her during her first pregnancy. She is normally pale but seemed to be unusually so and I was worried that she might be trying to do too much. At that time she was working for another family in the morning and I provided a snack lunch for her before she started her work. To build her up a little I made her nourishing soups which she enjoyed with fresh bread followed by some fruit or cheese and I decided that it would also do her good to have some Marmite which she viewed with some suspicion as she had not seen it before. I assured her that it was pleasant and left her to have her meal in peace.

Unfortunately, she spread the Marmite too thickly on her bread and took a large bite. When I returned I was reminded of the incident when A A Milne's Tigger ate some thistles. Poor Gregoria took a little time to recover and thereafter has treated British food with caution, but she loves lemon curd which was also new to her despite the fact that lemons cost next to nothing in Majorca when they are in season. Similarly she was unfamiliar with marmalade; oranges grow in abundance but the bitter Seville oranges used for marmalade are difficult to find in Majorca.

Tia, our Siamese, likes the quiet life and associates Gregoria with the noise of the vacuum, the movement of furniture and the general bustle of cleaning which she detests. She has come to know the sound of Gregoria's car and usually the first indication we have that Gregoria has arrived is when Tia gets up and trots purposefully to the utility room at the far end of the house where she remains until she hears her car depart some hours later.

One evening Tia failed to return. We called her at intervals throughout the night but by morning she was still missing and we started to search all of the places where she might have been shut in, including our own pool room, and a neighbour's cellar where she had twice spent a night. We also asked at all of the houses in the vicinity and contacted the animal refuges and the vet but nobody had seen her. After two days of worry we placed an advertisement in the Majorca Daily Bulletin and the local radio kindly broadcast a message, but we still had no news of her. My husband combed the mountain calling for her in case she had become trapped in a snare or up a tree, but to no avail.

By the sixth day we had virtually given up hope because we knew that she would have returned long before if she could. It was at ten thirty that night when we thought we heard her cry; we had deceived ourselves so many times before that we hardly dared believe that it was her, but on opening the door we found her lying exhausted on the mat. She was in a terrible state, very thin and hysterical and unable to stop crying; the pads of her paws were so sore that she lay on the bed with her legs hanging over the edge.

We have never discovered what happened to her or how she managed to find her way back, but within a week she had recovered completely.

The utility room is one of Tia's favourite spots because it contains the boiler; like all Siamese she loves warmth and on a cold day she will even sit directly on top of the metal box that contains the oil burner, despite the fact that it vibrates when it is working. In winter, for much of the day, she curls up and sleeps on a small table on which we have put an old cashmere jumper to provide her with a comfortable bed.

I went along there one morning to collect the washing and found the door had been left ajar all night. I took little notice of the cat asleep on the table until I realised with surprise that, although it was a Siamese, it was not Tia who is a chocolate point with an almost white coat. This was a young seal point male who woke and greeted me with tremendous affection, rubbing himself all around my legs and trying to climb up for me to hold him. I had just bent down to stroke him when Tia burst through the door and instantly leapt at him, boxing his ears and trying to get a grip on his neck, screaming at the top of her voice.

The stranger behaved perfectly and did not retaliate so I managed to prise Tia away. I shut him safely in the utility room while I carried Tia, rigid with fury, growling with rage and with her tail like a flue-brush, into the house where she paced the floor looking for a means of escape to continue the battle.

I took some food and water to our visitor which he much appreciated and I decided to hold him prisoner while I made some enquiries about him since he was in perfect condition and had obviously come from a good home. I telephoned our vet who promised to let it be known that we had found a Siamese. Meanwhile Tia was going berserk and I knew that I would have to find a safer place for the stray until his owner was located.

A young couple had recently moved into the professor's old house. They had no cat and I explained the situation to them and asked if they would be willing to provide a home for my captive even though it might only be temporary. They had always wanted a Siamese and gladly agreed, so I took him down to them in a basket. By evening they had completely fallen in love with him and he had made friends with their Collie.

It was not until nine that night that we had a telephone call from a young Spanish girl who said that she had lost her cat and the vet had told her that we had found one. It was soon obvious from her description that the cat was hers and I promised to meet her half an hour later. We collected him from his new friends, who were very sorry to see him go, and drove him down to the village where his entire family was waiting. The reunion was a joyous affair; they told us that his name was *Rubi* and that he had been missing for four days. They had no idea why he had walked the four kilometres up the mountain and were delighted to have him back as they had almost given up hope.

Although she is now nearly fourteen, Tia is still active enough to spring at anything that moves, but too sensitive and set in her ways to be put into a cattery. Our closest neighbours are an Englishman called George and his Spanish wife, Carmen; fortunately Carmen adores cats. so when we are going away we clear the house of fragile ornaments and Tia is free to roam in her familiar surroundings. Twice a day Carmen comes in to groom and feed her and take her for a walk on her collar and lead which she loves.

Tia walks like a dog although we have never trained her and some years ago when she was young she had a very pretty green collar with a bell of which she was especially fond. It incorporated a piece of elastic to enable her to slip it off if she caught it in a branch and one day she came home without it. We bought her another and forgot about the incident until she returned about a week later obviously delighted and proudly carrying the original collar in her mouth.

Like most Siamese she is a fussy eater and for years insisted on fresh chicken or meat. Attempts to feed her tinned food were treated with the ultimate insult of her trying to cover it up. Not long ago a manufacturer of cat food advertised on television showing two cats having a conversation. Tia, who is usually totally disinterested in TV, saw this commercial and her head stretched upwards as she took in every detail. She was so taken by it that we drew her attention to it whenever it was shown, always with the same reaction; sometimes she even got up and went nearer to the screen to study it in more detail and one evening curiosity overtook her completely and she leapt on top of the television in order to have a look behind.

Partly as a joke, we bought a tin of the product advertised and gave her some. She loved it and started eating as soon as her saucer was put in front of her, something she would never do with fresh food which has to be inspected and stalked from several directions before it is sampled. Since then she has lived largely on that particular brand although we are still mystified as to how this dietary transformation has come about.

Majorcan restaurants serve very generous portions and sometimes we are unable to finish them. The waiters never object to a request for *una bolsa por el perro* or doggy bag and Tia enjoys the highly flavoured samples of Majorcan cooking that come to her in this way. She even has her favourite establishment which cooks lamb to her idea of perfection.

Carmen gets on very well with Tia while we are absent, and Tia obviously likes and trusts her because she would never allow any stranger to groom her or take her out for walks. But as soon as we return she completely ignores her and walks across her terrace without a sideways glance while Carmen tries to attract her attention. We are very fortunate that Carmen is so forgiving and good hearted.

Carmen's husband, George, first came to live on the island with his parents in 1932. They were enchanted by Majorca and, soon after arriving on the island, bought a piece of land on the coast at Portals Nous where they built a house by the sea. George remembers those early days when his playmates would converse together in Majorcan and then turn to him and speak in Spanish because he was foreign and one did not speak Majorcan to foreigners. When cycling to and from school he would hitch a tow up the hills by hanging on to one of the horse-drawn carts that carried brushwood from the forests into Palma where it was used to fuel the bread ovens. This activity resulted in the constant clearing of the undergrowth and dead branches from beneath the trees and helped to prevent the spread of fires.

George's mother was Dina Moore Bowden, an American with a deep love for Majorca. Being Californian, she was greatly interested in the fact that Fray Junipero Serra 'the coloniser of California' was born at Petrá on the eastern side of the island. She founded a small modern progressive school in El Terreno in rooms above the old soda water factory that later housed the first Anglican church. Foreign children of several nationalities attended it until the early days of the Civil War when George and his family left Majorca aboard *HMS Repulse.* They returned in 1937 when it was evident that the island was unlikely to be involved in the conflict.

George was sent to study in the UK in 1938 and served in the Royal Navy during the Second World War during which his parents left Majorca and settled in Portugal where the Quaker Refugee relief organisation in Lisbon asked Dina Bowden to assist them in their work. She had studied music in Vienna and spoke fluent German which helped her to assist many refugees from Nazi occupied Europe to escape and find shelter in the new world. She also persuaded Americans to sponsor them so that they could enter the United States, but her success in these activities was terminated when the authorities forced her to leave Lisbon. Eventually the couple reached England where Dina was promptly enlisted into the YMCA/YWCA to organise and run a canteen near a Fleet Air Arm base on the Isle of Man.

When the war ended she returned with her husband to Majorca and resumed her efforts to promote the island. In 1949 she collected Majorcan artefacts, costumes and photographs of Fray Junipero Serra's birthplace in Petrá, packed them all into twelve suitcases and set off for California where the bi-centennial of his arrival in 1749 and the centennial of the Pioneers in 1849 were to be celebrated. Her Majorcan exhibition was exceptionally well-timed; it was shown in cultural centres in many cities where it attracted considerable interest and, on returning to Majorca, she found that she had received a great deal of publicity in the Majorcan press and was joyfully welcomed home.

To enable foreigners, and especially writers, musicians and artists who visited Majorca, to meet the local people Dina Bowden started *Los Amigos de Mallorca*, a social circle which held regular receptions in the restaurant at the popular local meeting place close to the Cathedral on Calle Conquistador which was known as the *Circulo Mallorquin.* These resulted in a great many interesting and valuable contacts being made and the receptions became very popular. Every year, shortly before Christmas, an especially large event was held to which the Civil Governor was invited; the proceeds were used to buy gifts for the 'Day of the Three Kings' when children traditionally receive their presents and they were personally handed to the children in one of Palma's orphanages by a member of *Los Amigos de Mallorca.* This work was recognised by the Spanish Government and Dina Bowden was decorated with the honour of the *Lazo de Dama por Merito Civil.*

In 1962 George, then living in Vancouver, assisted with the organisation of the Spanish exhibit at the World Fair in Seattle. His mother was much involved in the preparation of the displays which included a model of Junipero Serra's house in Petrá. George organised four groups of flamenco dancers and guitarists to liven up the exhibit and noted that by the time they returned to Spain they had all sold their guitars. It was evident that there was a ready market for Spanish guitars on the American Continent and in 1963 George decided to import good quality guitars and sell them in a shop in Vancouver. He employed teachers to operate a scheme whereby customers could pay $20 for the loan of a guitar and eight lessons to enable them to decide whether they wished to continue and, if so, which type of guitar to purchase.

Because he found that the performance of the guitars he imported varied greatly, George returned to Majorca in 1964 to organise the manufacture of instruments of more consistent quality. For a time he had a workshop in the then new Pueblo Español and later opened a shop close to Frank Short in the Avenida Antonio Maura. Sales to tourists soon absorbed all he could produce and the Canadian operation was eventually abandoned. Meanwhile his mother wrote many articles about Majorca and her excellent book giving an account of the early life of Junipero Serra was published in 1976. It is illustrated by superb photographs by Stefan Laszlo.

George has devoted much of his life to research into the design and construction of the guitar and he is one of the world's leading authorities on the subject. While there is no such thing as the perfect guitar and different qualities are required according to the intended use, it is possible to achieve equal performance from each string, coupled with great depth of tone and duration of note. By applying techniques that he has mastered by the minute study of historic instruments and much research into materials and the geometry of construction, George has made fine guitars for many leading players. It was only in 1994, some years after he retired, that he produced an instrument that totally satisfied him. He is confident that he is now capable of consistently reproducing the same quality because the superb performance is the result of applied knowledge rather than fortunate accident.

9. A Cinema under the Stars

The coastal area west of Palma comprises a series of bays, many of which originally had rocky beaches that have since been extended and replaced with sand. A motorway extends as far as Palma Nova and forms a division between the highly developed southern coastal strip and a range of hills – the *Sierra Burguesa* – a little way inland to the north. Although recently scarred in places by a severe fire, the hills are still largely pine-clad and they provide a perfect green back-drop to contrast with the clear blue sea and sky and the largely white hotels and apartment blocks. Even much maligned Magalluf looks very attractive when seen across the Bay of Palma from the motorway, especially at night.

Cala Major and Sant Agusti (usually listed in holiday brochures as Cala Mayor and San Agustin) are two of the earlier holiday resorts close to Palma that are working hard to recapture their former glory. Extensive roadworks have been undertaken to provide wide pavements enhanced by palms, and the area has certainly been improved, but it is still rather run-down in places and the Nixe Palace hotel, once one of the best on the island, stands forlorn and empty on its magnificent site adjoining the sea. Although it has lost some of its popularity as a holiday resort, the area abounds in apartments, bars and restaurants and is well served by public transport. Being close to Palma with a frequent bus service, it is particularly suitable for those who want a permanent or holiday home that does not involve the expense of a car.

There is a sandy beach at Cala Major which tends to be crowded during the day but most of the bathers had departed when we went there one summer evening to see a free film show arranged by the Palma Council. The film was to be shown in English with Spanish subtitles so we took two folding 'director' chairs and went along. Two towers had been erected close to the sea with a huge screen stretched between them and as it grew dark the audience, almost entirely Majorcan and mainly in beachwear, started to arrive until several hundred were sitting expectantly on the sand. We must have looked slightly odd, dressed in street clothes and seated in our chairs, but the sand was damp and nobody minds a little eccentricity in Majorca.

An enormous projector, looking like a small traction engine, was dragged into place. It had a chimney to cool its lamp while on each side a giant film spool resembled a wheel. The reels were big enough to hold two hours of film and thus avoid the need to have any break in the performance. The operator switched the lamp on and off several times and, appearing to be satisfied, commenced to thread the film through a complex path that started on one side of the machine, rose skywards over the top and descended to the take-up reel, passing through the film gate in the process.

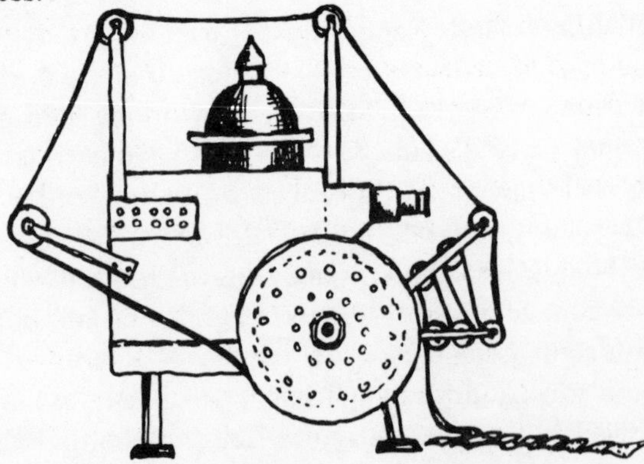

A short length of the film was shown to test the set-up and then rewound and we knew that the performance was about to begin. It was an excellent film and it was five minutes or so before I took my eyes off the screen to glance at the projector.

There was complete pandemonium. A couple had made themselves comfortable on the sand underneath the raised platform on which the projector was standing and soon after the start a snake of film had descended into their laps. Thereafter it had continued to pour onto them and they were desperately trying to keep many yards of it out of the sand while making frantic efforts to attract the attention of the operator who could not hear them above the noise of the sound-track. It was some time before matters were sorted out but in due course the film was correctly threaded and the performance continued without further trouble. We thoroughly enjoyed our unusual evening in the cinema under the stars.

After the film show we went a little further west to San Agusti which starts where Cala Major stops. It also is largely comprised of restaurants, cafés and bars including an Italian pizzeria, La Trattoria, which is one of our favourite places for an inexpensive meal as it has a terrace by the sea and serves some of the best pizzas on the island as well as other Italian dishes. It is very popular with the Majorcans who often come in large parties late in the evening.

We like to eat out on Sunday and one of the best places for a traditional English roast is Bennett's, also in San Agusti, just off the main road up a turning opposite the Yacht Club. It is British-run and offers delicious roast beef carved at the table.

The next resort is Illetas where two small sandy beaches are hard-pressed to serve the many hotels in the area. Nearby is The Anchorage, a very attractive large development of houses in an unusual architectural style which ideally suits the location; the actual address being Bendinat. A legend states that when King Jaime I of Aragon was victorious in a battle against the resident Moors, shortly after his landing at Santa Ponça, he rested in the tent of one of his supporters and ate a frugal meal after which he said '*Be hem dinat*' meaning 'We have eaten well'. This was corrupted into Bendinat.

The area now features a 9 hole golf course which has plans for extension to 18 holes. The Restaurante Hoyo 10 in the club house is open to non-members and offers a good fixed-price menu in a very pleasant setting with a view over the golf course. It was here that I held a dinner to celebrate the 75th anniversary of Save the Children Fund which is well supported by the British community on the island.

During the summer a series of free concerts are arranged on one of the greens near the club house which can be enjoyed by diners in the restaurant and anyone else who cares to come. These do not start until it is dark so those attending usually bring chairs or mats, because the grass can be damp, and some arrive with a complete picnic including wine. Although these concerts have now become very popular there is always plenty of room for everyone; they are advertised in the local press and details can also be obtained from any information centre on the island.

The next major development on the main coast road is Portals Nous which has a good sandy beach running west to Puerto Portals. This is a large and very attractive marina with all of the buildings painted ochre and white. Motor and sailing yachts of every size are packed into the harbour and there are many shops selling everything a yachtsman (or yachtswoman) might require, including several fashionable boutiques. There are also dozens of cafés and restaurants to suit every taste and pocket.

Continuing along the coast, just before Marineland, the French Coffee Shop is ideal for breakfast, morning coffee, afternoon tea or an inexpensive snack lunch. Marineland itself has earned an international reputation for its expertise in marine biology and is often involved when Mediterranean marine life is in danger. It is a very popular tourist attraction and packs a remarkable number of exhibits into a limited area, the highlight being a superbly presented dolphin display. There are also performances by parrots and sea-lions together with penguins, a small zoo and an aquarium.

Only a few hundred yards away the Sporting Tenis Playa development on the left offers a restaurant, eight good tennis courts which are illuminated in the evening, a gymnasium and sauna, a swimming pool, and access to a small beach. We attended a function held at the Tenis Restaurant during which a number of diners were seated at tables in a line close to a wall.

Suddenly a piercing yelp interrupted the lively buzz of conversation; a waiter, making difficult progress between the wall and the customers he was serving, had caught the button of his sleeve in the elaborate blonde coiffure of one of the ladies. Her exceptional concern was due to the fact that she was wearing a wig which she was about to lose at any moment. The waiter disentangled himself with difficulty, laughing so much that he nearly anointed her with the soup he was carrying. Thereafter, whenever he passed behind her she clutched her crowning glory.

A little after the Tenis complex the Hotel Punta Negra has two small semi-private beaches and serves fine meals in its restaurant. It enjoys a beautiful location on a headland and offers some welcome seclusion in an area which tends to be somewhat over-developed.

Next comes Son Caliu, easily identified by the huge Mercadona supermarket on the right which has excellent fish and meat counters. Almost opposite, the Restaurante Son Caliu is a firm favourite with both Majorcans and the expatriate community; in the evening it serves international meals in the medium price bracket, but at lunch time it excels with a superb Majorcan *menú del dia* which must be one of the best value-for-money meals on the island and it is necessary to go early to get a table in the courtyard in the summer. There is a small but attractive sandy beach at Son Caliu which is hidden behind the large hotel of the same name.

Continuing west, the next development is Palma Nova. The beach has recently been substantially widened to make this a very attractive area for bathing or just lying in the sun. The coast road is lined with restaurants, cafés and bars, but most are not very tall and as they are situated on the north side, away from the sea they can hardly be seen from the beach. At its eastern end, close to a little harbour, the Gran Dragon restaurant, which has a twin establishment in Palma, offers Chinese cooking, while to the west Ciro's, formerly an up-market restaurant, now offers meals in the medium price bracket.

Further to the west, the Playa de Palma Nova now comprises a long, wide sandy beach which stretches as far as Magalluf. Our most recent visit there was to attend a morning service in one of the hotels. After we left we stepped straight into the bustle of a popular holiday resort but it still had a human touch in the form of an old Majorcan riding a moped which had a grinding wheel fixed on the pillion. He tooted a bulb horn, set his machine on its stand and stretched a belt from a pulley on the engine to another pulley on the spindle of the grindstone; a turn of the pedals fired the motor and he was ready for business. Waiters hurried from the restaurants and hotels carrying knives to be sharpened and he seemed set for a busy morning.

The next town is Magalluf. Seldom has any resort suffered worse coverage in the British press and on television, but a visitor could be forgiven for thinking that this criticism related to some other place. We have been there many times and have never seen any disturbance. It is true that parts of it resemble a cross between Southend-on-Sea and Blackpool with a little bit of Soho thrown in; if one searches for sleazy bars and wet T-shirt contests they can be found, but we stayed at two hotels in the area while our house was being built and it was just like being in any other lively resort. The large hotels just outside the town enjoy excellent sea views and are well removed from the noise and bustle of the centre while the sea front has been greatly improved by a multi million pound investment in the construction of a pedestrian precinct and substantial widening of the beach.

A popular story on the island concerns an Englishman and a Spaniard who were putting the world to rights over a bottle of wine. The conversation turned to Gibraltar and the Spaniard suggested, since it was no longer of any significant military importance to Britain, that it might one day be returned to

Spanish sovereignty. The Englishman thought about this for a while and answered: 'I suppose that it is a possibility at some time in the distant future, but we will never give up Magalluf!'

There is entertainment of every kind in Magalluf and too many hotels, restaurants, cafés and bars to mention. Most cater for British tastes and a large number of the bars are British owned or managed. It is certainly not necessary to speak Spanish in order to eat there and the names of the establishments, which include the Benny Hill Pub, The Prince William Pub, The Mucky Duck, and Lady Diana's, reflect the market for which most of them cater. The area throbs with life in the season and the tour operators arrange concerts in the larger hotels to suit those visitors who are not attracted by the brightly lit bars and discos. Children love the beach, pédalos and boat trips, so Magalluf can truly claim to offer a fun-packed holiday for all age groups.

The BCM Disco in Magalluf is one of the largest in Europe. Nemo Submarines operate from offices in the town and take passengers by boat to the little island of Sech, a short way off the coast, from where they provide a 45 minute underwater ride in a submarine; other holiday entertainment close to Magalluf includes The Pirates, a dinner and show with much audience participation in a Caribbean setting; Go Karting on a large track close to The Pirates; and a huge Aquapark which features water slides of every description.

To the west of Magalluf a peninsular extends southwards and far down on its east side Portals Vells offers three small sandy beaches, one of which is nudist. The others are served by boat trips and can become very crowded in the afternoon, but there is usually some space until lunch time. Close by there is the only Casino on the island; in addition to the usual gambling facilities, it stages spectacular shows on one of the largest stages in the Mediterranean which can be enjoyed in the 2000 seat auditorium with or without dinner. It is necessary to show a passport or *residencia* before entering the gambling room but they are not required for the restaurant and floor show. In the centre of this area, near El Toro, the Golf de Poniente offers 18 holes in a fine location.

On the other side of the peninsular from Magalluf, Santa Ponça caters more for the family holiday, with a good sandy beach, plenty of shops, cafés, bars and restaurants, and entertainment including pédalos, water skiing and boat hire. There is a championship 18 hole golf course, the Club de Golf de Santa Ponça, and horse riding is also available in the area. There are many places to eat in and around Santa Ponça and for dinner in attractive surroundings we like the Restaurante Terraza Barbieri at the *Club Nautico* which specialises in fresh fish and shellfish. A little further on, the road climbs to the top of the cliff from where there is a fine view of the bay and the Isles de Los Conejos and Malgrats which are a prominent feature of the seascape.

A large cross on the point of Sa Caleta, on the promontory which divides Santa Ponça beach from its port, commemorates the landing of King Jaime I in 1229. The chapel nearby houses a stone which was used as an altar for the first mass celebrated by the Christian army after their invasion. The King then progressed eastwards and Palma surrendered to him on December 31st, effectively bringing to an end a period of Moorish rule which had lasted for over 300 years. His victory marked the start of a period of prosperity for Majorca but Muslim residents were persecuted and most of their possessions were divided amongst the victors.

The Jews, who had co-existed peacefully with the Arabs, were treated more kindly, mainly out of respect for their commercial connections and skills in crafts such as map-making, silverware and jewellery, but they were heavily taxed, wore prescribed clothing and had to live in Ghettos, mainly in areas behind the Cathedral in Palma.

The area from Illetas to Paguera is part of the Municipality of Calvià which is one of the wealthiest in Spain. Social activities continue throughout the year making it an excellent choice for a holiday during the winter months when some other resorts are closed.

The town of Calvià is the administrative centre for the Municipality but it is still little more than a village. Its importance being indicated only by its large church and immense new Town Hall. There are few shops and many of those that exist are unmarked. This is common in villages where most trade is local. It was over a year before we discovered that there was a butcher in the town as his door and shutters had been closed whenever we passed and there was no trace that a shop existed. It was only when we noticed a customer leaving the premises that we looked in and saw him at work.

We were told about the superior bread available from a baker at the top of the town almost next door to a little supermarket. On parting some chain curtains and looking in through the doorway of what appeared to be a private house we discovered a veritable Alladin's cave. Not just bread but *ensaimadas* and other pastries, wine, groceries, vegetables and fruit crammed the shelves. Through a curtain at the back the family could be seen watching television, totally undisturbed by the activity in the shop.

There are several restaurants in Calvià. For those requiring an inexpensive meal with a local flavour, Ses Forquetes, a small restaurant incorporated into the lowest floor of the Town Hall building, offers a good *menú del día.* Nearby Ca na Cucó specialises in Majorcan cuisine while Meson Ca'n Torrat, long established in the town, has moved to attractive new premises in the main street. It is a family-run restaurant serving local and international food and is very popular with the Majorcans.

Slightly harder to find, but well worth the effort, Es Comellà lies just north of the town. It is run by an English family and attracts many expatriates for dinner or Sunday lunch. I have used it for several dinners in aid of the Save the Children Fund and each one has sold out completely within a week or so of the venue being announced. Charity dinners provide a welcome opportunity for the British expatriates to make up parties and enjoy a pleasant evening with their friends in a convivial atmosphere while helping to raise money for a good cause.

10. Saints and Sinners

An ecumenical service is held every year in the Cathedral in Palma and it is always filled to capacity. On one occasion, although we arrived early, we still had to sit in the choir stalls as the entire nave was full. The majority of the churches in Majorca are, of course, Roman Catholic and the buildings and their contents are extensively described in most guide books but the Anglican Church also has a story that is not so well-documented.

Although Anglican services were held for some British construction workers near Alcudia in the 1860's, the history of the Anglican church in Majorca really commenced in 1925 in a tea-room run by Mr and Mrs Frank Short, the grandparents of the man who had so efficiently arranged the importation of our furniture. A Chaplain would come over occasionally from Barcelona to conduct services in the tea-room and this arrangement continued until 1934 when the first Anglican Church in Majorca was opened in a converted soda-water factory in Terreno.

Two years later when many British residents, including Robert Graves, were evacuated aboard *HMS Grenville* and *HMS Repulse* at the outbreak of the Spanish Civil War, the Anglican Church was used as a store room for many of their possessions. It was fortunate that the wife of the British Vice-Consul paid the rent throughout the period of the conflict because, when Generalísimo

Franco subsequently came to power, Anglicans were only permitted to have a church on the island as it was considered to have been in continuous existence before and during the war.

The first Chaplain, a retired priest who was already living on the island, received no stipend but his pension was augmented from the collections. The church was not allowed to advertise its existence in any way and a notice reading 'Please Close the Gate' served as a signal that a service was being held. It was quite normal for two armed members of the *Guardia Civil* to position themselves at the back of the room during the sermon and the Chaplain did not wear his collar or surplice outside the church. At the end of the service he would stand at the door to shake hands with his congregation, first taking care to ensure that an adequate quantity of Jeyes fluid had been poured down a particularly offensive drain near his feet.

The present Anglican Church of St Philip and St James in the Son Armadans district of Palma was completed in 1966 and financed from local contributions and a £5000 donation from the Benham Charitable Trust. It comes within the Diocese of Gibraltar in Europe but has to be self-supporting, receiving no subsidy of any kind from Britain. Its congregation is responsible for the full stipend of its Chaplain together with his insurance, accommodation, heating, lighting, telephone, car, petrol, travel, and other expenses and the current expenditure of about 8 million pesetas (£40,000) is met from the collections, interest on investments, sales of second-hand items in its Thrift Shop and conventional fund-raising activities such as bazaars and raffles.

We soon found ourselves involved in many of these events which can be enormous fun when there is a good team. For some years I was responsible for the accounts for the Thrift Shop which is well worth a visit by anyone with an hour or so to spare in Palma on a Thursday morning. It is held in the Coleman Hall below the church and it abounds with bargains, predominantly in women's clothing but also costume jewellery and bric-à-brac.

We have known three Chaplains, although we came to Majorca towards the end of the term of the first of them when some tension had developed between him and the Council. We never knew the full details but remember that when they attempted to present him with a small parting gift he shut himself in his house and refused to come out to accept it.

The next Chaplain was a very devout and retiring man who had no secretary but somehow managed to handle an immense amount of work without any fuss or publicity. At that time he was responsible for the Anglican services in Palma, Menorca, Puerto Andratx and Cala D'or as well as visiting the sick, conducting funerals and performing the many other duties expected of an Anglican priest. Incredibly, the total cost of running the church at that time, including his stipend, travel and other expenses, amounted to less than £25,000 a year.

He had a very strong Geordie accent and was preaching a sermon one Palm Sunday when he came to the point where Jesus rode into Jerusalem on an ass. Eyebrows shot up all around the church as he appeared to say 'There he was, not riding like a king on a fine horse, but sitting humbly on his arse.'

Shortly before he left, a windfall was received in the form of a gift of £100,000 from a landowner who first offered the money elsewhere but, when it was refused, elected to donate it to the Anglican Church. Unfortunately much of the extra income from this substantial capital sum has subsequently ben absorbed by greatly increased administrative expenditure.

Although he was also middle-aged and single, the next Chaplain was a total contrast to his predecessor. He had been born and raised in Northern Ireland and was utterly ruthless in his determination to modernise the church and obtain the maximum possible publicity for all of its activities. It was obvious that his coming would involve dramatic changes and we decided to assist him to the best of our ability; my husband became a Churchwarden, while I was elected to serve on the Council with the special task of organising a social programme to celebrate the 25th anniversary of the consecration of the present building.

The Chaplain knew that there were many wealthy people living on Majorca who might be sympathetic towards the

Anglican Church, even though they did not attend his services. He decided that a grand ball should be organised which he thought would attract them even if the price was exceptionally high and he hoped that it might become the main annual social event on the island. Our research soon indicated that this was a risky enterprise because many members of the expatriate community who were not regular churchgoers seemed willing to support any external charitable activity in which the church was involved but they were reluctant to finance its mounting internal expenditure. Several long-time residents, including members of our own circle of friends, were quick to resurrect details of its past that we had never heard mentioned, although my husband was busy producing a booklet on its history based on a lecture presented some years before by Neville Waters, a former Churchwarden. We were even told about an incident concerning a previous Chaplain who had eventually been defrocked by the Bishop.

The majority of the Council decided that the chance to wear anything up to a tiara would have irresistible appeal and a Grand Ball was scheduled for June 22nd. The ballroom of the Royal Yacht Club was reserved for the evening and we did our best to attract support, with full backing from the local paper and radio station, but it was obvious by mid-May that we had a turkey on our hands.

The Council was just considering how to cancel the project without too much loss of face, when an impresario announced that he had hired the Auditorium in Palma for the same night. He planned to stage a large concert supported by several famous artistes who would be coming out from Britain to perform in aid of charity. No time was lost in preparing a statement that the Church would reluctantly abandon its Grand Ball so as not to dilute the audience for such a worthwhile event. A banner headline in the Majorca Daily Bulletin the following day read '*Eight Months Of Work Go Up The Spout*' while a subhead stated '*Big night at yacht club won't go ahead because of clash*'.

A more successful project concerned the replacement of the plain windows in the church with stained glass. There had been insufficient money available for this when the church was built, but the concept was revived in time for its twenty fifth anniversary and the congregation, which averages around fifty regular supporters and a scattering of visitors, was asked to find the funds.

To our delight, our friend Nils Burwitz was selected as the artist for the design of the 1.2 metre high and 9 metre wide area of glass which stretches across the width of the church above the main door. His initial proposals, presented as water-colour sketches, were exhibited in the church and they attracted very favourable comment, so he prepared full sized panels in oil on canvas to give a better idea of the final effect. These panels were converted to stained glass by Nils who worked in Barcelona with a leading expert called Pere Canovas, the glass sections finally being cut in the Queixelos workshop. They show Christ, his twelve apostles and St Luke, all with their appropriate symbols, but the setting is unusual in that it depicts not the Holy Land but places and objects that are familiar features of the Balearics.

The church is a little difficult to find but a visit to inspect this unique example of modern stained glass is well worthwhile. It is situated in a small road called Nuñez de Balboa which leads off the Calle de Andrea Doria and it is marked on the Firestone map as *Iglesia Anglicana*, right alongside the telephone exchange which is shown as *Teléfonos*.

When the windows are viewed from the interior of the church the colours of the background run in a rainbow sequence from deep purple behind St Matthew in the left-hand panel to a strong red behind St John on the right. This is counterbalanced by another rainbow created by the colour of the robes the apostles are wearing, from the purple of St John to the ruby red of St Matthew's cloak. The yellows of the two rainbows meet in the centre panel, depicting Christ as the source of light.

It was during a visit to Chartres Cathedral that Nils saw a design in the form of a labyrinth on the floor of the nave.

Labyrinths symbolise the tortured path of the soul in its journey through life, ending with enlightenment at the centre. Nils has used one to form the halo around the head of Christ in the centre of his design; it is extended on both sides to link with halos around the heads of the saints.

The panels show St Matthew holding a book in which money bags are depicted to recall his position as a tax collector for King Herod, while above his head an angel blows a trumpet. Next comes St Matthias who replaced Judas Iscariot; he was martyred by being crucified and his body is said to have been mutilated afterwards, so he is shown with a cross and a double-sided axe. The Judas tree blooms behind his head and a hebrew candelabra at the right of the panel commemorates what is thought to have been the first Jewish service to be held in Spain for 500 years. It was held in the old Anglican Church in El Terreno in 1966, two years before the passing of the Law of Religious Liberty, and was arranged by Benjamin Roth who wrote a column in the Majorca Daily Bulletin for many years under the name of Benito.

The next panel shows St Thomas and St Simon. The former holds a builder's square in one hand because he is said to have been responsible for building a church in India and a halberd (symbolising the method of his martyrdom) in the other; while the Menorcan coat of arms rests against his knee. Beside him St Simon has a saw-toothed pattern running down the front of his cloak to symbolise the instrument with which he was martyred; he holds the Finnish coat of arms in his left hand because the Anglican Church was used by the Finnish community for their services in Majorca.

Next comes St Jude with a boat in the background because he was a missionary who travelled overseas. The cross in his panel is the one that can be seen on the road between Sa Pobla and the Albufera marshes where the first Anglican services were held in Majorca. Behind it is the Catholic Church at Cala D'or which is still loaned twice a month to the Anglican Chaplain for services in that area and in the foreground there is a hoopoe as an example of Majorcan birdlife.

The fifth panel shows St James the Less carrying scrolls and the coat of arms of Ibiza which used to come under the Chaplaincy of Palma. The waves in the coat of arms turn into a river as they enter the next narrow panel and run under the Roman bridge at Pollença with the little island of Sa Vedra in Ibiza in the background.

The centre panel depicts Christ. It is bordered by another small panel followed by one showing St Philip holding the escutcheon of Majorca in his right hand; his robes have a design of loaves and fishes because he was present at the feeding of the five thousand. The eighth panel shows St Peter with the bay of Palma in the background where fishermen are at work. His robes show his symbol of crossed keys; an inverted cross which is partly concealed behind the edge of the panel commemorates the belief that he asked to be crucified upside down so that he could look to heaven as he died.

Two figures in the next panel portray St Andrew (the brother of St Peter) and St James the Greater. St Andrew carries the X shaped cross on which he died. St James's symbols are the shepherds crook that he carries in his left hand and a conch shell on his robe; he is the patron saint of Spain and it is believed that after King Herod had him beheaded his body was taken to Santiago where his shrine is an object of pilgrimage

The tenth window shows St Luke in the background, as he was not an apostle, with St Bartholomew in the foreground standing in front of a palm tree with the outline of a bat (the national animal of Majorca) incorporated within its fronds; the flaying knives with which he was martyred are depicted on his robes.

The final panel shows St John, the younger brother of St James the Greater, with his symbols of a chalice and serpent which refer to the legend that he survived an attempt to kill him with a poisoned cup.

Nils was put under tremendous pressure to complete the windows in time for the 25th anniversary celebrations in October 1991 and he just managed to make the date. Those depicting the saints were financed by members of the congregation to commemorate loved ones, but the cost of the three centre panels depicting Christ and the expense of fitting the windows and setting up lights to illuminate them was met from church funds.

During August 1991 a team from British Channel Four TV visited Majorca to make a programme in their 'As it Happens' series. This followed the approach frequently adopted for TV coverage of Majorca and consisted of little more than a procession from bar to bar, an interview with a wet T-shirt judge and a mobbing by chanting English lager louts. Some members of the church were surprised, however, by a scene shot late one night in the slightly seedy area of Palma known as the Apuntadores. The camera travelled to the far end of a bar where the Anglican Chaplain, flanked by his blonde Sunday School teacher and the Editor of the local paper, could be seen standing with glasses in their hands.

The Chaplain's attempt to suggest that his glass was filled with lemonade was not entirely convincing, especially to those who knew that he could usually be found at his favourite drinking spot long after the majority of his congregation had retired for the night. The Majorca Daily Bulletin reported the incident by stating that their Editor and '*his boozing buddy*' the Chaplain had been '*caught telling outrageous anecdotes in Whispers Bar.*'

The 25th anniversary celebrations were enjoyed by all members of the congregation as there was something for everyone. There were naturally several religious services including a Confirmation and the dedication of the new windows by Bishop John Satterthwaite, then Bishop of Gibraltar in Europe.

The festivities commenced with the first Harvest Supper to be held at the church for many years. After the meal the amateur entertainment revealed some unsuspected talent, including a poem which was written and presented by the Churchwarden responsible for construction work. It was greeted with tumultuous applause by an appreciative audience, many of whom were starting to suffer from exhaustion following a period during which the church had acquired a new organ, a new font, new choir stalls, new vestments and, of course, the new windows. The theme concerned a flash of inspiration which came to the Chaplain one day in his bath when he realised that the church was complete apart from a bell and the subsequent efforts by the congregation to 'cast a bell, design a belfry – and all before the Bishop's birthday.'

The Chaplain decided that the Coleman Hall beneath the Church represented a potential source of revenue that was not being exploited. It was decided that it should be fully equipped with china, cutlery, tables and chairs in time for the Harvest Supper and then made available to any groups willing to make a donation to the church for the use of its fine new facilities. The Council thought it best for the tables to be specially constructed so that they could be folded away easily and so leave the hall clear for other activities. Every member made a suggestion concerning their design and the outcome was similar to the camel that resulted when a committee designed a horse.

After many delays the tables were delivered, unvarnished, just in time for the Harvest Supper. The concept had been to have light folding tables that could be put away when not required, but these were so heavy that it took two people to lift one. Unfortunately, they had been made from unseasoned wood and warped in the heat of the hall. When I saw them the morning before the event they appeared to be cocking their legs against the walls. In some cases the warp was so bad that one leg was about two inches off the ground while the tops, instead of being flat, looked more like aircraft propellers.

There was little time for any elaborate solution to the problem so slices were simply sawn off the legs until the tables were stable. It was an odd sensation for anyone at the head of one of the worst affected examples because the nearest bottles and glasses leaned to the left, those in the centre were upright while those at the far end canted over to the right resulting in some members of the congregation thinking that they had drunk a little too much before taking their seats.

The booklet my husband had prepared on the history of the church, excluding the gossip that had come to our ears during our efforts to promote the ball, was delivered from the printer just in time for the celebrations and it is still on sale at the church. Other events included a fine concert by a Majorcan choir; a talk by Nils on his thinking behind his design for the windows; a Council lunch and a party for children. The climax was a very successful dinner and dance attended by Bishop John Satterthwaite which was held at the Royal Yacht Club but with a more reasonable ticket price than the aborted June event.

The dinner was held on October 12th which happened to be my husband's 60th birthday and he still treasures an oil painting which Nils presented to him on the night. It depicts a sunset, but close examination reveals that the sun is surrounded by a halo based on the labyrinth pattern in the stained glass windows. Another unexpected present was an olive wood bowl with an inscription that had been beautifully carved by one of his fellow Churchwardens.

The following day we took our family, who had come over from England for the 25th anniversary celebrations, to lunch at a restaurant near Calvià. The Bishop happened to be sitting at a nearby table so, when we were leaving, I went over to greet him. As I bent to speak to him, he suddenly plucked a large strawberry from his bowl and popped it into my mouth saying 'Food of the angels for an angel!' It was a real conversation stopper, but I eventually managed to swallow it and wish him a safe journey home.

We always enjoyed a visit from the Bishop who preached with great sincerity but also knew how to enjoy life and was excellent company on any social occasion with a huge fund of amusing experiences. His diocese covered an immense area which was still extending because churches in Russia and Eastern Europe were then being returned to the Anglican Church and he travelled constantly throughout his diocese. It was while he was on the Spanish mainland that he was involved in a serious car crash in which he nearly lost his life. A rib had punctured his lung and it was fortunate that the accident happened near a hospital which was able to give him immediate treatment. He suffered other injuries and it was some time before he was able to return to England.

He made an amazing recovery and when he came to have lunch with us some months later, we were delighted to find that his sense of humour was totally unaffected. He described his experiences in the Spanish hospital where a Catholic nun, who was nursing him, was a little overwhelmed by having to tend an Anglican Bishop and always crossed herself several times before washing him.

Another story concerned his transportation home by air. Because of his injuries he was to be carried in a contraption not unlike an open coffin so that he could travel well-supported and flat on his back. The method adopted to insert him in the box was to turn him face downwards while it was placed over him, after which both he and the box would be inverted. While he was lying on the bed waiting for it to cover him the nun said 'Oh my Lord Bishop, has anyone ever told you that you have a bottom like Princess Di's!'

In addition to Palma, there is a resident Chaplain at Puerto Pollença and Anglican services are held every Sunday in the Roman Catholic church in the main square. Twice a month a similar arrangement applies when the Chaplain from Palma holds an Anglican service in the Roman Catholic church at Cala D'or.

Recently, after a period of heavy rain during late October and early November, we woke to a perfect Sunday morning without a trace of cloud in an incredibly blue sky. The pines were proudly displaying their fresh green needles and not a breath of wind disturbed them.

We drove down the hill in brilliant sunshine and headed for the coast to attend Morning Praise at an hotel in Palma Nova. We had heard about a scheme operated by the Intercontinental Church Society which supplies a succession of Anglican priests from October to April in the Magalluf area. It is sponsored in Majorca by Thomson Holidays who provide board and accommodation for the visiting priests. They each spend about six weeks on the island conducting a Sunday morning service at the Hotel Santa Lucia in Palma Nova and in the afternoon Songs of Praise at the Hotel Trinidad in Magalluf. Each Wednesday morning there is a service of Holy Communion at the Hotel Son Matias in Palma Nova.

We expected a small gathering in a corner of the huge lounge of the hotel, but more and more people came to attend the service until about 150 were seated around a little stage where the priest's wife was skilfully operating a sound system. It was a very moving service, the priest's fine Welsh voice being enhanced by an excellent choice of hymns. We particularly welcomed his inclusion of a reading from the old testament, something we very seldom hear these days. The collection went to assist the work of the Intercontinental Church Society which stretches as far as the Falkland Islands, maintaining numerous permanent Chaplaincies in Europe, North Africa and South America.

It was refreshing to discover that a simple service in an hotel lounge, with hymns accompanied by canned music, could be so moving and informative. Talking to the priest afterwards we learned that the previous week about 400 people had packed into his service on Remembrance Sunday.

It seems a little strange that we are able to live in the middle of the Mediterranean and still attend a traditional British Remembrance Day service every November. In fact so many poppies are worn that the Majorcans have become quite familiar with the custom and no longer enquire about their significance.

One Christmas we went to a popular service of carols that the Salvation Army holds every year at an hotel in Magalluf. Their band from Maidstone came over for the event which was very well attended. It prompted us to find out a little more about their activity and we were surprised to discover how much they were doing to assist those in need in Majorca.

In Cala Major the Salvation Army have a centre where they hold regular Sunday morning services. On the first Sunday in each month the service is followed by a 'faith lunch' when members of the congregation bring food which is shared at a communal meal. The centre is well-equipped and currently receives some financial support from the UK although this is reducing and will eventually cease. Much of their work concerns English speaking victims of poverty on the island. Sadly these cases now exist because many long-term residents came when prices were a fraction of those that apply today and some elderly people find that their fixed incomes are no longer sufficient to maintain them. Youngsters who come to the island to find work and fail to do so also frequently end up in need of help.

The Salvation Army has a charity shop at Palma Nova run by volunteers. It can usually spare clothing for those in distress and suitable cases are offered food, given a bed for the night or even assisted with a passage back to the UK. At Christmas a hot meal is provided for about 50 people who might otherwise eat alone or even go hungry and two families are under virtually constant care. Two hospitals are regularly visited and known patients are seen at others. Like the Anglican Church, the Salvation Army does not perform marriage ceremonies in Spain but it conducts funerals. Other activities include a Sunday school, a bible study group, a youth programme for children of eight to fifteen and a youth band. Three hours are set aside each Tuesday morning when anyone in trouble can call for help and advice and find a shoulder to cry on if needed.

The Roman Catholic church of San Lorenzo in Palma Nova is one of several which celebrates Mass in English every Sunday morning, and many other religions are represented on the island including the Jewish community who have a Synagogue at Calle Monseñor Palmer 3 just off the Paseo Maritimo in Palma. It is a moving sight to see the great Cathedral filled every year by members of the congregations of most of these churches at the annual ecumenical service.

11. Fiestas

Unlike the tourist attractions in the form of dancing displays, concerts and other performances that are specially staged for visitors, the traditional fiestas of Majorca have a long history and many have a religious origin. They are organised by Majorcans for Majorcans and seldom get much advance publicity because a whole town will have been working for months to prepare for its fiesta and everyone in the locality is well aware of the dates and times. Visitors are welcome, but the crowd that attends these events is mainly composed of local residents so there is often nothing to inform the stranger about the significance of the ritual. We have usually been fortunate and found ourselves beside a Majorcan willing to explain what was taking place.

The first of the major religious festivals, and the one most looked forward to by the children, is *Tres Reyes* or the Three Kings which is celebrated on January 5th, the eve of Epiphany. This is the day on which Spanish children traditionally used to receive their Christmas gifts. Christmas Day is now also observed as a gift day, so parents have considerable expense at this time of year.

The arrival of the Three Kings, Melchor, Gaspar and the black Baltasar, is usually celebrated by a procession which varies in scale depending on the town where it takes place. Palma stages a very spectacular parade that commences with the kings, all wearing rich robes, being ferried across the bay which is illuminated by fireworks. They step ashore opposite La Lonja and then ride to Plaza Cort where they enter the Town Hall to be greeted by the dignitaries who escort them to the balcony overlooking the square to wave to the crowd. They then parade through the city followed by a procession of thirty or more highly decorated floats.

The last time we went to see this we took some folding chairs and sat opposite Galerías Preciados in Avenida Rey Jaime III. There was a buzz of excitement in the crowd as a squad of police motorcyclists appeared with lights flashing and cleared those who had surged forward back on to the pavement. They were followed by mounted police wearing scarlet coats with white epaulettes, white breeches and gold helmets with white plumes, some on jet black horses and others on magnificent greys with green saddle cloths.

Soon we saw the kings also riding on fine horses and then the elaborate floats. A giant butterfly with illuminated wings was followed by an enormous goose flying over a group of children dressed as toy soldiers. There were gigantic models of the white pottery whistles decorated with red and green stripes that are sold throughout Majorca; a full sized elephant bedecked with jewels; a scene from the Arabian Nights; flying dolphins pulling a chariot in which Neptune rode in splendour; a group of sailors in a small boat towing, for no obvious reason, a brightly coloured hot-air balloon; a turkey all of eight feet high; gnomes in toadstool houses; the scene in the manger surmounted by a giant star, and many more. As they went slowly by, the brightly costumed boys and girls in the floats scattered sweets which were quickly gathered up by the crowd.

A smaller procession in Calvià again featured the three ornately dressed kings on horseback who made their way to the local cinema which had been decorated with balloons and tinsel and took their places on thrones on the stage; behind them a mountain of presents awaited delivery. In many towns and villages parcels, clearly marked with the child's name, can be left at some suitable point where children can gather for the kings to deliver them. In Calvià an expectant audience of excited youngsters filled the seats in the auditorium waiting for the kings to call out their names. It took a long time for them to work through the list and we were sorry for those who had to wait until the end before receiving their gifts, while all around them packages were being opened with shouts of joy.

The evening of January 16th, *San Antonio Abad,* is celebrated by bonfires in the streets of many towns to mark the eve of St Anthony who is the patron saint of animals.

January 17th, the actual Saint's day, is when a large number of household pets and many farm animals are paraded from Palma Cathedral to the church of San Antonio in Calle de San Miguel to receive a blessing. This is one of the major processions in Palma and as the route is relatively short a dense crowd fills the pavements and the squares of Plaza Cort and Plaza Mayor through which it passes. St Anthony spent much of his life as a recluse and fought temptation by prayer and fasting. He is associated with protection against the diseases in animals and he has altars dedicated to him in the Cathedral and at several churches on the island.

The parade is accompanied by devils, demons and characters wearing grotesque masks representing the tempters of the Saint. Most of the *galeras*, the horse-drawn carriages that ply for hire in Palma, are decorated for the event and filled with young children in Majorcan costume. Animals of every kind walk or ride in the parade and the most recent event included sheep, pigs, goats, innumerable cats and dogs and even two penguins from Marineland and a Peregrine falcon. Decorated floats and two bands further enlivened the occasion.

Similar parades to bless animals are held in Artà, Costitx, Muro, Sant Joan and also in Puerto de Andratx where we went to the Roman Catholic church behind the port to observe the ceremony. The priest stood on the steps adjoining the road and the animals paraded past him, stopping to be sprinkled with holy water. The dogs did not object, but some of the horses became alarmed and one rider seemed to be having difficulty controlling his mount until we realised what he was instructing it to do. A moment later it knelt on its bent forelegs before the priest to receive its blessing. In the evening, down by the fishermen's quay, there was music and dancing while sardines were barbecued and later distributed to the crowd.

A popular event on St Anthony's Day in Puerto Pollença is called *Pi de Sant Antoni*, St Anthony's Pine. It starts in the morning when a tall pine tree is cut down in Formentor; all but the topmost branches are removed and the pole is brought by sea towed behind a boat to the shore in Puerto Pollença amidst music, dancing and the eating of *butifarron*, sausage, and toasted bread. After being well greased it is set up in the square in front of the church and young men attempt to climb it to reach a bag of confetti and burst it to shower the crowd below. The tree for a similar ceremony in Pollença is brought from Ternelles. This is quite a common custom, the traditional prize at the top of the pole being a cockerel in a cage.

It was only by chance that I learned of a ceremony in Calvià connected with the St Anthony festivities. I swim every morning at the local sports centre and one of my Majorcan friends asked whether I would be at the fiesta that evening; she was helping with the catering and was able to provide full details of the event which had not been publicised in the English press or on the radio. It took place on a net-ball pitch behind the large church in Calvià and was typical of similar affairs that take place throughout the island at this time of year. A large load of sand had been dumped on the pitch and a tall bonfire, with a stuffed effigy on top, illuminated the crowd that had assembled by the time we arrived. Smaller bonfires had been lit on other piles of sand and a long table down one side of the pitch was laden with *cocas*, several types of uncooked sausages, bread rolls, cakes and tarts and jugs of sangria.

One of the pleasures of events of this kind is sharing the fun with people we know and meeting many of our neighbours. The young folk danced in circles to Majorcan tunes while burning logs were extracted from the bonfires and set under metal grids. Bunches of wire skewers were placed in the sand and before long people bought sausages and rolls from the refreshment table and then barbecued them on the grids. We soon mastered the art of holding a cut roll in a paper napkin and dropping a cooked sausage into the open V of the roll which was then pinched together by one hand while the other extracted the skewer.

When we moved to one of the other barbecues we were welcomed by our old friend Mateo who had helped so much with the construction of the terrace around our pool. He was there with his wife and son and his mother-in-law, who was a fine old Majorcan lady, very alert and interested in what was going on. Mateo and my husband were soon deep in discussion while I talked to his wife and her mother about life in the village and how it had changed over the years.

January 20th is the day of San Sebastian, a Roman soldier who embraced Christianity and was sentenced to be shot to death with arrows. He survived and was nursed back to health, but was later martyred for preaching his faith. He is the patron saint of Palma and he is remembered during a week of fiestas in the city. On the eve there is music in six of the larger squares and thousands join in the dancing until the early hours. On the day a painting depicting the Saint is hung over the balcony of the Town Hall in Plaza Cort. The original used to be displayed until it was discovered that it was possibly by Van Dyke and a copy is now used. A recent innovation for this fiesta is a cycle ride around the city when around 10,000 cyclists on machines ranging from racing and mountain bikes to ancient boneshakers set off from Plaza Cort to ride to the Sports Stadium.

Immediately prior to Lent there are carnivals in many towns and children compete in fancy dress parades wearing costumes that must take months to prepare. The children's event, known as *Sa Rueta*, is held in the Borne in Palma during the morning and proud parents stroll around the city long after it has ended giving their offspring more time in which to show off their elaborate outfits until the enormous carnival parade called *Sa Rua* commences later in the day. It progresses around the city and one of the best places from which to see it is the Borne because it turns from Avenida Rey Jaime III into the Borne, passes down one side, turns around the Plaza de la Reina and comes back up the other side to turn into La Unió.

The noise is deafening because nearly all of those participating have whistles and there are many bands, amplified music from the floats, the tooting of horns and occasional firecrackers, while the road is soon deep in confetti and coloured streamers. The colourful parade takes nearly two hours to pass, watched by thousands of people some of whom are also dressed in carnival costumes. This is followed by dancing until the small hours by those with sufficient stamina.

On the last Thursday before Lent, *Dijous Llader*, a figure is hung outside the town hall in some towns. The effigy is blamed for all of the misfortunes that have affected the town during the previous year and it is subsequently tried and executed. Another Lenten custom concerns *Jaia Serrada* a model of a woman with seven legs poking out below her skirt. A leg is cut off during each week of Lent.

The town of Sant Joan celebrates the feeding of the five thousand with a fiesta called *Pa i el Peix,* the Bread and the Fishes, on the fourth Sunday in Lent when there is a special church service, dancing, bonfires and a parade during which hundreds of fish pies are eaten.

Romerías, pilgrimages involving a picnic, are held in conjunction with several festivals including *El Pan Caritat* at the Hermitage of Crestaix in Sa Pobla on the third day of Easter; the Hermitage of Santa Magdalena at Inca on the first Sunday after Easter; and at Marratxi on June 30th to mark the day of Sant Marcial, when there is also a market with stalls selling pottery and handicrafts.

Easter is marked by many religious parades, the most solemn and impressive being the procession of the penitents, known as *La Sang,* in Palma on Maundy Thursday. The name, which means the blood, actually refers to a very large cross which is carried in the procession behind thousands of representatives from religious groups who wear robes and curious pointed hoods. They carry candles and walk barefoot to the sound of muffled drums. Floats carry representations of Easter scenes and the entire procession takes several hours to pass by.

Pollença, Felanitx and some other towns observe Good Friday with a procession called *Devallment del Calvari* to mark the taking down of Christ's body from the cross. In Pollença, late in the evening, an effigy of the body is carried silently down the 365 steps of the cypress-bordered stairway known as the *Calvario* and taken to the church.

An important series of fiestas relates to Santa Catalina Tomás who is Majorca's only Saint. She was born in Valldemossa in 1533, beatified in 1792 by Pope Pius VI and canonised by Pope Pius X in 1935. Her symbol is a white cake of fig bread which is often included in her portraits. Many stories are told about her piety. She is reputed to have mixed sand with her soup as a precaution against gluttony and to have eaten only one meal a day. The devil was said to rise up from the hole in her sink and tempt her as she did the washing up. Robert Graves claimed to have the very sink in his house; it came from a cottage in Deià, where she lived for a time with an aunt, and Robert rescued it when the building was being demolished in 1931.

Fiestas to celebrate the life of Santa Catalina are held in Valldemossa on July 28th; in Santa Margalida (where she is the town's patron saint) on the first Sunday in September; and also in Palma, where she lived in the Convent of Santa Magdalena and where she died in 1574. The Palma event is held close to the day of Santa Margarita, which is October 16th, to commemorate the anniversary of her taking her vows at the Convent.

We went to Valldemossa in the afternoon of her fiesta in July and found the entire town swept clean and decorated. Arches of palm fronds had been crossed above the doorways of the houses in most of the narrow streets, with blue, white, yellow and red paper flowers attached to them. The square near the *Cartuja* had a ceiling of white paper streamers from which a central wreath incorporating a picture of the Saint hung as a centrepiece.

We sat at a café table in the square and ordered *tortillas* to keep us going for the long evening ahead. Directly opposite, a row of chairs had been set out for the local dignitaries and behind them more chairs suggested that there would be a band, so we were certain that we had selected a good observation point. Spectators began to line the streets and children in traditional dress were scampering everywhere. It was not long before the sound of music was followed by the appearance of a procession of beautifully decorated donkey carts going to fetch the Saint.

There was a burst of cheering from the crowd as a small group walked down the main street and turned up to the *Cartuja*; to our surprise we saw that it included King Juan Carlos and Queen Sofía. About half an hour later they walked back to the square and seated themselves on the chairs directly in front of us. Security men whispered into their portable radios as the light slowly faded, the waiters took their last orders before the event and a cluster of press photographers, each with several cameras and numerous assorted lenses dangling from his shoulders, formed an untidy group between us and the royal party.

Once more we heard music, but this time it was the beat of the drum and the sound of the Majorcan bagpipe. Soon the carts, drawn by immaculately groomed donkeys, again filed past, stopping briefly for the occupants to salute their king. The procession is known as the *Carro Triunfal* or Triumphal Cart and it portrays the early years of the Saint who is represented by a six year old elected from the children of the municipality.

The carts, each beautifully decorated by an arch of flowers, contained young children in folk-dance costume or dressed as angels. Strings of lights powered by a hidden battery illuminated the carts and as they passed the crowd sang the Saint's traditional song known as *Sor Tomasseta* while the children in the carts distributed sweets, some of which seemed to be deliberately aimed at the Royal couple who obviously greatly enjoyed the ceremony.

The final cart contained the Saint surrounded by at least twelve other young children dressed as cherubs. The sides and rear of their cart were covered with yellow flowers and a large golden halo was suspended over the head of the young girl portraying Santa Catalina Tomás who is popularly known in Valldemossa as the *Beateta* or little Saint.

Our next encounter with the Saint was at Santa Margalida the following September. The *Processó de la Beata* is one of the major festivals in Majorca attracting many hundreds of participants. Stalls selling food and toys had been set up in the centre of the town from which all traffic had been excluded and chairs extended along both sides of the wide street leading to the Town Hall. In the evening we sat and listened to a concert of light music superbly played by the local band. Soon the crowd grew thicker, an occasional firework exploded, and the sound of bells, rather like sleigh bells, could be heard from time to time. By nine it was obvious that something was about to happen as more bands started to assemble in the roadway. There were twelve in total, from Petrá, Montuiri, C'an Picafort, Llucmajor, Sineu and other towns in the area; each accompanied by groups of dancers in folk costume. One by one they were called to order and they marched from the Town Hall at five minute intervals to join up with several decorative floats that had assembled at the church. They were followed by a procession of town councillors who had been brought to the Town Hall in large chauffeur driven cars that had been specially permitted to enter the town to drop off their distinguished passengers.

After about an hour it began to grow dark and two men walked down the street, one carrying a watering can filled with fuel while the other held long paper tapers. With these they lit fires in tall braziers set at intervals along the pavement, each with a neat stack of logs beside it for re-fuelling. Soon the haunting melody of *Sor Tomasseta* could again be heard and the procession came into view. The floats were magnificent, each representing a scene from the life of the Saint. Many were drawn by horses, but the larger ones were built around lorries or farm tractors and trailers, huge sprays of flowers covered all traces of the structure beneath and girls in elaborate costumes rode on the floats.

One depicted the embroidery with which the Saint must have occupied much of her time; it featured an enormous thimble about four feet in height, an equally large cotton reel, a gigantic needle and an embroidery frame at least six feet in diameter containing some partly finished work; another represented the interior of a church with nuns at prayer.

The most elaborate float showed the Saint in white with a lighted halo over her head and flanked by angels, one holding a harp and another a dove; the entire float was covered in ruched white material embellished with silver stars and hearts while streamers extending from the rear were held by eight more angels. The bands marched between the floats and large groups of Majorcan dancers walked in procession behind each band.

Many of the dancers carried clay pitchers about eighteen inches high with a narrow neck and two large handles. We soon had an explanation for the sound of jingling bells that we had heard earlier. Groups of boys dressed as devils, with brown hoods sporting brown horns, black shirts, red pantaloons, black shoes and a belt hung with bells, charged into the groups of dancers whenever they spotted a clay pot.

The dancers attempted to smuggle their pots past the devils by hiding them, usually under the girls' aprons or even their skirts. So long as they yielded them up without a struggle all was well, but if they resisted the devils would try to wrench them away and good-natured scuffles were frequent.

On one occasion a mother of one of the girls obviously thought that a devil had been a little too enthusiastic so she took him to one side and gave him a real dressing down. We watched with amusement as the strongly-built devil slowly wilted under her flow of invective.

At the rear of the procession a young woman, dressed as the Saint, walked with her attendants. Periodically the head devil, a big man considerably older than his assistants, would rise up in front of her holding a pot in either hand. He then jumped into the air and hurled the pots to the ground where they smashed with a tremendous crash while he bowed in supplication. Our Majorcan neighbour explained that the devils represented the tempters who lead people astray and the smashed pots symbolised the temptations that the Saint successfully resisted during her lifetime; several thousand are broken during the course of the evening. When the procession reached the church there was a ceremony called the *trencadissa* when more clay pots filled with sweets and other surprises were smashed, their contents being gathered by the eager spectators.

By midnight a dance had started in the main square with a modern orchestra and an excellent lead singer who sang in English, French and Spanish. We sat outside a café in the warm night air and drank coffee while couples drifted in to the dance area. As we had a long drive ahead of us, we reluctantly had to leave the people of Santa Margalida enjoying their big day which obviously still had several more hours to run.

In mid-October we went to Palma to see the last and largest of the three annual processions commemorating Santa Catalina.The parade started dramatically with five mounted policemen in their fine uniforms; they were followed by eight drummers of the *Tambores de la Sala* wearing long blue coats trimmed in red and matching red stockings, and a mace bearer in splendid robes. After them came a horseman carrying a banner, then a group of dancers in Majorcan folk costume and behind them a band; the sequence of a banner carrier, dancers and a band was repeated as town after town was represented in the procession.

In total there were more than twenty bands, some played traditional instruments including the pipe, drum, tambourine, *bandurria*, guitar, violin and the curious Majorcan bagpipe. Others were full sized orchestras with forty or more players and modern instruments. We remembered seeing one of the large brass bands in the parade at Santa Margalida; we first recognised it by its distinctive sound but were able to positively identify it by the huge white euphoniums, prominently bearing the word Yamaha, coiled around two of the players like friendly boa constrictors. Another large band was also familiar because it was from our home town of Calvià.

All of the bands played three initial notes followed by the same two-part tune that we had first heard in Valldemossa. After the three note warning the dancers sprang into action to perform first a slow and then a rapid dance which caused the girls' skirts to flare out and reveal their long white pantalets while the crowd applauded their efforts.

Between many of the groups of bands and dancers there were a few decorated *galeras* and motorised floats. We smiled as the driver of one carriage desperately tried to prevent his horse eating the greenery from the one in front. The floats were good but not as elaborate as those we had seen at Santa Margalida. The theme was olden times; one float portrayed a laundry scene with washing hanging out to dry at the back; others showed dressmaking with an old tailor's dummy and an early sewing machine; old farm machinery; a model of a church; and a very well presented tableau of charcoal burning and grain harvesting. One was dominated by a giant red-headed devil towering over an angel imprisoned in a large version of one of the clay pitchers we had seen smashed during the previous procession. There was a kitchen scene showing sausage making and finally six men, splendidly dressed in long yellow coats, red breeches and soft red and yellow hats walking in front of a large carriage drawn by four horses which carried the Saint and her companions.

Interspersed between the bands, dancers and floats, groups of devils, dressed like those we had seen at Santa Margalida, made mischief by darting at the crowd. One swept a girl off her feet and kissed her. She seemed to like it and posed with her arms around the devil while her companion took a photograph.

A few of the devils wore highly polished red or green masks presenting grotesque faces which must have been very hot and heavy. As the procession paused in front of us one of these devils removed his 'head' to mop himself with a large red handkerchief, smiled a little guiltily at us, and then replaced his headgear before resuming his prodding of the crowd with a wooden trident.

June 24th is the day of St John the Baptist; on its eve bonfires are lit in many towns with Sa Pobla and Muro staging the largest displays. An odd custom in Manacor relates to a willow tree that is said to have the power to cure hernias in children. Early in the morning of the feast day the affected child is passed through the branches of the tree into which cuts have been made so that sap flows out. The sap is rubbed onto the hernia and the cut branches are bound together; tradition states that, if the branches heal, the hernia will be cured.

During this week another curious event is held in the town of Sant Juan called the *Festa d'es Sol que Balla,* the Festival of the Sun that Dances. It involves processions, dances and bonfires and commemorates a belief that the sun danced on St John's night.

Another series of fiestas relates to the fishing industry which was once of great importance to the island. On July 16th, the day of our lady of Carmen, major events take place in Porto Colom, Puerto de Andratx, Cala Ratjada and Sa Rapita.

We joined the crowd attending the *Fiesta de la Virgen del Carmen* in Puerto de Andratx which commenced in the late afternoon with a parade by drum majorettes and the town band, all very well turned out for the occasion. The girls, aged between nine and twelve, wore white costumes with short pleated skirts and emerald green cuffs, matching green capes and white military style hats with a red front panel and a white peak lined with green on its underside; gold trimmings and white boots completed their very smart outfits. The band was also dressed in white. They processed along the waterfront playing lively marches, turned up to the church and attended a short service.

When they emerged a procession formed. The majorettes again accompanied the band, now playing solemn music, then came a statue of the Virgin and Child carried shoulder high on a bier adorned with white gladioli and red and white tiger lilies, followed by the congregation. They all walked down from the church to a highly decorated fishing boat moored at the waterfront and the Virgin was carefully transferred to a floral bower that had been prepared for her on the deck.

The harbour was packed with boats, most of which had also been decorated for the occasion. Some were merely enlivened with flags and coloured paper streamers, but many were really ornate, with liberal use of myrtle, pine branches, flowers and lights. Eventually the fishing fleet, followed by dozens of large and small pleasure craft, sailed out of the harbour, not to return until dusk.

When the colourful boats came back into the harbour there was much hooting of sirens followed by another procession to take the Virgin back to her place in the church; then an elaborate firework display and finally a play in Majorcan which we found rather hard to follow.

Over a *cerveza* an old Majorcan, so wrinkled that he must have been approaching his century, told us a little more about the fishing festivals. Apart from those of the *Virgin del Carmen* on July 16th, most fishing ports, especially Palma, celebrate the feast of St Peter their patron saint on June 29th. Decorated trawlers, the leading one carrying a statue of the Saint, sail in procession around the bay to the sound of sirens and rockets while the fishermen's families watch from the quay. When they return the statue is paraded around the fishing port and there is then a concert given by a brass band.

The eve of the feast of Saint Ursula, October 20th, is celebrated as the night of the virgins. This is when young men serenade their sweethearts and hope to be invited into their houses to partake of a *buñuelo* which is a fried bun, somewhat similar to a doughnut in texture.

In times gone by girls would hope for several such serenades, just as in Britain they longed for numerous Valentine cards. If their daughter was unlikely to attract such attention unaided, parents would sometimes pay a youth to sing to her and enable her to retain her pride. This tradition dates back to the Middle Ages but the reason why Saint Ursula became involved is unknown.

November 1st, *Todos Santos,* All Saints Day, is a national holiday throughout Spain. It is marked by giving children rosaries of sweets and it is when the Majorcans visit their dead, taking flowers, especially chrysanthemums, to the graves. The demand is so great that some growers cultivate the flowers mainly for sale on this day; chrysanthemums are not widely purchased by the Majorcans at other times because of their association with death. By six in the morning the stall-holders on the Ramblas in Palma are busy preparing wreaths and by mid-day few flowers remain unsold. An ecumenical service is held in the main city cemetery in Calle Jesus which is always well attended.

A custom which is almost unique to Majorca takes place on Christmas Eve when a poem recalling the prophecy of the coming of Jesus, known as the *Cant de la Sibil.la* or Sybil's song is sung in some churches by a young boy dressed in a red and green tunic and wearing a sword. It was originally a lengthy poem but only eight verses, telling of the coming of judgement day, are now used; the last being a prayer to the Virgin to intercede when the day of judgement comes.

Not all of the festivals have religious origins. Towards the end of January we went to Bellver Castle and walked down into the woods where the mounted police have their barracks. A crowd of about 400 assembled to see an outstanding display of dressage which is presented every year by the police in their full ceremonial dress, and bare-back riding by a police team comprising two men and a girl.

There was also a demonstration by the local fire brigade who put out a fire in an old car and then showed how foam was produced until a huge pyramid almost covered the parade ground. The crowd was then invited to a picnic served on tables loaded with *cocas* which resemble pizzas, sandwiches, cake, nuts and crisps washed down with unlimited Coca-Cola and lemonade. The whole event provided well over an hour of first class entertainment and it was all entirely free.

Several annual fiestas relate to agriculture and wine growing. In early September the little town of Vilafranca holds a festival to mark the local melon harvest. There is a competition to find the largest melon, dancing until the small hours and a melon fair which also includes exhibitions of farm machinery, wood carvings, carrier pigeons and a dog show.

On the evening before the judging we were particularly attracted by a procession of children, each carrying a lantern made by hollowing out a melon and inserting a candle. Intricate patterns were carved into the skins of the melons and the candles illuminated them from within. This charming little event was followed by traditional folk dances performed on a stage in the Town Hall square.

The dancers, who were all young and enthusiastic, carefully preserved the traditional steps and arm movements and we were delighted to see that there were so many of them in such a small town. Virtually the entire population turned out to watch and applaud the dancers, many of whom must have been related, and we felt a little like intruders at a family party even though we were made very welcome.

The melon fair is only a little over twenty years old and it is a low budget affair, but it provides a fascinating glimpse of Majorcan country life. The melon that won the competition weighed over 12 kilos. Sweetness is also measured; the norm on a graded scale being 12 degrees. The 1994 crop was exceptional with melons registering levels of 14 to 16 degrees of sweetness and the town mayor is working to obtain a *denominación de origen* for the Vilafranca crop.

On a much larger scale, the annual *Festa d'es Vermar* - Festival of the Wine Harvest is held in Binissalem, the main events take place on the last Sunday in September although there is a free supper called *Fideus de Vermar* on the previous Thursday evening which involves a walk to the nearby estate of Can Arabi where *fideus,* a dish of lamb and noodles, is served to anyone with the foresight to bring a plate and cutlery, while a band provides music to accompany the meal. On the Saturday there is a parade of decorated floats and an evening concert.

On Sunday we found the entire town centre closed to traffic, and market stalls set up in the roads leading to the church square were selling bottles of local wine, sweets, candy floss, inexpensive jewellery, toys, leather goods and other trinkets.

At noon there was a competition to judge bunches of grapes grown in the local vineyards. This was held close to the church and we joined the crowd waiting for the judges to arrive. Applause announced their approach and we saw two very dissimilar characters, one dressed in a pink and white floral shirt and baggy blue trousers while the other was very smartly turned out in a well-cut grey suit with shirt and tie.

Huge bunches of grapes were displayed in boxes on a long line of trestle tables and grey suit carefully lifted the first bunch from its box and hung it on the hook of a pair of old fashioned balance-scales which floral shirt held in one hand, keeping the other free to slide a weight along a bar engraved with numbers. They made their way slowly from box to box weighing each bunch, grey suit using a gold pen to record details on a note-pad. As the weight was announced the crowd applauded if the previous best had been exceeded and everyone became quite excited as the final bunches were judged. The victor received his award with tears of joy and we wondered how many days he had spent nursing his prize-winning grapes to such perfection.

Stalls in the square sold plastic cups filled with grapes and these were in great demand, perhaps because they were being sold by some exceptionally pretty girls in Majorcan costumes and also because, when empty, the cups could be used for the free wine that would be available later.

A parade of dancers, led by a flag bearer, marched up the steps to the terrace in front of the church and several bands of musicians prepared to accompany them on traditional instruments. The bagpipe and drum players are known as *Xeremiés* and on this occasion they were joined by others playing guitars and flutes. Soon a display of traditional Majorcan dances was in progress and we found that we were becoming able to recognise some of the tunes and movements which have been carefully preserved for many centuries.

When the formal dancing ended, another band started to play traditional tunes from a raised platform in the centre of the square and free wine was poured into the plastic cups in which grapes had been sold from large barrels set up at each corner. Lights strung from the trees illuminated a very merry scene as the people of Binissalem danced their traditional steps in groups of two, four, six, eight or in large circles. This was no set display, it was an opportunity for the youth of the town to release some of its seemingly inexhaustible energy; dancing as their forefathers must have danced for hundreds of years before them.

Some details had changed; the girls almost universally wore jeans and T shirts and the men were similarly dressed, but even when it grew late, they still observed the correct movements which involved the arms and hands almost as much as the feet. Much wine was consumed but nobody got drunk, nobody was rowdy and, as in Vilafranca, we felt as if we had been invited to attend a large private party.

These are but a small selection of the fiestas that regularly enliven the Majorcan scene. In addition to those mentioned, every town has its own fiesta which usually spreads over a week and often includes several church services, sports events, plays, dancing, concerts, cycle rides, exhibitions of vintage cars or motor cycles, communal meals and outings with a picnic lunch.

The town of Calvià holds its fiesta around the time of the feast of its patron saint St James the Apostle on July 25th. In 1994 it included most of the above events plus an exhibition of paintings, a display of aeromodels with a fully working helicopter, film shows, a coach tour, a photographic competition, and a demonstration of the construction of traditional musical instruments, including the *Ximbomba* which is an unusual type of drum that is played at many fiestas. It is often made out of an old wooden bucket from a waterwheel or a clay pot with a cured sheepskin stretched over the open top; a reed in the centre of the skin is rubbed with a wet hand to produce a distinctive sound.

One evening during the Calvià fiesta we went to the church square to see the *Nit de Foc* or night of fire. It started with the sound of a distant drum and the explosion of thunderflashes some way down the hill near the Town Hall.

The insistent, repetitive beat of the drum grew louder and louder until a group of men dressed as devils exploded into the square in a shower of fireworks. Some had wheelbarrows loaded with firecrackers with which they rushed at the crowd, rockets shot upwards from concealed launching tubes and a golden rain of fire cascaded down from fireworks strung across the square.

Firecrackers were everywhere and it was a night for old clothes, though nobody actually suffered burns. It lasted for nearly an hour; with the devils taking turns to maintain a frantic drumming from the relative safety of a small stage, which was also used as the launch pad for a wide variety of fireworks. Other devils ran amongst the crowd which scattered at their approach.

Spectators in houses adjoining the square were armed with buckets of water with which they attempted to soak the devils when they were incautious enough to walk below them. It was a riot of fun and noise and by the time it ended the devils and the crowd were quite exhausted.

The Calvià fiesta also included a fine concert by the *Sant Jaume Banda de Música de Calviá* comprising about forty amateur musicians who played superbly in the square below the church. Chairs that had been set out earlier soon filled with local residents and, as we live near the town, we soon recognised the baker, the ironmonger and many other trades-people and their families.

The programme was popular/classical, commencing with a Beatles medley followed by In a Persian Garden, a march by Penders and a very pretty piece which was new to us called Goyescas by Granados. Each of the pieces in the first half of the concert had a different conductor, some were young girls and they made the nice gesture of kissing one another on both cheeks as they handed over the baton. All were good but a young man who conducted the final item before the interval was outstanding. I see from a note on my programme that I marked him down as a future Colin Davis.

The second half was entirely conducted by the band's director who drew out its full potential. It started with a chorus from Tannhauser sung by a well-rehearsed group of local children and included selections from several shows including West Side Story.

The following evening we joined a much larger audience in the new gardens that had recently been completed in the town. As is common in Majorca, the performance was not scheduled to start until ten in the evening and actually commenced rather later. Clever use had been made of lighting to illuminate the trees and give the effect of a giant theatre; a stage had been built on which there was a grand piano and an excellent sound system ensured that the very large audience could hear every note. The pianist, Marta Pujol was a perfect accompanist for the four professional opera singers who had come over from the mainland to present the concert. It was of the highest possible standard but, like all of the other events in the fiesta, it was absolutely free.

Many fiestas mark historical events such as one in Soller in May which commemorates a raid on May 11th 1561 by corsairs in twenty-two ships under the command of the pirate Ochali who had sailed from Algiers and put in at Ibiza for water. The Governor of Ibiza warned Majorca of the danger of an attack on Soller and the garrison there was strengthened.

Eventually 1700 Moors attacked; during the fight two sisters, Francisca and Catalina Casanovas, killed two pirates with the crossbar of their door after they entered the house via a window. Now known as *Ses Valentes Dones de Ca'n Tamany* they are remembered each year at this fiesta. The Moors split into two groups; one was defeated and the raiders were chased back to their ships by the defenders, but the other group attacked the town and finding it unprotected took many women and children as prisoners.

Early in August the town of Pollença recalls a similar raid in 1550 by pirates led by *En Dragut* who was one of the fiercest of the corsairs. Although the town is about five kilometres inland from its port, it was not immune from attack by Turkish and Barbary raiders, probably because the land from the port to the town is very flat.

The festival is known as *Fiesta de Nuestra Señora de Los Ángeles* and, in glorious weather, we spent a day there enjoying the spectacle. After a religious procession known as *Mare de Deu dels Angels,* a mock battle commenced in the afternoon with the firing of rockets and ringing of bells. The leading actors are elected by popular vote and much time is spent making costumes and rehearsing the fighting.

The Christians wore white shirts and baggy pants and their womenfolk wore nightgowns because the actual battle took place at night. The Moors wore turbans, decorative waistcoats and wide cummerbunds. Juan Mas, the Christian commander, waited in the Plaza de la Almoina with his supporters, armed with staves and a few old guns.

The Moorish raiders, brandishing swords, were led by the infamous corsair. They attacked from all directions and battle raged for several hours, ending with a Christian victory at midnight in the football ground. There was then a huge firework display while exhausted Christians and Moors sat happily sipping beer together and planning improvements for the event the following year.

The landing of King Jaime I in September 1229, to liberate Majorca from the Moors, is marked in Santa Ponça by festivities which include a main event when a Mass is held at the foot of the stone cross that commemorates the landing. The service is followed by a procession and a series of performances lasting well into the night includes pipers, dancers, singers and even rock groups.

King Jaime's subsequent conquest is celebrated in Palma on December 31st at the *Festa de l'Estandard*, the Festival of the Standard. We joined the crowd in Plaza Cort at ten o'clock and found the Town Hall already decorated with three banners hung over its balconies and a large portrait of the Conqueror, over which the flags of Majorca, Spain and the Balearic Community were flying. A fine old olive tree at the side of the square was surrounded by red poinsettias and the giant figures of a man and a woman in traditional dress, which normally live inside the town hall, had been brought out and placed one at each corner of the building; the female figure wore a wimple, black top and regency striped skirt and the male smoked a long 'churchwarden' pipe while wearing a wide-brimmed black hat, a black jacket and baggy pants.

The ground immediately in front of the Town Hall was strewn with green leaves and on the left side of the square eight mounted policemen, in the costumes we had seen when they led the procession of Santa Catalina Tomás, were in line abreast holding lances topped with the flags of Spain and Majorca.

It was only when I used a telephoto-lens to take a close-up picture of the assembled 'horsemen' that I realised that one was the very attractive girl who had demonstrated her skill as a bare-back rider when we went to the police display in Bellver Woods. She was wearing exactly the same red jacket, white breeches and shiny black boots as her male companions and attracted a considerable amount of attention from the crowd.

On the far side of the square, facing the Town Hall, a military band and about fifty soldiers with rifles were on parade, some with highly polished picks, shovels or axes strapped to their backs.

Other participants then entered the square including a group of women and children in folk attire and some dancers in elaborate costumes. A Majorcan gentleman was standing next to us somewhat unusually dressed in a purple cloak, puce shirt, bright cravat and mountain boots. We asked him whether the dancers were the famous Cossiers who perform at Algaida and Montuiri during July and August. He thought that they were, but a woman in front thought that they were a local group. Other members of the crowd also had differing opinions and there was quite a commotion for a few minutes while the matter was hotly debated without any positive identification being established.

The next group to arrive were unmistakable as they had very realistic horse costumes attached around their waists and we knew that they were *es cavallets* who dance in Felanitx in the third week of July; at Pollença on August 2nd for the feast of Our Lady of Los Angeles; and in Felanitx again on August 28th for the feast of San Agustin.

The police riders formed into line two abreast and rode slowly across the square to halt in the road leading to the Cathedral and await the main procession. This emerged from the Town Hall led by the town drummers in their long blue coats trimmed with red and a man carrying a glass case containing the crown worn by Jaime I. The civic dignitaries followed, bearing on their shoulders a six metre pole clad in green foliage and draped with a long red and yellow pennant. This was quickly erected in the centre of Plaza Court and two military guards with lances stood beside the Standard as sentinels, while the rest of the procession formed up behind the horses and marched slowly towards the Cathedral to attend a service. The crown in its case was left below the portrait of King Jaime and the military band remained in the square to entertain the crowd. Chairs were arranged in a semi-circle facing the Town Hall to await the return of the dignitaries, padded ones in the front for those of highest rank and slatted ones at the back for less important posteriors.

An hour later, the sound of pipes and drums heralded the return of the procession and the soldiers sprang to attention in response to a trumpet call and then aimed their guns skywards. The salute from thirty or more rifles was so well-timed that it sounded like one large explosion and the returning horses reared slightly in alarm as the procession entered the square.

The dignitaries lowered the Standard from its position in the centre of Plaza Cort and, to loud applause from the crowd, they again carried it on their shoulders, this time back into the Town Hall. They then returned to the square to fill the semi-circle of chairs while the soldiers marched off in quick-time.

The whole of Plaza Cort was soon packed to capacity and people came out onto the balconies of the surrounding houses to listen to a poem by Pere Alcantara Penay, recalling the origins of the feast, recited by the actress Aina Segura in the centre of a group of children who joined in loudly for each chorus.

The crowd then drifted away, but only for a few hours. It was New Year's Eve and by midnight the square, together with Plaza Mayor, Plaza Santa Eulalia and the Borne would again be packed with revellers who would listen to bands and bring twelve grapes to be eaten while the clock above the Town Hall struck midnight.

And so the year of fiestas in Majorca came to a close, only to commence again on January 5th with the great processions of the Three Kings.

12. *Flora and Fauna.*

On waking I throw open the *persianas* and survey the scene from our balcony filled with gratitude for the series of coincidences that eventually led to our living two thousand feet up a mountain overlooking a stretch of spectacular Mediterranean coast. From such an elevated viewpoint the horizon is high in a sky which is so often blue that I feel a little surprised if the day dawns with rain, a sea mist or cloud. Even if the morning is misty I am compensated by the sight of a surrealist landscape. The little hills dotted along the coast become islands in a white sea which runs up every valley and obscures familiar landmarks.

From this eyrie I can see many of the elements that make up the Majorcan countryside. Pine trees in their thousands cover the slopes of the mountains and stretch down to parts of the coastal strip while holm oaks, olives, carobs, figs and almond trees grow in profusion.

Unlike Britain where winter is the period when many trees shed their leaves and hibernate until the spring; most Majorcan trees only survive the hot summer months by cutting down on water loss by shedding leaves, reducing their surface area by curling them or coating them with wax. This results in a reversal of the British seasons with surplus leaves falling during the hot summer and fresh green growth appearing in the autumn, ready to exploit the eagerly awaited rain.

On uncultivated land, shrubs fill the spaces between the trees, lentisks abound with their resinous scent and shrubby growth while rock roses give the impression that they have escaped from cultivation with their quite large pink flowers and grey sticky leaves. Between the rocks wild gladioli add a splash of colour and again produce the effect of a neglected garden. A scattering of wild lavender reinforces the illusion.

In the more productive areas fig, almond, orange, lemon, pear, pomegranate, apple and apricot trees are common. Some old farm houses have two tall palms standing like guardians one on either side of the drive and many have tall, slender, dark green cypress trees to add height and shade.

We are too high for fruit, but the almond can survive even at our altitude. A visit to Majorca in February when seven million almond trees are in blossom offers a sight that will never be forgotten. This is a subject that artists return to again and again although it is hard to capture on canvas or film. Unfortunately one has to be there at the right time, because all too soon the wind blows the blossom away. The area around Calvià is particularly beautiful at this time when the fields are abundantly dressed in pink and white.

Wild flowers grow in profusion, especially in the spring. Bright yellow cape sorrel covers the fields from February onwards and yellow broom sprouts from any convenient crevice at the roadside. In June many orchards are red with poppies, another favourite subject for artists, and in the autumn bright blue morning glory winds itself over fences and walls. In neglected corners prickly pears and pink bignonias soon gain a foothold and spread to an enormous size.

The local authorities make imaginative use of shrubs and trees on the verges and central reservations of roads where mimosa, broom, and oleander bloom throughout the year. Many roundabouts feature lush green grass often shaded by a mixture of date and fan palms irrigated by elaborate sprinkler systems. In the warmer parts of the coastal strip palms abound and survive remarkably well in very small beds in the pavements, while rubber trees grow to an immense size to fill up larger areas. Hibiscus and orange trees are planted in many parks and squares and the flowers and fruit are never vandalised.

We thought that we were experienced gardeners having twice turned bare English ground into a pleasing mixture of sweeping lawns, herbaceous borders, rose beds and well trimmed hedges. Our garden at Munstead had formed part of the grounds of one of Britain's greatest gardeners, Gertrude Jekyll, and we spent ten years restoring its acres of yew hedges, lawns and borders to something of their former glory, but we were totally unprepared for gardening on top of a mountain in Majorca.

Much of the land in front of our new house had been scattered with rubble from the excavation work to present us with a daunting task because many tons were involved. We soon noticed, however, that the stones had been chipped out leaving each with at least one relatively flat face and providing us with plenty of suitable material with which to build walls to hold back the earth we would have to import.

We progressed slowly, building a retaining wall, breaking up the ground with a pick to provide drainage and then getting earth delivered by Juan who skilfully manoeuvred his lorry to tip soil to a depth of about two feet behind it. We discovered that the golden rule is not to fight nature. A plant in the wrong location can be kept alive by constant attention, but it is much better to experiment and find where things do well without being too demanding.

I have a few temperamental plants that repay the care they insist on, including a fine stephanotis and also a very happy hydrangea for which I eventually found just the right spot in a corner of a covered terrace; but our initial plantings resulted in many failures because we underestimated the difficulty of providing sufficient water during the summer and shelter from the strong winds that sweep across our exposed site in spring.

In our rather harsh habitat we are too high for some varieties that grow in profusion in the fields and gardens lower down. We can grow hibiscus, but only the sturdy red species; we tried growing hybrids but sooner or later they all succumbed to the chill spring winds. Similarly, the common purple bougainvillaea does best, although we do grow hybrid varieties in a few sheltered spots. Shrubs and trees that thrive include red and pink bignonias, daturas with long white trumpets and a wonderful scent in the evening air, yellow and white jasmine, powder blue plumbago, pink and white oleanders, yellow mimosa, yuccas and phoenix palms. We have to nurse our roses, clematis, rubber trees, and jacarandas which present few problems in the gardens in the village below, but we have no difficulty with some climbers such as the passion flower and honeysuckle.

Geraniums and pelargoniums provide colour and withstand drought. I have seen some growing in a small urn on top of a gatepost that are never watered and seldom lack flowers. In Majorca they can suffer from attack by a moth grub and if neglected they display holes in their stems and rot back, but when regularly sprayed with an insecticide such as *Lancord* they happily survive the winter and can eventually grow into sizeable shrubs with quite thick trunks.

Other trouble-free plants include alyssum, begonias, dianthus, carnations, wallflowers, marigolds, freesias, pansies, petunias, salvias, stocks, and mesembryanthemums that open to greet the sun with cushions of flowers in all shades of pink to crimson and close in the evening.

Gardening is all about climate and the climate in Majorca is complex. We have often been on the beach watching holiday-makers dressed in little more than a shoe lace soaking up the bright sunshine and then noticed heavy cloud inland. Although we are only four kilometres from the coast as the Majorcan kestrel flies, we have a completely different climate. We are cooler in summer, which is a bonus, but we also have cooler winters and much more wind. Frost is rare and it is the wind that does most damage to plants which can not withstand its chill touch.

Overall, we have a higher rainfall than the coastal strip, but rain falls very locally on the island and it is common to be drenched in Palma only to find that not a drop has fallen on our garden. From our high observation point we can often see rain clouds discharging on parts of the land spread out before us while other areas are bathed in sunshine.

When a sea mist rolls in we are usually above it, but when there is a thunderstorm it is often all around us. Storms can be quite frightening because the rain is so intense that the level of water in the swimming pool can rise three inches in the space of an hour or so. We have gutters at the rear of the house to take water to our *cisterna*, but no gutter can handle the full volume of a rainstorm and the water pours over the sides.

The balcony outside our bedroom is built out from the house to form a porch over the front door. Rain comes off the roof and onto the balcony which would quickly flood if it were not for a large spout that the builder has thoughtfully provided to allow it to escape in a cascade. Unfortunately it has been placed directly over the line of approach to the door so that visitors sometimes receive a very damp welcome.

After long periods of drought, which can last for many months in the summer, the ground is baked hard and gentle rain would evaporate without penetrating the surface. The heavy downpours are essential, but they lead to flash floods as water rushes down from the mountains. Soon after we arrived a heavy storm caused a flood which tore down the valley from Capdella to the coast causing considerable damage and cutting a wide channel through the beach in Paguera. High winds in the same storm ripped tiles from our roof and lifted a heavy teak sun-burst table over a wall to be smashed to pieces on the terrace below.

There is an old windmill at the roundabout where the main coast road joins with the one leading to Santa Ponça. It was painstakingly restored over a long period but the new sails had only just been fitted when a hurricane ripped them off. Another high wind sank some boats in the harbour in Palma and caused considerable damage to others, so the winds are not unique to our mountain location.

The most colourful time for gardens in Majorca is the spring, before the summer heat comes. After the temperature rises the native plants use a variety of methods to survive. Some simply die back to a bulb to await cooler conditions, some die completely after spreading seeds to ensure next year's crop, while others reduce their leaves to a bare minimum. Roses, for example, flower in spring and become almost totally defoliated by August, only to make fresh growth and flower again in the autumn. We find it relatively easy to have a good display of flowers from March until early July, but we have to rely on the bougainvillaea, hibiscus, geraniums, pelargoniums and begonias for colour in high summer. By September the yellow and orange mesembryanthemums are in flower soon to be joined by the plumbagos and bignonias.

Once the rains are over, autumn is a particularly pleasant time in Majorca. The days are still warm enough for light clothing but it is not too hot for walking or sightseeing. In the garden it is a time for rooting cuttings and planting to enable the new stock to make good roots before the heat of the following summer. Providing the ground is clear of weeds by mid-May none will be seen until September when the rain turns the ground green almost overnight, so autumn is also a time when we are busy again with the hoe.

The rose is never the easiest of plants to cultivate, but it is particularly difficult in Majorca because it really hates the full heat of summer and becomes exhausted by its double flowering season. Everyone has their own preferred method of rose pruning but we find it best to give the bushes a light trim after their first flowering and then a full pruning in December or January to prevent them being rocked by the spring winds. Red bugs which live in the mastic trees find new rose shoots irresistible, ants disturb the roots, while sawflies and leaf-cutter bees chop up the leaves. We have the usual complement of aphids and a moth which bores into young flower buds. Mildew attacks some varieties and others are prone to a rust on their leaves, but we love our roses which repay our efforts with a glorious display.

Fruit and almonds are grown on the western side of Palma, but the main agricultural area is the flat *pla* or plain that extends east of Palma from the mountains in the north to the coast in the south. This is dotted with old windmills, some of which have been restored. There are two types; wind pumps, usually with square bases and circular hoops holding metal sails which were used for irrigation; and older circular towers with six sails which were mainly used for grinding grain although some broke down clay for making pottery.

The fields are often used to grow several crops in a year, mainly potatoes, tomatoes, green vegetables and strawberries. Cereals are also cultivated on the plain and there are many orchards growing oranges and other citrus fruit. Apples are grown on the cooler ground to the north, particularly around the villages of Orient and Puigpuñent while vines are mainly confined to the areas around Binissalem and Felanitx although there are small vineyards near Andratx and Banyalbufar.

The lower slopes of the northern mountains are covered in pine and oak woods which used to be kept clean by the efforts of charcoal burners, the gathering of brushwood to fuel bread ovens and by pigs which were allowed to roam in the woods to forage for acorns. The cessation of these activities has increased the danger of forest fires in the dry summer months and the island has recently experienced some serious outbreaks.

The noise and general disturbance of our building operations scared away many of the local birds and animals but when the work was completed they started to return. The sparrows took it all in their stride and never left, but soon they were joined by warblers, thrushes, nightingales, redstarts, finches, crossbills and linnets.

K J Stoba's excellent book *Birdwatching in Mallorca,* lists about 280 different birds that have been sighted on Majorca. Fewer than 60 are residents but the island is on the migratory path for many species which pass through in spring and autumn and it provides a wide variety of habitat, from the sparsely populated northern mountains to the eastern marshes and salt lakes.

Not all of the feathered visitors are welcome. Starlings arrive by the thousand in October and stay until spring when they fly off to central and northern Europe. During their stay they are a pest in Palma and other towns, covering cars, statues and buildings with their droppings. Many deterrents have been employed to discourage them, including fireworks and amplified music, but they have not proved very effective.

It was not long before a kestrel rode the air currents over our mountain, hovering for several minutes virtually motionless and then plunging to the ground to seize an unsuspecting mouse. A family of partridges wearing smart green coats with red stockings walked in single file along the rear terrace chatting to one another as they passed the kitchen window. The red-legged partridge is said to have been brought to the island by the asthmatic King Sancho. A very large pheasant spent a day in our woodland before travelling on and hoopoes, quite large birds with crested heads, pinky-brown necks, and distinctive black and white striped wings, became a common sight as they looked for the *geckos,* wall lizards, that the Majorcans often call *dragós* or little dragons.

One night we were awakened by what seemed to be a burglar on the roof of our bedroom. Nearly all Majorcan roofs are covered by two layers of pantiles; the first layer is laid upside down to form troughs, the tiles being overlapped to conduct water down the roof; the second layer is set the right way up to bridge the gaps between the troughs. Only a few rows along the edge of the roof are cemented so anyone moving over the others causes them to rattle. We heard the 'burglar' along the length of the house and then to our surprise, he started to roll marbles down the valleys in the tiles. They took some time to travel from the ridge to the eaves and we lay in bed listening and wondering whether to take action ourselves or call the police. My husband considered that anyone on the roof was at a disadvantage and could be tackled without assistance, so he went onto our balcony, calling first in English and then in Spanish for the burglar to come down.

There was total silence. Further calls still produced no response and we decided that we might make more progress if we could see what was on the roof which was impossible from the balcony. One way would have been to go down into the garden, but my husband had a better idea involving a shaving mirror lashed to a walking-stick which he made into a primitive periscope. He scanned the entire roof but saw nothing.

We had hardly settled down again before more marbles rolled down the tiles. This time my husband exploded in anger and shouted to the intruder to give himself up, but once again there was silence. We never did establish exactly what had happened, but we think that the large white owl which we had seen flying around the house at night had found a method of cracking snails by rolling them down the roof to smash on the concrete path below.

We sometimes hear a strange single note endlessly repeated at night. It is a little like the torture of the dripping tap except that the rhythm is broken by pauses just long enough to persuade us that it has stopped, only to start again just as we are dropping off to sleep. We have been told that it is made by a Scops owl which emits the monotonous beep while it hunts for its dinner.

Ornithologists come in considerable numbers to Majorca and good facilities are available for birdwatchers, particularly in the reedbeds of the *Albufera* near Alcudia. Other popular areas are the salt lakes around Campos, Cabrera Island, Porto Colom, Artà, Formentor, Pollença, Lluc, Gorg Blau, Orient and Andratx.

Rabbits abound on our mountain and Tia, our Siamese cat, is adept at catching them, sometimes bringing one inside to show us and letting it escape to provide us with a little entertainment. We have shrews and mice, and *geckos* who become quite friendly and often enter the house where we catch them in a trap made from an ice cream box and a piece of cardboard. The trick is to place the open box over the *gecko* and slide the cardboard between the box and the wall, trapping the *gecko* so that it can be released outside the house.

We were about to have breakfast on the terrace one lovely sunny morning only to find it alive with frogs. We had never seen any on our land before, and have very seldom seen one since, but there must have been thirty or more. Tia found that if she put a paw on a frog's back it jumped like a tiddlywink and started the others hopping too; we had to shut her in the house while we collected them up and took them to safety.

It was only a few weeks later that we performed another rescue. This time it was a small mouse who had fallen into the swimming pool in the night and found himself unable to climb out. He would have drowned if he had not been sensible enough to swim to a floating thermometer and cling to it like a shipwrecked sailor clutching at a buoy. We soon scooped him out with the pool net and he scampered away with no obvious ill effects.

Curious scratchings in the ceiling warned us that we had other visitors. Outside, by the light of a torch, we could see two little faces peering at us from the top of the chimney, so we borrowed a cage-trap and baited it with cheese. Our success was phenomenal; every night without fail there was a mouse-like creature sitting in the trap waiting for a car-ride down the hill. On several occasions we found that two had entered the trap together and both were awaiting transport.

We lost count after we reached fifty and still have to set the trap from time to time when we hear noises in the ceiling. The problem is that they have a taste for the plastic that coats electrical wiring and can cause damage to the cables, and themselves, when they nibble through.

These little animals have tufted tails and large ears with a black stripe running from the eye to the ear, the upper body is grey/brown but the underside is white. Juan's son, Carlos, assures us that they are *lirons,* dormice, but they are more like a gerbil than an English dormouse. Tia's attitude to them is extraordinary in that she studiously ignores them when they chatter in their cage; no mouse is normally safe within a mile of her, but she absolutely refuses to take any interest in them once they are captive.

Dormice seldom enter the house itself, but one day I saw one crouching in a corner by the stairs. I called my husband who armed himself with the ice-cream box trap and crept slowly up behind it until he could drop the box over it. When he did so there was a whirring sound and we realised that we had trapped Tia's favourite clockwork mouse.

One warm night I rested my arm on top of the sheet and touched fur which promptly vanished. I was still half-asleep but woke my husband to tell him about it. 'Don't be silly,' he replied. 'You imagined it, go back to sleep.' About an hour later, however, there was a tremendous shout at he leapt from the bed saying that something furry had run over his hand. We put on the light but could see nothing. Not knowing what it was, we acted with caution and explored the bedclothes to ensure that we had not caught whatever it was in them, but there was nothing there. We then peeped over the side of the bed and met two eyes looking at us from underneath. A *liron* had climbed up and entered our first-floor bedroom where it had become trapped when we closed the doors to the balcony. As soon as we opened them it quickly made its escape, scampering without difficulty down the vertical wall.

The tortoise is fairly common in Majorca and at least two live somewhere in our garden. An association called *Amics de las Tortugues,* Friends of the Tortoise, has been formed to look after their preservation as they are threatened by forest fires and continual development of their habitat. We have been told not to touch them because it makes them agitated and they lose liquid which they may be unable to replace on a hot day. Most are brown but a scarce dark green variety with white spots and a long tail lives in the wetlands of Albufera.

A friend of ours was driving on a fairly quiet road when he was stopped by a policeman. As he had been exceeding a short 50 kph speed limit on a hill, he assumed that he would have to pay an on-the-spot fine, but the policeman just pointed to a tortoise that was crossing the road. He stood and guarded it until it had safely reached the opposite verge and then waved the traffic on.

Other wildlife we see occasionally includes hares, hedgehogs, pipistrelle bats, weasels and the harmless grass snakes than can grow up to six feet long. None of the three snakes found in Majorca is poisonous, although grass snakes can bite if they are picked up; the others are the viperine and cowl which are smaller and not often seen. Once a pine marten like a big shaggy cat walked along the wall at the back of our property. It has a thick-set larger cousin living on the island called a *genet* which has a ringed tail and mottled coat but we have never seen one.

After it rains the snails come out and also curious worm-like creatures which can be up to three inches long, they curl into a spiral when touched and Majorcans call them *serpientes.* They love to crawl between the slats of *percianas* and drop on your hand as you open a window; they also get squashed inside door frames and make a horrible mess – I dislike them intensely.

Insect life is varied and specimens are often much larger than their counterparts in Britain. We have some stag beetles that look like a 747 coming in to land. There are bright green bugs five inches long not counting the tail (it may or may not be a sting, we have never risked finding out) and a few small scorpions that are probably relatively harmless, although we notice that Gregoria treats them with extreme caution.

Soon after we moved in we heard a buzzing rather like a bad electrical connection. Day by day it grew louder until we could almost feel it as well as hear it. We discovered that it was made by the grasshopper-like creature known as the cicida or harvest bug which the Spanish call the *cigarra* or *chicharra* and the Majorcans call *cigales.* After a while we were able to ignore the noise and suddenly, some time in late summer, we realised that it had stopped. This was because the adults die around September but not before laying several hundred eggs in the branch of a tree. In December these hatch into yellow larvae which spin threads to let themselves down to the ground into which they burrow to find a root. For four years they live on sap taken from the root to emerge in June, shed their skin and become adult insects.

We have many varieties of butterfly, including the lovely black and yellow swallowtail; others include the red admiral, the long tailed blue and the Cleopatra. Dragonflies are common as well as large humming-bird hawk moths which hover in front of flowers to take the nectar without alighting.

One of the 'nasties' is the processionary moth. Traps are set for these in the form of a lure which attracts the males with the scent of the female. The female lays a hundred or more eggs in a pine tree and the larvae weave a nest that looks like a large white ball of cotton-wool, leaving it at night to feed on pine needles. When they are mature in February or March, they crawl in procession down the trunk and along the ground to find a suitable spot in which to bury themselves; the *procesiónares* look like a long brown cord as the caterpillars march nose to tail. They emerge in July or August to change into moths which only have a short life during which the females lay eggs to repeat the cycle.

The offensive thing about the processionary moth is its caterpillar which has hairs that cause intense irritation, especially if they get into an eye. We have many pines on our land and we get rid of the nests by cutting them down with long pruning shears if they are low enough to reach; if they are high up we ask our neighbour to shoot them out of the trees. It is very important not to touch the nests or the caterpillars and we find that the best way to dispose of them is to burn the nests on a hard surface to prevent the caterpillars escaping by burrowing into the ground. We transport them on the prongs of a long fork and wear gloves and long sleeves throughout the operation.

One morning we awoke to a strong smell of burning wood and when we went out onto our balcony we found it covered with ash. There was smoke across the valley to the south of the house and the flames spread rapidly until the north side of the range of hills running parallel to the coast above Portals Nous and Palma Nova, known as Na Burguesa, was alight for several kilometres.

An appeal was broadcast for local volunteers to assist in fighting the fire and my husband was away all day helping to tackle the blaze which, at its height, covered a 12 kilometre front. Two seaplanes and several small single-engined planes have been equipped for fire-fighting; the twin-engined Canadair seaplanes can scoop water from the sea, store it and drop it like a bomb on the fire, but the smaller planes must return to Son Bonet airport to reload. All of the pilots distinguished themselves with some very skilful flying, and the outbreak was eventually brought under control, but only after the area had suffered very severe damage.

My husband returned at nine that evening, black from head to toe and totally exhausted as he had been hauling heavy fire hoses up and down the near vertical slopes. Fire engines had come from all over the island and he had been working with a team from Inca, but the terrain prevented the vehicles getting close to the fire and very long lengths of hose were required. He had just enough energy left to drop into a hot bath and then went straight to bed.

The Council gave a small party for the helpers and my husband still has a T-shirt printed with the message *salvem Na Burguesa* with which he was presented as a token of thanks, but their gratitude was short-lived. Shortly afterwards he went back to the council offices to pay our *Impuesto Sobre Bienes Inmuebles,* local rates, which had always been due in September. He was promptly fined 20% for being late as the time for settlement had been advanced to July without our receiving any prior notification.

In recent years, forest fires have been a serious problem and teams of volunteers have been formed to clear the debris and tidy up as much as possible. The authorities are encouraging the planting of new trees and aircraft are even being used to distribute seed over the affected areas. Watch-towers have been erected across the island which are manned constantly to quickly detect any new outbreak of fire.

13. Rules and Regulations

It took a little while for us to adapt to the habits of our Majorcan hosts. People from northern climes tend to suffer from what has been described as Malady of Supposed Urgency – MSU. This causes them to rush when they could easily afford to stroll and to fret if delayed by a queue. The problem is almost non-existent on the island apart from on the roads. Majorcans never seem to be in a hurry when you are waiting behind one in a shop or outside a phone booth, but once in a car they suffer severe MSU and are sometimes unable to find time to stop at red lights.

Initially we thought it curious that these same drivers were slow off the mark when the lights changed to green, until we realised that experience had taught them that there was a high statistical probability that one of their number would be dashing through on the red and a quick start could lead to one of the dramatic accidents that are still far too frequent. Some cyclists and riders of motor-scooters consider themselves absolved from the highway code and regularly shoot lights or even proceed the wrong way down one-way streets.

On the motorway we are often passed by two cars travelling at over 120 kilometres per hour with only a few feet between the leader and the one behind. It is common for a car to overtake on the left and then shoot across to the right in front of one's bonnet, tyres screaming at the limit of their adhesion as it turns off the motorway into a slip road. We asked a Majorcan friend why there was so much amateur driving and he explained it by saying: 'It is because many of us are amateurs; most of those driving high-powered hatchbacks today were riding a moped only a few years ago.'

Six months after we arrived it was necessary for us to have new driving licences. Until then it had been legal for us to drive using our British ones, but we were now residents and could not operate a Spanish-plated car without a Spanish driving licence. We understood that the process would involve a medical inspection, so we went to our doctor for a certificate but he could not help us. Special independent centres have been established where one must report for the test. We found one close to the *Tráfico* building which deals with the issue of licences.

The staff were pleasant but spoke no English so we had a little difficulty understanding what was required of us in the examinations which covered eyesight, hearing, reaction times, co-ordination and general health. One test involved a computer which displayed two moving 'roads' on each of which a black line represented a car. They moved at increasing speed while we attempted to keep each 'car' on its respective road by manipulating two levers, one in each hand. It was easy at first as the roads ran parallel, but when they started to diverge and then come together it became almost impossible. I left what must have represented two complete wrecks behind me and my husband did little better.

I then went on to have my hearing tested. This might have gone quite well if the test had been conducted in English as all I had to do was indicate in which ear I could hear first a high and then a low pitched note, but as I did not understand the rapid flow of Spanish and said *perdón* every time the tester began the routine the result was probably inconclusive.

I was a little worried about the medical as I had only recently had my coronary by-pass. I had since undergone many examinations in London and my heart was probably in better condition than most of those being tested, but nerves caused it to pound and I was sure I would fail. I thought it best if the doctor did not see my scar and he must have thought me unduly modest as I frantically clutched my blouse and prevented him opening it to examine my chest, but he did not persist and, to my relief I was told that I was considered fit to drive. However, I had not fooled him for a moment, because when I went to renew my licence he looked at me and said 'Ah, the lady with the bypass.'

A Spanish driving licence, known as a *Permiso de Conducción* is virtually an identity card as it contains a photograph, a specimen signature and an address which must be updated if one moves. We use ours constantly to guarantee our cheques and credit cards.

When they are two years old, all Spanish registered cars are subjected to mechanical inspections similar to those in Britain but much more stringent. The tests cannot be performed by ordinary garages; cars must be taken to special government appointed centres where their drivers are expected to assist by staying with their vehicles and working the brakes, lights or steering as the testers require.

The equipment is comprehensive and each test commences with an analysis of exhaust fumes followed by inspection of the lights, wipers, screen-washers, horn, indicators and tyres. When our car was due for its first test my husband managed quite well initially, but misunderstood a command in Spanish and almost wrecked the brake-testing machine by doing an emergency stop when he was supposed to apply gentle but increasing pressure; the car shot upwards and sideways, forcing the tester to leap to safety. This was followed by an inspection of the steering, suspension and exhaust with the car stationary above a pit. From time to time commands in Spanish from the depths below called for the steering wheel to be moved or the hand-brake applied and my husband did his best to co-operate, but he was unprepared when the front of the car was suddenly shaken quite violently from side to side by a machine to reveal any play in the axles. He came home and needed a strong drink before describing his experiences, but the car was given the vital coloured sticker for its windscreen to show that it had passed.

We are totally in favour of such inspections as they have virtually eliminated the old bangers that used to crawl around the island with doubtful brakes and steering. The only really shabby cars seen today are a few old crocks that still display foreign plates, although they have obviously been on the island for many years. A genuine British car on a visit to Majorca would be displaying a current UK tax disk on its windscreen, so the ancient cars running on British plates that do not display such a disk are probably paying no road tax and not being regularly tested.

To encourage owners to buy new cars the government recently introduced an excellent scheme whereby they contributed £500 if a car at least ten years old was traded in for a new one. The dealers matched the offer with another £500 or more and the total saving of over £1000 was too attractive for us to resist, because the Citroen we had purchased from the 'professor' qualified under the scheme.

We had no problems, but heard of a couple who were not so lucky. Their car was twelve years old, so they handed it in and ordered a new one which should have been delivered by the time they returned from a short holiday. The colour they had chosen proved difficult to obtain and, after some weeks without a car, they decided that the only thing to do was collect their old car, re-insure it and run it until their new one eventually arrived.

Unfortunately the garage had removed various body parts from their car in the belief that it would soon be scrapped and could not obtain a colour match when replacing them. It looked very odd by the time it was back on the road and the final straw came when it did not qualify for the £500 contribution. It had initially been run on tourist plates and had only recently been converted to full Spanish plates, so despite its considerable age it was legally only two years old.

One day I went to collect our post and the postmaster, with a wry smile, said 'I think, *señora*, that you have a *multa.*' Amongst my letters there was an official looking envelope containing a form that told me that I had been observed turning left where such a manoeuvre was not permitted. The fine was 5000 pesetas but a discount of 20% applied if I paid promptly. This was the first I knew of the matter, the incident had happened several weeks before and I had not been stopped by a policeman. I believe myself to be an observant driver and could not remember committing any such offence so I did what any sensible wife would do and handed the notice to my husband saying: 'You must have been driving the car that day.'

He knew that he was not guilty, but the important thing was to pay the fine quickly. The internal post in Majorca is subject to mysterious delays that can result in a letter taking two weeks to travel two miles; our *multa* had been posted many days before and we only had a few hours to spare if we were to take advantage of the discount. We thought that we would have to make a special trip to Palma until the postman informed us that such fines were commonplace and payment could be made at any bank. We went to one in Calvià and in a matter of moments the *multa* was paid, but we still argue about which one of us was driving the car at the time.

In our bank, when cashing a cheque, it used to be necessary for us to stand in one line to hand it to a clerk who would then issue us with a numbered slip and post the cheque with a duplicate into a slot in the cashier's cage. We then had to join a queue in front of the cashier who would hold up his copy of the numbered slip to signal us to approach him. We never did discover what useful function the first clerk performed and one day when we visited the bank we found that he had vanished. Thereafter cashing a cheque took half the time.

The Calvià post office seldom stays in one place for long. The first question that friends ask when they come out to their holiday homes is: 'Has the post office moved?' It has had six addresses in as many years, one was in a garage with an up-and-over door and when it was opened the wind blew the letters everywhere.

About three years ago we were asked whether we would like to have a PO Box in Calvià. There is no postal delivery up our mountain so we have to visit the post office to collect our mail. Up to that time it had been placed in a folder in a suspended file where anyone had access to it; the system worked reasonably efficiently but we thought that a locked box would be an improvement and were the first to sign up for the service. In due course a large metal array of 50 lockable boxes was placed on a table in the post office and we were presented with the key to our box. I asked whether the post office had a spare key in case we lost ours or forgot to bring it and the postman said that it would present no problem. All we had to do was walk round to the other side of the table where there was unlimited entry to all of the boxes because the contraption had no back panel!

Collecting the mail is a major logistical problem. In theory the post office is open from ten in the morning until one, but that is subject to certain variables. The post must be collected from the bus, which may be delayed; the postman has deliveries to make in the village and may not get back to his office by ten; it may be fiesta, or it may have been fiesta yesterday and, as tomorrow is Saturday, a *puente* may be taken to avoid opening for just one day. Our own preferences also create difficulties.

If we are going to Palma we like to set off early. It is important to finish our shopping during the morning because, if everything we need has not been purchased by one-thirty, it is three hours before the shops are open again and the entire day is wasted. To collect our post we must either delay our departure, in which case we will not be in Palma before ten-thirty or leave Palma by twelve-thirty and hope that we have not chosen a day when the postman decides to shut early.

One day we dashed back and arrived at the post office well before it was due to close, but the door was locked. A young Spanish couple were waiting for the postman to return and we talked to them for about ten minutes before we noticed that the window of the post office was slightly open and a chair was conveniently located just below it. We hoisted the very law-abiding Spaniard up to the window. He was rather reluctant to assist us to rob the mail but the fact that we had the key to our box enabled him to salve his conscience and we returned home with our post.

My consultant suggested that I should try to swim every day as it is excellent exercise but our own pool is at a comfortable temperature only during July, August and September. Our daughters go in at other times, but even if I am feeling brave I find the water too cold by October in most years. We were therefore delighted when the local Council constructed a fine new sports complex just outside Calvià which included a superb pool in which I would be able to swim throughout the year.

We decided that having contributed to its cost as ratepayers, we might as well enjoy the use of its excellent swimming pool, tennis courts and gymnasium at the discount available to local residents. The Spanish passion for paper-work has long since ceased to surprise us, but we were totally unprepared for what was to follow.

We commenced logically, as we thought, by driving to the sports complex and asking for a membership form. The clerk explained that it was not for him to handle such important matters: he could provide a brochure but our application would have to be made to the Town Hall in Calvià. Thither we went, armed with our *residencias* which included our photographs and address and confirmed our right to live on the island. We explained that we would like to make regular use of the *Palau d'Esports* and produced our most recent computer-generated rates receipt to prove that we were indeed bona fide ratepayers. The young lady was most helpful, but she explained that the arbiter in this matter must be the computer. If our names appeared when she tapped the appropriate keys all would be well, if not then the first stage must be to have our data inscribed in its magnetic memory. She tapped but nothing happened. She explained that this was possibly due to the fact that we were not Spanish citizens but all we had to do was complete the appropriate form.

This form was impressive. In A3 landscape format, it commenced with boxes in which we were each asked to provide details of our mothers' maiden names and all of their forenames and went on to request similar details of other relatives before demanding extensive information about us, such as our academic qualifications and our present and previous addresses.

By straining our memories, and using invention when the correct answer eluded us, we completed the form, returned it and asked if we could now apply for our tickets for the sports centre. We also enquired as to the cost of membership and were informed that it would be 5,000 pesetas for one year but, to the infinite regret of the charming clerk, no more progress could be made that day. In due course the data would be processed, the computer would confirm that we existed, and a ticket could be issued. We would hear more in due course.

It so happened that we were troubled at that time by a stray sheep. Very pregnant, it had taken possession of a half-completed house not far from our villa and like many Majorcan sheep it wore a bell. The soft, hollow tinkling of sheep and goat bells on the distant hills in the still evening air of Majorca is delightful, but when the sound came from our newly planted herb garden it was more akin to a fire alarm. On several occasions the expectant mother wandered into the garden, but the last straw was when I opened the door to the rear terrace one morning and found her with the remainder of our carefully nurtured English curled parsley drooping from either side of her mouth.

We decided that someone must own the sheep and would wish to take possession of the lamb when it was born, so we called the police and explained the position. They promised to make enquiries and a day or so later a member of the *Policía Municipal* drove up while my husband was repairing the damage to the herb garden. We welcomed the representative of the law and led him across the road to the place where we knew that the sheep usually spent most of the day; there was evidence of recent occupation in the form of compressed grass, but no sheep. The officer looked puzzled and my husband explained in his inadequate Spanish that the 'mutton' had gone but would probably not be far away.

The policeman assured us that he had no immediate interest in the sheep. As we had recently completed a form which would result in our being entered on the Town Hall computer, he had come to inspect our documents and assure himself that we really were living where we claimed. Fortunately he did not require any more details of our family connections, but he examined our passports with care before pronouncing himself satisfied. We asked when we might expect the computer to be updated and he told us that there was a backlog, but that it would be worth enquiring in about two weeks.

After several visits to the Town Hall the time came when the computer acknowledged our existence as Calvià ratepayers. Its lack of such information had never prevented it issuing rate bills or providing receipts, but now it was fully informed and was able to issue a printout confirming the fact; it also made a small charge for its labour in printing the vital certificates.

We returned to our friendly clerk with the precious papers and asked if we could now pay for our tickets and enjoy the use of the sports complex. The answer was a qualified affirmative. The certificates were in order, but payments for the sports centre were not handled at the Town Hall. Not far away, in another building, we would find an accounts department which would handle the matter. We found it after a few enquiries and entered, carrying our passports, residencias, a 5,000 peseta note (Spanish government and local government offices seldom accept cheques), two completed application forms and our new certificates. These were all accepted by the clerk except for the 5,000 pesetas because the annual subscription price had risen since our initial attempt to join. I turned to my husband for the additional money but he had not been to the bank and his wallet was empty.

Later in the week, armed with sufficient funds, we went back to the accounts office and asked for our tickets. The reply was that these would be issued to us at the sports centre, all that was required was the production of the receipt which we were promptly given. We hurried to the sports centre confident that this must be our last hurdle, the clerk took the receipt and our application forms, shook his head and raised his eyebrows. 'But where are your photographs?' he asked. The pictures were required so that they could be incorporated in our admission badges. A visit to Palma was needed to obtain some colour passport photographs and these had then to be taken back to the sports centre. In total about three months elapsed between our initial approach and our admission badges eventually being issued.

Many foreign residents were caught when the date for payment of rates in our area was changed without warning, but the Majorcans seem to have an efficient grape vine to alert them to such traps. No apology was offered for the lack of any notice or the fact that we had only ten months' service instead of twelve for our previous rates payment.

We exercised our right to vote in Majorca for the first time in the 1994 elections to the European Parliament. The organisation was excellent; the system being based on proportional representation. Each party offers a list of candidates whose names appear in the order by which they will qualify for election. Votes are for a party not an individual. If a party gains enough votes to win four seats, the initial four candidates on its list are elected.

The first foreign voters were a novelty which attracted the press, so we were interviewed when we left the polling booth and had our pictures taken. It may have been the light or the camera angle, but the photographs were to say the least unflattering and on the day the picture appeared we had numerous calls from friends asking if we were ill.

Officialdom has changed greatly during the time that we have lived on the island. Many regulations were swept away after Spain joined the EEC and Customs formalities were abolished for the importation of goods, including furniture and effects, from anywhere within the Community. When *residencias* have to be renewed, computers now efficiently handle in a few minutes what used to involve hours in a queue at the police station.

Most of the previous red tape applied just as much to Spanish nationals as foreign residents, but they were better able to handle it, being accustomed to the complex procedures and unhampered by language problems. There has recently been a positive effort to improve efficiency and cut out pointless paperwork so that life as an expatriate in Majorca is much simpler today than it was only a few years ago.

14. Around the City of Palma

Visitors to a city walk with guidebook in hand observing its attractions and taking photographs as a record of their holiday; but residents tend to hurry past the same buildings, squares and monuments intent on reaching the bank before it closes and barely sparing a glance at the magnificent architecture or a thought for its historical associations. To us, Palma is an important centre for shopping and for visits to our lawyer or insurance agent; nevertheless we have never quite lost the enthusiasm of the tourist and find the city a source of endless interest.

Palma is home to around 325,000 of the 614,000 residents of Majorca. The main part still lies within the old boundary of its former 17th Century walls which no longer exist but have left their mark in the layout of the *Ronda* or ring road. The *Ronda* commences at the sea on its western end in Avenida Argentina and progresses in a zigzag pattern around the city until it returns to the sea on the eastern side. The curiously angled layout of its roads is a relic of the pattern of ramparts which were so constructed as to permit crossfire from two sides during any attack.

The layout of the streets is somewhat confusing. Until we got to know Palma well, we mentally divided the city into two halves, split vertically by a line running up from the sea along

Avenida Antonio Maura, continuing up the Borne and then north up Calle San Jaime to the Plaza Santa Magdalena. The two areas thus created used to be known as the *Vila d'Amunt* or high town to the east and the *Vila de Baix* or low town to the west.

When friends come to stay with us they always want to explore Palma and, whether we act as guides or leave them to find their own way around the city, the first problem is the practical one of where to leave the car. Anyone living on the island knows a few places where it is sometimes possible to find a space in the roads and squares, but we advise friends intending to spend more than an hour or so in the city to park their car where it will not have to be moved every 90 minutes, which is the maximum permitted in the streets under a system of pay and display known as ORA. There is a large car park under the Parque del Mar with no time limit, the entrance to which is at the sea end of Avenida Antonio Maura. It is ideal for strangers because it does not involve driving through the heart of the city and makes an ideal starting point from which to see the older part of Palma.

When we emerge from the darkness of the car park into the Parque del Mar we always pause to admire the exquisite scene before us. The Parque includes a large lake which reflects two of the most beautiful structures on the island, the Cathedral and the Almudaina Palace. They are completely different in design; the Cathedral being a mass of Gothic detail and spires while the palace is sturdy and square in the style of a fortress with castellated towers, but they harmonise perfectly and their elevated position makes them the central feature of the waterfront.

Once we reach the Avenida Antonio Maura the Almudaina Palace dominates our attention. Beautifully trimmed trees and delightful arches of water are features of the gardens of S'Hort del Rei which fill the space between the road and the Palace and we usually walk through them in preference to the pavement. The Palace was originally constructed by the Arab rulers of Majorca on the site of an old mosque and the name is Arabic for citadel. It was reformed at the end of the 13th Century in the reign of King Jaime II by Pere Salvà, who was also responsible for Bellver Castle. The architecture is similar to that of the Castle of the Kings at Perpignan; the window detail in particular being almost identical.

Our favourite feature of the Almudaina Palace is the 14th Century angel by Camprodon high above the central tower. George Sand mentions this in her book *Winter in Majorca* and in a footnote to his translation Robert Graves adds a little more information when he writes: '*It acts as a weather cock, and the Majorcans describe an unstable man as being like the Palace Angel.*' It was struck by lightning in 1431 and later damaged by fireworks but still stands proudly above the Palace.

At the end of the gardens there is a little triangular park from which wide steps lead up by the Palace wall and into the road leading to the main entrance. Today it houses the Captaincy General of the Balearics, but part of it is open to the public including the old Santa Ana chapel which is virtually in its original form.

Directly opposite the Almudaina Palace the great west door of the Cathedral features some beautiful stonework. The Cathedral, known locally as *La Seo* was constructed over a period of about three hundred years and was completed in the early 17th Century. I have only a superficial knowledge of architecture, but none is needed to appreciate the beauty of this perfect Gothic building in its superb location. Externally, it is a symphony of honey-coloured stone, ornate doorways and flying buttresses; superbly sited near the waterfront and visible from most approaches to the city, even at night when it is very effectively floodlit.

Internally, octagonal columns forty-five metres high support the vaulted roof over the nave which is seventy-five metres in length. A rose window eleven metres in diameter dominates the uncluttered interior, its theme being the star of David. The unusual *baldoquino,* canopy, over the altar, which was designed by Antonio Gaudí, reminds me of the crown of thorns. There are seventeen side chapels and King Jaime II and King Jaime III are buried in the Trinity Chapel. The Cathedral houses an interesting museum and there is another in the Archbishop's Palace close by.

This is the oldest part of the city and it is a delight for lovers of architecture as virtually all of the many narrow streets contain at least one interesting building. Many old palaces built by noble families between the 15th and 18th centuries are located in this area and they are well described and illustrated in most guide books.

I am just able to differentiate between Gothic and baroque but I derive great pleasure from a glimpse through a wide archway into one of the courtyards that are a common feature of most of these fine houses. Traditionally the main rooms are on the first floor which is reached by an open staircase that leads to a gallery supported by arches. An ornate well often forms the centrepiece of the courtyard and the whole effect is of coolness, calm and symmetry. Wherever we are in Palma, we always look into any open gateway and seldom fail to spot another gem which is normally hidden from view.

It is said that if you waited long enough you would meet everyone you know at Piccadilly Circus. In terms of one's friends in Majorca this certainly applies to the Borne which is the northern extension of Avenida Antonio Maura. Guarded by four Sphinxes known as *Ses Lleonès* it dates in its present form from the 19th Century and provides a delightful area of shade in the heat of the summer. At the top, in Plaza Weyler, stands the old Grand Hotel. This was the first luxury hotel in Palma; it was built in 1903 but closed at the outbreak of the Spanish Civil War. It has now been perfectly restored by the *Fundació La Caixa* and now incorporates a bar, a bookshop, an exhibition gallery and a concert hall. Not long ago we visited the gallery which was displaying an exhibition of sketches and watercolours by local artists and were delighted to see one by Nils Burwitz and another by the son of a former neighbour in Surrey who now lives on the island.

Across the road, the new Court of Justice is in the impressive building that was formerly the Palace of the Berga family. It features two tiers of arches in its courtyard, the lower ones have sturdy columns while the upper gallery is supported on thinner and taller pillars.

The Teatro Principal is only a little way farther along on the right. The interior is delightfully original with plenty of gilt and red plush. We like to go and see one of the operas that are beautifully presented during a season which commences in March and runs through to June. Leading performers come from the mainland to participate and an elaborate simultaneous translation system displays the dialogue in Spanish and Majorcan. Although tickets are quite expensive, there is seldom an empty seat in the house.

A little north of the theatre two statues in Roman costume guard the start of La Rambla; an attractive tree-lined promenade dating from the same period as the Borne. It is often a riot of colour because it is where the flower sellers have their stalls, conveniently located for those visiting friends in the two large hospitals in the area.

Some elaborate steps at the south end of the Rambla lead up to the Plaza Mayor. This was once the main market area but it is now a large and very attractive square where there is a craft fair on Saturday mornings in the summer. When Queen Elizabeth visited the island on *Britannia*, the Royal Marine band from the yacht played there, attracting a huge crowd of curious Majorcans.

More recently the *plaza* has featured some unusual performers who paint themselves white and then 'freeze' like statues, remaining motionless for long periods while curious passers-by wonder whether they are really alive. There is always something going on in Plaza Mayor and it is an ideal place for sitting in the sun to have a coffee and enjoy the atmosphere.

About half way along the south side of the square a smaller square known as the Plaza Marqués del Palmer leads into Calle Jaime II which is one of Palma's major shopping streets. Plaza Cort is near its southern end, dominated by *La Sala,* the Town Hall, a 16th Century renaissance-style building in three distinct layers. The ground floor has an unusually wide central doorway with an ornate pediment, while above it an iron balcony runs along the entire length of the first floor. Tall double doors open onto the balcony in the centre and there are three deep windows on either side, all with pediments. The second floor is relatively plain, but it is relieved by a large clock and the roof projects for three metres. Plaza Cort is the hub of civil events including many of the fiestas and parades in Palma and also the exuberant New Year celebrations.

A narrow street on the left side of the Town Hall ends in Plaza Santa Eulalia where the church of the same name is one of the oldest in the City. It was constructed in the Gothic style in the 14th Century not long after the Conquest and contains some fine mediaeval wooden panels. Nearby is the magnificent palace of the Vivot family in Calle Zavella, part of which is open to the public.

Only a little way further east is the Convent of San Francisco. It was founded in 1281 under Royal patronage but was later damaged by lightning after which some baroque elements were introduced including the main façade. The doorway portrays the Virgin surrounded by cherubs and two figures who are both theologians, the one with the book being Ramón Llull whose tomb lies behind the altar. The beautiful four-galleried Gothic cloister is a national monument; it encloses a garden of lemon trees with a well in the centre which was built to the order of Bishop Fray Juan de Santander in the mid-17th Century.

In her excellent book on Fray Junípero Serra, who studied at the Convent, Dina Moore Bowden mentions the well stating: '*Fray Junípero and his friends, Fathers Palou and Crespí, must often have found refreshment from its limpid depths as they paced the cloister in meditation or friendly discussion*'. Fray Junípero was later to found the missions in California which grew to become the cities of San Diego, San Francisco and Los Angeles. My husband's work used to involve frequent visits to California and from time to time families he met there come to stay with us. They are always fascinated when we take them to places on the island that have close links with their homeland.

Ramón Llull, who is buried in the church, was another of the great figures of Majorca. He was born in 1233 in the reign of King Jaime I and was the son of a Catalonian knight who had come to Majorca with the Conqueror. Ramón Llull was Lord High Steward to King Jaime II and, although married with two sons, he was constantly unfaithful.

There is a story that his conversion came at the age of 40 when he lusted after a beautiful girl who bared her bosom and revealed a severe cancer telling him that he should stop chasing attractions that could prove to be false and turn instead to the truth of religion. Another legend suggests that he had visions which convinced him that he should change his ways. Whatever the true reason may have been, he totally abandoned his former life and became a scholar at the hermitage at Randa and later a teacher.

He opened a school for oriental languages near Valldemossa to train priests who would be working in the east and wrote over 200 books, mainly on philosophy and theology. He became a missionary and was martyred in Africa. Accounts differ as to whether he was found alive or dead after being stoned, but his body was brought back to Majorca by the merchants who found him and he now rests peacefully in Palma.

The Archive of the Kingdom of Majorca is located in the Calle Ramón Llull which leads off one side of the Plaza San Francisco and is a rich source of information about the history of Majorca but, if our guests are not students, we usually walk to the narrow street known as Almudaina that is bridged by an Arab arch with rooms above it. This is one of the few undisputed relics of the Moorish domination of Majorca and it formed one of the gates in the ramparts that fortified the old Arab Palace. In the same street stands the old British Consulate building where I attended the wedding of the Seymour-Smiths on my first visit to the island; it has now been renumbered 7A and accommodates the Cultural Department of the Palma Council.

By this point our visitors are usually ready for a rest, but one more stop is worth while before returning to the car. This is at the Arab Baths in Calle Serra. As so often happens, the authenticity of these has been questioned; some believing that they were actually built by the Jews whose quarter was centred on Santa Domingo Street when under Moslem rule. (Later there were two Jewish areas, one behind La Lonja and the other between Plaza Cort and Plaza Mayor).

The baths are certainly Arabic in style with a domed roof supported on twelve columns which are not all identical, suggesting that they may have come from other buildings. There are also several horseshoe-shaped arches which suggest an Arab influence. The two chambers are the calderium used for steam baths and the tepiderium for tepid baths. Close by, in a restored

mansion in Calle Portella, is the Museum of Majorca with a fine collection of paintings.

If all of this has been packed into one morning we are more than ready for a late lunch. There is unlimited choice as Palma is full of excellent restaurants catering for every taste, but my husband prefers to return again and again to those that have previously provided us with fine food and fair value and where the staff have come to know us. One of these is a simple cafe in Avenida Antonio Maura called Iska. It has the air of a tourist trap with tables set out under an awning on the pavement and food displayed on plates in a glass-fronted refrigerated cabinet, but we have been eating there for eight years and have never been overcharged or had a bad meal. My special favourite is their half lobster which must be the best value in Palma.

Shortly after we arrived to live in Majorca we had an afternoon appointment with our *abogado*, lawyer, and went to Iska for lunch. The friendly owner joined us at the end of the meal and ordered the waiter to bring a bottle of *hierbas,* the green liqueur that is made on the island. It seemed innocuous but by the time I arrived at our lawyer's office around the corner in Calle Cayetano I was feeling its full effect and found it very hard to concentrate.

For an excellent meal in more luxurious surroundings we like to go to the Real Club Nautico which is located at the end of the pier overlooking the yacht harbour. The restaurant is upstairs and open to non-members. It has a superb setting and is cool in the summer. An additional advantage is that it is still possible to park outside which was why I chose it as the location for the 25th anniversary celebration dinner dance for the Anglican Church.

When entertaining guests, another of our regular tours, from the same convenient starting point, takes in some of the features of the other half of the city. We cross the Avenida Antonio Maura, pausing to look at the fine statue of Ramón Llull at the point where it joins the Paseo Maritimo, but instead of walking along the Maritimo itself we take the lovely palm-lined road that runs parallel with it called the Paseo Sagrera. It was named after a famous Majorcan architect, Guillermo Sagrera, who was born in Felanitx and is best known for the beautiful building nearby called La Llonja del Mar, a maritime trading exchange in the Gothic style which was finished in 1452. Built of Santanyi stone on a simple oblong plan, it has an octagonal tower at each corner, three smaller towers on the long sides and two on each of the shorter sides.

Internally it looks a little like a palm grove with six tall spirally fluted columns branching out into the vaulting of the roof. The bosses where the vaulting intersects are ornamented with coloured shields of the merchants, the custodian angel and the shield of Majorca. Externally an open gallery connects the towers and there is considerable decoration, especially over the eastern doorway where the custodian angel, the patron of the merchants, is beautifully carved with hair flying in the breeze.

The Merchants' Association ceased to exist at the end of the 18th century and La Lonja became a museum of fine art until 1974 when its collection was transferred to the Museum of Majorca. Nowadays it is the exhibition centre for the *Conselleria de Cultura, Educació i Esports,* Council of Culture, Education and Sport, of the Baleares Government. We went there recently to see some charcoal sketches by Ellis Jacobson and almost the first one we came to was a powerful portrait of Robert Graves.

Next to La Lonja another impressive building, marked as the *Museo Naval* or Naval Museum on the Firestone map, is actually the old Sea Consulate built in the 17th Century in the renaissance style as a registry for ships and a court of maritime law. It is now used by the local government and is not open to the public, but I was fortunate enough to be invited to a reception there when I was able to admire the interior with its fine panelled ceiling.

In a narrow road behind La Lonja is Giovanni's, one of the best small Italian restaurants in the city where we have enjoyed many excellent meals. Next to it, a virtually unmarked door opens into the extraordinary interior of Abaco, located in an old residence, part of which has been preserved in its original form as a museum. The sight that greets visitors as they enter the main hall is difficult to adequately describe. Huge piles of fruit are scattered on the floor, ready to be used in the delicious but rather expensive cocktails that are a feature of the establishment and everywhere there are elaborate displays of fresh flowers which are changed daily.

Attractive new gardens are being laid out between the Torrente La Riera and the Avenida Argentina where there is a massive rampart on the corner that has a small tower which reminds us of one overlooking the harbour in Valetta in Malta. Below it an attractive stone bridge, a popular subject for artists, crosses the Torrente and on the other side of Avenida Argentina some old windmills have recently been restored in Es Jonquet.

This area became very run-down but it is being renovated and, in the attractive stone-paved square called Plaza Vapor, there is an excellent Italian Pizzeria called Mangiafuoco which means 'eat fire' in Italian and refers to Pinoccio's puppet master who was a fire-eater in a circus. Nearby the *mercado* or market of Santa Catalina is open every morning and worth visiting for fresh fish, meat, fruit and vegetables.

Recrossing the Avenida Argentina we come to the Avenida Rey Jaime III, which is Palma's counterpart of London's Bond Street, with some very smart shops and what is at present the only department store, Galerías Preciados. In these days of the Common Market many Spanish products can easily be purchased in Britain, but Lladró china figures, Majorcan pearls and leatherware of all kinds make excellent gifts and are usually less expensive on the island. At Number 10 in Jaime III there is a well-stocked Government Tourist Office where the helpful staff will supply maps and details of future events.

For additional shopping one of the best areas is the pedestrian street called Calle de San Miguel which is lined with inexpensive shops and leads off Plaza Mayor. It also contains the church of San Antonio outside which the animals are blessed after their procession from the Cathedral.

Nearby is the Olivar market, the biggest in Palma; which is the scene of intense activity every morning, although many supermarkets can now match the prices asked at the stalls. Behind it lies Plaza España, a very large square containing a fine statue of King Jaime I on horseback, a Tourist Office, many of the bus termini and two railway stations.

The station on the left of the square serves the train to Soller and, for a day out with a difference, we take our guests by train and tram to Puerto de Soller. The train thinks that it is a tram for the initial part of the journey because it runs along the centre of a busy road. The line was established in 1912; the original British steam-engine being replaced by the present electric train in 1929. Its twenty-seven kilometre track which runs through Bunyola required thirteen tunnels and is quite an engineering feat that includes a loop above Soller which provides a preview of the town from above and a stop for photography.

The train normally comprises an engine, five carriages and a van for mail and goods and, at little extra cost, it is possible to travel in a delightful antique first-class compartment, the journey taking about an hour. Two new carriages have recently been built at a cost of twelve million pesetas but they retain the characteristics of the older rolling stock complete with wooden panelling. At Soller the old electric tram, on which we rode with Pedro during our honeymoon in 1954, provides a connection to the port. An excursion on these ancient vehicles from Palma to Puerto de Soller, a leisurely lunch by the sea, and the return journey by tram and train makes an enjoyable and unusual day.

The other station in Plaza España serves a more modern train which goes to Inca via Santa Maria, Consell, Binissalem and Lloseta. The map still shows the line continuing through Sineu, Petrá and Manacor to Artà but that section has been closed for many years. On Thursdays it is an excellent means of getting to the huge market in Inca and avoiding the parking problem in the town.

There are dozens of galleries and exhibition halls in Palma and we rely on the Tourist Office to provide us with details of their exhibits. In addition to the many Government-sponsored displays of arts and crafts, twenty-five independent galleries regularly present collections of sculpture, paintings and photographs, including many by local artists.

The impressive Paseo Maritimo runs largely along land reclaimed from the sea and forms the main route to the west from the City. It is lined with hundreds of yachts in the marinas on its south side and large hotels on the north. Sandwiched between the hotels is the Auditorium, with each storey projecting a little further than the one below until it looks as if it might fall on its face. It is an important centre for concerts and ballet and also for occasional shows presented in English by two lively amateur groups who stage them to raise money for charity.

Close to the Auditorium, my favourite restaurant is the Bahia Mediterraneo, situated high up in an attractive white building that was once one of the leading hotels but which has now been converted into apartments. The views over the bay from its terrace are fantastic, especially at night. Dinner in the high-ceilinged pink and white dining room is an occasion to remember and the service is always faultless. It fully justifies its above-average prices and advance booking is virtually essential to get a table.

To the north of the Paseo Maritimo there is a most unusual miniature walled city called the Pueblo Español which is entirely composed of scaled-down reproductions of famous Spanish buildings. In all about one hundred national monuments are reproduced and the area is attractively laid out with walks, squares and shops selling local craftwork, some of which is produced on the premises. It was there that George, our neighbour, once had a workshop where he made and sold his fine guitars. There are several restaurants and the complex also incorporates a large conference and banqueting hall.

A little further west, the *Castillo de Bellver* towers above the city in a delightful park. Although it can be seen from many points our initial attempts to reach it by car failed because the map is slightly misleading. The trick is to head for the Calle Camilo José Cela and pass through the impressive gates at the top. The road swings through the grounds in a wide arc, circling the castle as it climbs the hill, and at the top there is a large car park.

Bellver Castle is a unique example of Gothic military architecture using a circular plan. It was built between 1300 and 1311 in the reign of King Jaime II, the moat being added in 1330. The large round keep has three circular towers attached to it and an unusual 33 metre high fourth tower, called the Homage Tower, which is also circular but divorced from the main structure and joined to it only by a narrow arched bridge. The interior of the main castle features a circular courtyard with a well in the centre. It is surrounded by a double gallery with rounded lower arches below and twice the number of pointed arches above. The castle has been used as a palace, a prison, a mint and a place of refuge. It is now a museum and a venue for delightful open air concerts which are held in the courtyard. At night it stands floodlit and visible for many miles.

We have become very interested in the complex history of Majorca and Bellver Castle has been linked with many major events since the 14th Century. When King Jaime II died in 1311 at the age of 71, he was succeeded by his second son, Sancho; his first son having retired to a monastery. King Sancho was not an absolute monarch as he was forced to pay homage to the King of Aragon, but the period was one of extensive trade. He suffered from athsma and to alleviate it he constructed a palace on high ground adjoining *La Cartuja* at Valldemossa that can still be visited.

The death of King Sancho in 1324 marked the start of a decline in the fortunes of the monarchy and of Majorca itself. He was buried at Perpignan and, as he had no direct heir, he left the throne to his nephew Jaime III with a regency council. This Jaime was not a strong ruler and is usually remembered for his *Leyes Palatininas* which governed the customs and etiquette of the Court. Eventually a dispute developed between Majorca and Aragon where King Pedro IV, the brother-in-law of King Jaime III, laid claim to the island and invaded it in 1343. Jaime III resisted and died in a battle at Llucmajor in 1349 when attempting to regain power. His body was taken to Valencia but was later returned to Majorca and now lies in the Cathedral. His family were imprisoned for a time at Bellver Castle.

There followed a depressed period under the rule of Aragon. Epidemics of plague in 1348, 1375 and 1384 killed more than 60,000 people on the island. In 1391 King Juan and his court came to stay at Bellver Castle for three months to escape an epidemic of typhoid that was ravaging Catalonia, further straining Palma's limited finances.

In 1747 a massive levy was placed on Majorca to pay for Spanish wars and all unmarried men found on the streets were press-ganged to serve in the army. They were held in terrible conditions at Bellver Castle before being sent off to fight in Naples. Early in the 19th Century the castle was used as a prison for French officers taken at Bailen in the war with Napoleon. They fared better than their men who were sent to the island of Cabrera and virtually abandoned to their fate.

Bellver Castle is on the western edge of Palma. The city is now encircled by a new motorway which had to be built because the *Ronda* became inadequate. This *Via Cintura* links the motorway from Palma Nova in the west to the one leading to the airport and El Arenal to the east and is a great improvement for both residents and tourists. All of the exits are clearly marked and it is no longer necessary for strangers to thread their way through Palma to reach its environs.

One area now easily reached from the *Via Cintura* is Son Vida with its fine hotels and golf course. It is one of the best residential areas near Palma with large houses surrounding the well-known Son Vida golf course. The Hotel Son Vida was once called the Sheraton and it is one of the few five-star hotels on the island. Today it is challenged by the Arabella Hotel, also overlooking the golf course and much favoured by German visitors. Both hotels offer international cuisine in the higher price band.

Located at the Golf Club, the Restaurante El Pato is well worth a visit. Although in the upper-middle price range, the food is perfectly prepared and presented for lunch or dinner. *El Pato* means the duck, and their duck in orange sauce is memorable. The eighteen-hole championship course is very popular and reservations are essential for non-members.

Another turning off the *Via Cintura* leads to La Vileta with a restaurant of the same name in a converted *finca* that has been run by the English owner, Bob Edwardes, for many years. Every summer I organise a dinner there in aid of the Save the Children Fund which is always well-supported. It is held in the cool gardens and lights strung from the trees make it a very attractive setting.

Also on the outskirts of Palma, the Poligono Victoria consists of warehouses stocking anything that might be required for building construction, ship repairing and civil engineering, as well as the main showrooms for most makes of car. One warehouse that we often visit is called Central Mimbrera where over an acre of floor space is filled with a huge variety of cane furniture of every description together with mats, baskets and artificial flowers.

A little further out, on the other side of the international airport, lies the little town of Sant Jordi (not to be confused with Colonia Sant Jordi which is on the coast a long way further south). It is a perfect little Majorcan village, situated on a hill and neatly arranged around its main square. Just off the square lies the Restaurante Ca'n Quirante which is run by a Majorcan who has established it, despite its rather out-of-the-way location, by offering excellent food, attractive prices and original marketing methods.

There are two good night spots on the fringe of Palma. Es Foguero, quite close to Sant Jordi, and Son Amar on the road to Soller. Both offer well-staged floor shows in huge theatre-restaurants which have been added to restored farmhouses. The price of the show includes dinner and at Son Amar you can dance and enjoy drinks in the gardens after the performance. World-famous acts are engaged for these shows which are presented to huge audiences because tour operators promote them to the tourists and organise coach trips from the holiday hotels. The noise level comes close to the threshold of pain but the shows are very spectacular. The last one we saw at Son Amar included the *Drifters* (famous for their recording of *On the Broadwalk*); one of the best illusionist acts I have ever seen on or off television; Spanish dancers in breathtaking costumes; a performing horse; and many supporting acts.

Son Bonet airport, where the Viscount landed when we first flew to the island, is also off the *Via Cintura* and it has been used for private flying since the international airport was opened at Son San Juan. Opposite the entrance is an old farmhouse which has been converted into one of the best Majorcan restaurants on the island called Meson Tio Pepe where we have had some outstanding meals. A superb *bodega* is a feature of the restaurant and its prices are very reasonable considering the quality and variety of the menu. At lunch time they serve an excellent *menú del dia* which is tremendous value as it includes a good *rioja* house wine.

We went to Meson Tio Pepe for a dinner-dance in support of *Ciudadanos Europeos,* an association which is active in strengthening integration and collaboration between foreign communities and Majorcan public and social life, advising expatriates of any changes in Spanish legislation and protecting their interests, particularly in matters such as voting and taxation. The membership currently embraces eleven different nationalities and includes many Majorcans. The local branch is headed by Kate Mentink, a very live wire who lives quite near us in Calvià.

The dinner commenced with *entreméses* consisting of smoked salmon roses, prawns, baked mussels, croquettes and an endive salad with roquefort sauce. We were then served with an excellent white wine and delightful purses, rather like small Dorothy bags, made from a pancake base and filled with a mixture of three different fish in a delicious sauce. A mint sorbet refreshed our palates and then we enjoyed a generous helping of tender entrecôte in a port wine sauce with small roasted potatoes and a good red *rioja*. Next came a lemon and champagne sorbet followed by a slice from the celebration gateau, so large that it required four waiters to carry it, champagne, coffee and flaming rum with hand-made chocolates. All of this, including dancing to a live band and drinks in the garden before the meal, cost about £15 each.

Our evening did not end there. We had been unable to shut Tia in the house when we left and in such circumstances we normally see her eyes reflected in the car lights as we return, but on this occasion she was nowhere to be seen. In response to our calls we eventually heard a faint reply but could not locate her until my husband got a torch and walked down the road where he found her high up in a pine tree outside a house which was then owned by rather an odd couple. We always knew when the rubbish lorry had reached their gate because instead of the usual dull thud of *basura* being collected there was only a loud clanking of empty bottles.

Tia was very distressed and it was obvious that she had been chased up the tree by a dog and could not get down unaided. As my husband returned to tell me that he had found her and to fetch a ladder, she screamed loudly thinking that we were not going to come to her rescue.

So, at two in the morning, in full evening dress, we walked down the road carrying a long aluminium ladder between us, my husband remarking that he felt rather like Raffles, the gentleman burglar. Even when fully extended, the ladder did not quite reach the branch to which Tia was clinging but, by the light of the torch, I climbed right to the top and level with the bedroom window of the house. I prayed that nobody would open it to find a Peeping Tom outside and, holding on with one hand, while talking to her to calm her, I just managed to reach out and grab Tia and bring her down. As soon as she was safely on the ground she trotted off and took a short cut back to the house while we walked the longer way along the road with the ladder. By the time we returned she was waiting at the door trying hard to look as if nothing unusual had happened.

15. Too Much Talk

We enjoy entertaining friends who come to Majorca on holiday, but are less enthusiastic about friends of friends. The problem often strikes without prior warning; the telephone rings and a voice we have never heard before gushes brightly 'I believe you know the Browns, we told them that we were visiting Majorca and they gave us your number and asked to be remembered to you.' If the conversation could only end there we should be delighted but we know what will inevitably follow. 'Perhaps we can meet you while we are here and you might like to show us some of the sights.'

If we were retired and living a lonely existence on our mountain-top, this might provide a welcome relief but my husband has press deadlines to meet; we have an active social life and I am heavily involved with charity work, so it can be a problem to find a free day at short notice.

Diana and Michael were recent examples. After the usual telephone introduction, when they told us that they had brought some Stilton and English Cheddar as a gift from some mutual friends, we arranged to meet them at their hotel in Paguera to have a drink and exchange news. We met them for the first time in the bar. He was tall and thin with a military bearing while she could only be described as blonde and fluffy. They would not let us go after a couple of drinks and insisted that we joined them for dinner when we soon discovered that Diana suffered from verbal diarrhoea. The meal seemed to last for an eternity as Diana had a maddening habit of loading her fork, raising it until it almost touched her lips, and then lowering it back to her plate because she had remembered some anecdote that took priority over the food. When the stories she recounted involved other people, she mimicked their voices which protracted her delivery and confused her and her audience so much that the point of the tale was entirely lost.

Michael was thoughtful and almost mute, his conversation being limited to acting as an interpreter to explain what Diana was trying to convey. He usually succeeded but sometimes he too got lost in her verbal labyrinth whereupon they would embark on an argument, totally oblivious to our presence. We realised that the jar of Stilton and the wedge of farmhouse Cheddar which our friends in England had sent us were more of a peace offering than a gift!

Having committed ourselves to showing them some of the features of the island we debated where to take them and decided that, in view of Diana's affliction, the more breathtaking the scenery the better. Nowhere on Majorca offers more dramatic views than the northern mountain range with its rugged landscapes, but the tour is definitely not for the nervous or inexperienced driver as it involves many miles of narrow twisting roads and some very steep climbs and descents.

As we could not predict where we would be at lunch time I decided to prepare a picnic. It had to be cold food because we were not taking any cooking equipment with us, unlike the Majorcans who like to gather in large family groups at the week-ends in the summer and cook enormous meals in a party atmosphere on makeshift barbecues. We had a folding table and four chairs that fitted easily into the boot of our car and were able to pack plates, glasses and cutlery and a checked tablecloth to lift the meal above the level of plastic forks and paper plates. As I wanted to maximise the difference from an English picnic I chose typical Majorcan fare.

I bought a *pan Mallorquin,* a round flat loaf of heavy-textured bread; a string of *tomate de ramellet,* pulpy thick-skinned Majorcan tomatoes used mainly for cooking; and a bottle of good quality *virgen* olive oil to make *pa amb oli.* For the next course I made a large thick *tortilla española* with nothing but eggs, potatoes, onion and olive oil. The Spanish omelettes served in Britain often contain peas, peppers and corn which are never seen in a Majorcan version. I also cooked some *empanadas,* small pies consisting of pastry filled with lamb which are traditionally eaten at Easter when the lamb is at its best. With these we would have a salad made from *cogollos*, small lettuces grown like asparagus with soil heaped around them to keep away the light and prevent them turning green; huge Majorcan tomatoes and some sliced white onion.

As a *postre*, I prepared a *tarta de almendras,* almond cake, and also packed some *Galletes d'Inca,* round salty biscuits that are a local speciality, and some Mahon cheese which is the only one in the Balearics with a *denominación de origen*. It is made from cow's milk and is available fresh, semi-cured or well-cured. If the curing extends beyond ten months it is called *Mahon añejo*. I also packed a bottle of white *Vina Veritas* from the Ferrer bodega at Binissalem which would keep at the right temperature in our insulated cold box.

We collected Diana and Michael from their hotel, drove to Palma and headed north for Soller through Bunyola and Alfabia after which the first series of hairpin bends commenced as we climbed over the Sierra de Alfabia to the Coll de Soller. There are some superb views from this road but they are a mere foretaste of what is to come. The decent into Soller is so tortuous that it was a relief to enter the town and have a few kilometres of relatively straight road before turning off for Biniaraix and Fornalutx, two very attractive and slightly similar towns which nestle quietly in the shelter of the mountains. Their features include stone façades with wooden balconies and verandas, crooked sloping streets, some with steps, and endless terraces of orange and lemon trees.

After Fornalutx we rejoined the main road and twisted up to the Mirador Ses Barques where we stopped to admire the fine view over Puerto de Soller. Diana who had been talking non-stop since we left Paguera was rendered speechless. The sheer beauty of Majorca seemed to strike her dumb and for the next hour she was completely silent as she drank in the incredible mountain scenery. The road snakes through the Sierra de Torrellas and is dominated on the left by the Puig Major which is the highest point on Majorca at 1445 metres.

This is wild country, the home of the black vulture, a paradise for experienced walkers and a graveyard for fools who do not respect its dangers. It mellows a little as one approaches the reservoirs at Pla de Cubert and Gorg Blau. Both are filled with trout and carp and fishing is permitted but a permit must first be obtained from ICONA in Palma.

Just after the reservoirs we tested the brakes along twelve kilometres of twists and turns on the road down to Sa Calobra which is so steep that at one point it curves and runs underneath itself. Later is just manages to squeeze between a massive rock face and a huge monolith eroded into curious formations. Calobra is possibly a corruption of *colobra* which is Majorcan for snake and this word perfectly describes the route down to the sea.

The 'English' edition of one illustrated guidebook to Majorca loquaciously describes this descent to the coast as: '*Phantasmal, bristling in a rough sea, the rough wounding rocks, creating a mythology of hallucination, tense, overflowing, finding its culmination and surprise at the same time in the crack of the Bretxa (opening), from whose lookout point one can contemplate the most charming view, like a flower of light amid thorny thistles. So is the Calobra village and its beach, rising thaumaturgically from the abrupt rocky place*'. Even if this description is a little over the top, the views certainly are sensational with towering rocks, pines and tantalising glimpses of the sea. Sa Calobra itself is not too developed and has a small harbour, an hotel and some restaurants.

We left the car and walked down to the beach where a path, which goes through two tunnels hewn out of the solid rock and a cave, brought us out by the Torrent de Pareis. The scale of the cliffs at this spot is gargantuan and the view north looking up into the path of the Torrent is unforgettable; the great depth of the ravine being emphasised by its narrowness. The sandy beach is the location for a choral concert in July which attracts a huge audience to this Wagnerian setting.

The beach was crowded because it is served by boats from Puerto de Soller as well as coaches that include Sa Calobra on their tours, so for a peaceful picnic lunch we retraced the road to a turning leading to the much quieter beach of Cala Tuent. It consists of shingle instead of the fine sand of Sa Calobra but the pines come almost to the water which is always crystal clear. It is said to be one of the finest places from which to watch the sun set on Majorca, but we suspected that its magic would wear off long before then and Diana would start to remember anecdotes that she had mercifully buried at the back of her mind while she stored memories of mountains, pines, rocks and sea.

The spell was evaporating even as we unpacked the picnic basket. She was reminded of an outing in Wales when her uncle had fallen into some nettles and her aunt, who was related to some titled family, who had a magnificent house in Norfolk, which caught fire and the insurance did not cover the cost which was just what happened when her friend in London was burgled and lost a ring which had been in her family for generations and was unusual because....We had already lost her train of thought and even Michael was unable to translate for us.

We carried the table, chairs and picnic basket to the beach and I distracted Diana by giving her the cloth and cutlery and asking her to lay the table. While my husband opened the wine and water, I prepared the *pa amb oli* by cutting slices from the loaf and rubbing and squeezing a halved ramellet tomato over the surface, particularly the crust, so that the juice was absorbed. I then dribbled olive oil over the bread, spreading it with the used half of one of the tomatoes. This served to take the edge of our appetites while we relaxed in the sunshine.

The meal continued as planned with the *tortilla* followed by the *empanadas* and salad, the almond cake which I served with *fresas y nata*, strawberries and cream, and finally the cheese from the nearby island of Menorca.

Although the return ascent was by the same route, the views were completely different when seen from the reverse direction. Instead of valleys sloping downwards to the sea, we were conscious of the sheer height of the near vertical rock faces with trees clinging precariously wherever they could find space for their roots. After regaining the main road, we headed for Lluc and its famous monastery which nestles in a wooded mountain valley.

Lluc is the home of *La Moreneta* or the small brown lady, a statue which certainly dates from earlier than 1238 when it was found in a cleft in the rock at this spot by a shepherd boy. It was placed in the Oratory of San Pedro in the nearby town of Escorca but is said to have disappeared only to be found again at Lluc. After this had happened three times it was considered to have miraculous powers and a chapel was built for it at Lluc. Our Lady of Lluc is the patron saint of Majorca and *La Moreneta* is the object of many pilgrimages; the most famous being the annual one from Palma which takes place during a night in August and is called the *marxa a peu.* In 1884 the population of Majorca donated a crown for the statue containing over 100 jewels and 600 pearls.

Over eighty miracles have been attributed to Our Lady of Lluc, one of which concerned a man and his wife who were making their way to Lluc from Inca. The man had become tired of his wife and pushed her over a cliff, leaving her to die and intending to say that she had met with an accident. He was astonished on reaching Lluc to find her alive and praying at the altar at the feet of the Virgin.

The present monastery dates from the 17th Century with 18th Century additions and is in the shape of a Latin cross with a single nave and chapels on each side. The centre of the roof is surmounted by a dome and elsewhere the barrel vaulting is supported on polished jasper pillars which were quarried locally.

Henry Shelley in his book published in 1926 records that hospitality was then provided without charge. He writes: '*Rarely can the mountain road thither be traversed without passing numerous small and large domestic parties either trudging on foot or slowly wending their way upward in the family mule cart. The ground floor apartments are specially reserved for these peasant pilgrims, and as they usually prepare their meals in their rooms it is not surprising that those apartments are but barely furnished. Markedly otherwise are the rooms reserved for the use of "those of the superior rank". These are situated on the first floor and are approached by wide stone stairways and open off spacious stone-paved corridors. These guest chambers are really self-contained suites comprising usually a salon or sitting-room, and several bedrooms. The suites are admirably furnished in a simple style, are provided with a full supply of bed and other linen, are lighted by electricity, and are kept scrupulously clean. There is no charge whatever for these suites, or for light and service, and there is practically no restriction as to the length of time they may be occupied.'* Today pleasant accommodation is still available at the monastery but, as it is in great demand, stays are limited to two days and a modest payment is requested.

Another feature of Lluc is the internationally famous boys choir, *Los Blauets*; dressed in blue cassocks with white surplices, they are all students at the music and choir school at the monastery. There is also an interesting and quite extensive museum, a restaurant, which now charges a little more than the ten pesetas a day that was asked when Henry Shelley wrote his book, and the inevitable souvenir shop.

The grounds are possibly more attractive than the architecture of the building, which tends to be functional rather than ornamental. There are many walks, one of which passes a series of bronze plaques embedded in the rock depicting the five mysteries of the Rosary.

From Lluc we took the old road south to Inca. To our right the double peaked Puig de Massanella, the second-highest mountain on the island, rose to 1348 metres. This is a region of oak forests, where the charcoal burners spent many months in the mountains, living in crude huts. The only traces of their activity today are circles edged with stones, called *sitjas;* that formed a base for mounds of oak logs which were covered in earth and moss and burned slowly until the wood was converted to charcoal. Lime burning in the same area was a similar process but it required greater heat so a cylindrical oven known as a *forn de calç* was constructed, partly below ground, which was lined with stones. Near the top of the Puig there is a huge snow-pit, about twenty metres deep, where snow was packed in the winter and covered with a layer of salt or ash and branches to preserve it as ice for use in the manufacture of ice cream and medicines. Prior to the availability of refrigerators it was cut into blocks, brought down the mountain by mules and then transported to Palma.

Our descent took us through the pretty town of Selva with steps flanked by cypresses leading to its Gothic-fronted church and on to Inca from where our route home ran through the northern edge of the *Pla*, the plain dotted with square windmills, and the villages of Consell and Santa María. It must be admitted that these would come fairly low in a contest for the most attractive town on Majorca and Diana, who had been remarkably quiet until we reached Inca, hardly paused for breath from there to the point when we reached the hotel in Paguera where she and Michael were staying. As we entered the lobby Diana, who had spotted an elderly lady holding court to some other guests, turned to us saying: 'There is old Mrs Peters, don't let her see us, she talks incessantly and I can never get a word in edgeways!'

The friends who had given our names to Diana and Michael came over to Majorca later in the year. They had stayed with us previously but for this visit they wished to be based on the other side of the island and we recommended Cala San Vicente which is a pretty cove with a sandy beach on the north coast near Pollença. We arranged to drive over one Sunday and take them to church in Puerto Pollença where there is an Anglican Chaplain but no Anglican Church. The service is held in the Catholic Church in the large square on the north side of the town and it is virtually a case of the Anglicans going in as the Catholics depart.

We set off early, collected our friends, and took them for a stroll before church around the narrow streets of Pollença itself where most of the houses are built from the same warm stone giving it an air of quiet harmony. The attractive Convent of Santo Domingo has a beautiful cloister where, during the Festival of Pollença now in its 33rd season, a fine series of concerts is presented in August and September. The Convent houses the tomb of Juan Mas who led the successful battle against invading pirates that is commemorated in a fiesta every August.

In the main square we showed them an old *noria* or water wheel with clay pots attached to it which illustrated very clearly how water was brought up from a well in former times. The showpiece of Pollença is the magnificent stairway, known as the Calvario, that leads to a small chapel at the top of the Puig des Calvari one of the two hills that shelter the town; it has 365 steps and is flanked by tall cypress trees.

We then walked as far as the Roman Bridge. Like most objects of antiquity, its authenticity has been questioned and no doubt it has been repaired many times since it was constructed, but its double arches with an unusual small centre arch to reduce the pressure of flood water probably reflect the original design.

To the south of Pollença there is an interesting walk of about three kilometres through pine and oak woods to the Ermita de la Mare de Deu at the top of the Puig de Maria. The hermitage offers visitors modest but very clean accommodation and has fine views over the town and the bays of Alcudia and Pollença but, as it was nearly time for church, we could not make the climb that morning and our friends resolved to go there the next day.

We drove the five kilometres to Puerto Pollença which is said to have been the Roman settlement of Bocchoris, although no remains are now visible. The Catholic Church is relatively modern with an attractive and almost bare interior in natural stone and a large dome over the altar. After the service the congregation assembled for coffee and a chat at Maxim's café in the square and we were joined by the Chaplain, who knew us from previous visits. He has a flourishing Anglican flock in his parish and there must have been 100 or more worshippers in the church that day. Our friends were particularly impressed by his sermon which was delivered with obvious sincerity and admirable brevity.

The Puerto is now a popular holiday resort and much of the promenade beside the curved and sandy bay has been turned into a tree-shaded pedestrian precinct with cafés, restaurants and hotels on the landward side. It is the ideal starting point for exploration of the lovely Formentor peninsular to the east, but that day we headed south, hugging the bay of Pollença with only the sands of the Playa de la Cuarassa between us and the sea.

The next town was Alcudia which has strong Roman connections. The old Roman town of Pollentia on this site, or very close to it, was founded by Consul Quintus Caecilius Metellus over 100 years before the birth of Christ. The largest single example of the Roman occupation of Majorca is the amphitheatre, still in remarkable condition considering its age, that lies between the town and its port. Alcudia has two fine gateways, the Puerta de San Sebastián and the smaller Puerta de la Xera, both flanked by tall towers. The passenger ferry sails to Menorca from the nearby port which also handles transporter services to Tarragona and Sagunto.

Although Alcudia was very crowded we soon found peace and quiet on the road heading into the peninsular and just after Bon Aire, the sandy beach at Mal Pas was nearly deserted, despite its charming position looking across the bay to Formentor and backed by pines. We spent some time admiring this lovely view before continuing on to the Ermita de la Victoria which looks more like a fort than a church because it stands in an area which was once infested by pirates. In July there is a service at the hermitage followed by wine and *buñuelos* accompanied by dancing. This is perfect walking country with pine forests and fine views, especially from the top of the Atalaya de Alcudia which is over 400 metres high. On the other side of the peninsular, and reached by a road leading from the Puerto, the beach at Aucanada is sandy, quiet and edged by pines, with added interest provided by a small island on which there is a lighthouse.

We continued south, still following the coast with the great bay of Alcudia on our left. To our right stretched the interesting marsh lands of La Albufera which swarm with the eels that are regarded as a delicacy by the Majorcans and which form an important ingredient in *espinagades*, the pastries that are sold in Sa Pobla. Our friends are keen birdwatchers and they immediately decided to spend a day there later in the week.

The reserve covers more than 4000 acres and is now protected by the local ornithological society which maintains full facilities including hides. Visitors permits are required, but these are available at the reserve. As well as an exceptional range of birds including falcons, plovers, terns, lapwings, kingfishers, bitterns, wagtails and moorhens, the reserve houses freshwater crayfish, green pond tortoises and several varieties of orchid.

The entrance to the Albufera Visitors Centre is close to a bridge, known as the English Bridge because it was constructed by a British company managed by a devout Anglican called John Bateman and his partner, William Hope, when they were draining part of the marshland by means of canals. Bateman lived in a farmhouse on the marsh and it was there in the early 1860's that he conducted what may possibly have been the first Anglican services to be held on the island.

We soon reached Ca'n Picafort where we turned inland for Santa Margalida, also known as Santa Margarita, the large town where we had seen the fascinating procession of Santa Catalina Tomás with the devils breaking the pots.

Our drive then took us through Muro which has an unusual bull-ring cut out of the rock and the *Museo Etnológico* a museum of furniture, old tools and kitchen equipment. Then to Sa Pobla where rice was once grown commercially and from where up to three crops of potatoes are now grown every year, many being exported to Britain. An important fiesta is held in Sa Pobla on January 16th for the *Revetla de Sant Antoni Abat*, the eve of the day of Saint Anthony, when *foguerons* or bonfires are lit in the streets and the people in elaborate costumes eat *espinagades*, eel pies, to the curious sound of the drum-like *ximbomba* and the tambourine.

Our next stop was at Campanet to see its fine caves which were only discovered in 1945. They are not quite as dramatic as those on the east coast as they lack an internal lake, but they are nearly a mile long, sympathetically lit to emphasise their stalactites and stalagmites and well worth a visit; especially in the summer when they tend to be far less crowded with tourists than the more popular caves of Drachs, Hams and Artà. From Campanet we had an easy run through Pollença and back to Cala San Vicente where the sunbathers were just gathering up their inflatable beds and umbrellas and preparing to return to their hotels as the shadows lengthened.

Over dinner our friends told us of a five hour walk they had enjoyed the previous day to the Castell del Rei which defended Pollença from its position at the top of a 400 metre high cliff. They were captivated by the scenery and were able to see the island of Menorca quite clearly from the now ruined castle which was built during the 13th Century by King Jaime I and destroyed in the mid-14th Century by King Pedro of Aragon after a three month siege.

We were many miles from home so we bid farewell to our friends soon after dinner and returned on the old Roman road that runs almost straight from Alcudia to Palma. As we chatted on the long drive home we agreed that the north-east area contains some of the most dramatic scenery on the island.

16 Recycled Rubbish and Desperate Doggies

My first encounter with the insatiable demand that exists on Majorca for second-hand goods was when I worked as a volunteer handling the finances of the Anglican Church thrift-shop. Each Wednesday goods would be brought in and prices would be agreed with the owners; the church taking a small commission on any subsequent sales. On Thursday mornings these goods were displayed on tables and dress rails in the Coleman Hall and, by the time the doors closed at lunch time, the shop would usually have taken well over 100,000 pesetas. This has been going on for twenty years and it still continues, with no sign of any decline in sales.

If this were a unique operation its continued success might not be remarkable, but it is only one of many outlets for used clothing and household effects. Busy charity shops are run by the Lions and the Salvation Army, while hardly a week goes by without there being a bazaar or jumble sale in aid of a school, club, church or charity. Nor is that all, frequent fashion shows are presented where selected used garments are modelled and auctioned to an enthusiastic audience.

Car boot sales are a more recent introduction. One is held on Sunday mornings on the Poligono Industrial at Consell in aid of the Balearic branch of Age Concern Spain and another takes place every Saturday morning in a car park in Genova which benefits several charities including the animal shelters and Save the Children Fund. As early as seven-thirty in the morning, cars loaded to the roof with an extraordinary assortment of used items can be seen making their way to the sale; their drivers intent on securing a good pitch. By nine trading is well under way and it continues until lunch time. The concept is that anyone with surplus items can load them into a car; pay the organiser 1000 pesetas for a pitch and sell them for the best price they can obtain. Inevitably, this has become partly commercialised and several cars can be seen week after week, their owners effectively using the sales as a market, but there are still some genuine private sellers offering jumble found when clearing out the loft or garage. Car boot sales are also a very useful facility for those planning to return to the UK who wish to dispose of items not worth shipping back.

Some friends of ours were selling their house and decided to get rid of some surplus furniture and effects, so they attached a roof-rack and loaded their car with as much as it could carry. They told us later that, as soon as they arrived at the boot sale, it was like entering a safari park when a car is often swamped by baboons prising loose every detachable item. Before they had even switched off the engine the ropes securing their load were being untied by regular bargain hunters who had spotted that this was a genuine house clearance and not just another dealer.

Because experts with a sharp eye for items of real value are likely to snap them up as soon as they arrive, it is unlikely that any priceless antiques will be obtained for a few pesetas at these events, but genuine bargains can be found. In particular the sales are a good source of old records, books, ornaments, pictures, tools, costume jewellery, china and glass, and clothing of every description. It is important to remember that much of the island was, until quite recently, on a 120 volt supply; many of the older 'bargains' in electrical goods are likely to be wired for this voltage and require a transformer before they can be used.

The largest genuine jumble sale is organised in aid of the *Sociedad Protectora de Animales y Plantas de Mallorca*, one of two charities on the island which care for stray animals. It is held every November in the main stadium of the track for trotting races in Palma which is called Son Pardo. The policy of the Society is to return animals to their owners whenever possible but, if they are unclaimed, to find someone willing to give them a good home or look after them for the rest of their lives at their kennels. They are put down only if they are fierce or incurable.

When we last went to this event we parked easily in the large car park and joined a crowd, composed almost equally of Majorcans and expatriates, walking to the entrance where a large grey shaggy dog sat in a chair holding a ladle. As we approached the ladle was held out to us and some coins we placed in it were tipped into a bucket by his side. Several people greeted him with a cheery 'Hello Russell' because the occupant of the dog-suit is well known and has been collecting for this event for many years.

Once through the gate we could see ten trotting horses being exercised on the track, the beautifully groomed animals pulled skeleton carts consisting of little more than two wheels and a frame, never breaking into a canter as they trotted round and round. Trotting races are popular in Majorca and they are held in Manacor as well as Palma.

On entering the enormous covered stadium the scale of the jumble sale became evident. The steps up to the main hall served as racks for hundreds of pairs of shoes, many in almost new condition; inside, tables were strewn with used clothing, separate sections being devoted to jumpers, underwear, jackets and skirts, jeans and trousers, dresses, menswear and more handbags than would be found in the average leather shop. Electrical goods displayed on tables along the back wall included irons, lamps, hair-dryers and curlers, radios, clocks, record players, heaters, air conditioners, fans, vacuums, hotplates and coffee makers. There were toys of every description with several tables devoted exclusively to dolls and new soft toys including an adorable panda and a very large teddy bear. Other tables displayed bicycle parts, records, tapes, videos, car spares, sports goods, china, glass, baskets, carved wooden items, seeds, plants, wine-making equipment, painted tiles, perfumes and soaps, typewriters, photo frames, cameras, sewing machines, key cases, wallets and purses, perfumed candles, and thousands of books. Larger items included furniture, ironing boards, a tailor's dummy, baby buggies, curtain rails, a stack of briefcases and holdalls, and a few curiosities such as an old sink with one tap and a single ski boot. The event produced a profit of about one million pesetas because all of the items had been donated.

Money is also raised for the care of animals and other charities through fashion shows which tend to follow a repetitive pattern. The audience is almost totally female and the same avid supporters seem to turn up at most events. They are seated on chairs arranged before a stage or cat-walk and volunteer models parade the clothes while a compère describes and then auctions them. One of the most popular compères is Peter, a disk jockey on the local radio station, who has now presented the show at the British American Club for seven years. This year it attracted an audience of over a hundred women and bids went quite high with one fur coat fetching about 100,000 pesetas. The Anglican Church also holds regular fashion shows in its Coleman Hall when selected items from its Thrift Shop are modelled and auctioned to similar audiences.

Books in English are always in demand. My husband ran a book sale for the church for several years with a policy of 'pile them high and sell them cheap'. Hardback books were priced at 100 pesetas while paperbacks were 50 pesetas each and thousands changed hands during the day. Those who purchased them often gave them back to the Church after they had read them and some became quite familiar, being resold year after year. It was amusing to see the reaction of some elderly parishioners to the lurid covers on some paperbacks but most eventually found a buyer; however one set of three hard-bound volumes that nobody had enough courage to purchase was an illustrated encyclopaedia of sex.

Bazaars are another important source of revenue for charity. They usually feature games such as a tombola, a competition to guess the weight of a cake, and raffles. Home made jams and pastries are popular and handicrafts of all kinds are sold, especially as Christmas approaches when there is a brisk demand for table decorations and unusual small presents. We went to a very lively one in aid of the Harbour View nursing home and were met in the street by the Pink Panther, Mother Goose and a gorgeous lady in a striking black and white outfit with a huge black and white hat who turned out to be the Matron. Many of the helpers were in costumes which, we later discovered, had been loaned by the local dramatic society; Matron's outfit having been used in the Ascot Gavotte scene from My Fair Lady.

Once inside the mixture was fairly traditional, several stalls offering used clothing were finding plenty of custom. Gwen D'Arcy, a popular columnist in the local paper, had a novel version of lucky-dip with small presents set out on playing cards; participants paid for an opportunity to pick a card from a pack and won the gift on the corresponding card on the table. We went home with a very pretty pincushion and some nail clippers which we find ideal for Tia's sharp claws although she prefers to have them done professionally by her vet. Other stalls were selling beautiful hand-made chocolates, books, colourful hand-made Christmas decorations, and there were also several competitions. One comprised a map of Majorca into which we were asked to stick a pin to indicate where we thought there might be buried treasure; we were amused to note that one pin had been inserted into the approximate location of our house.

Other popular bazaars are organised by schools and clubs, all offering much the same selection of donated items. The Salvation Army have found an original way of clearing surplus clothing left over from their regular bazaars by selling large dustbin bags for the equivalent of a few pounds and allowing purchasers to fill them to capacity without extra charge. Many items acquired on impulse are later donated to other events and so the recycling continues.

17. A Party at Porto Cristo

We had been invited to a party at a *finca* a few kilometres from Porto Cristo on the east coast. Our friends Tony and Amanda had restored it over a period of three years and had managed to convert it from a ruined farmhouse to a beautiful home with all modern facilities without sacrificing its original character. The party was to be a housewarming to mark the end of the major constructional work and it was due to start at eight in the evening.

Tony and Amanda kindly suggested that we spend the night to enable us to really enjoy the party and avoid a long drive home in the early hours. As we had not been to the eastern side of the island for some time, we decided to set off early, with our party clothes packed in the boot, and take advantage of the opportunity to spend a day there without having to allow for the return journey. Distances in Majorca are greater than they seem from a glance at the map.

We headed for Manacor and passed the Restaurante C'an Matias y Miquel soon after turning off the Via Cintura. It is famous throughout the island for its lamb and is popular at all times but particularly so with Majorcans for Sunday lunch when it is absolutely essential to book in order to get a table.

Nobody could call Manacor an attractive town. The main road tries to skirt around it as quickly as possible and we had some difficulty reaching its centre. References to it date back as far as

1129 and it may even have been the Roman town of Cunici. King Jaime II founded the present Manacor early in the 14th Century and had a summer palace there, but all that remains of it is one tower close to the church of Santa Maria. The church is neo-gothic and somewhat pyramidical in outline that has a tall tower which looks as if it has swallowed its large clock and is having difficulty digesting it. There is a museum of miniature furniture and an archaeological museum in the Torre dels Enagistes.

Manacor is a manufacturing town supplying furniture, fine cabinet work, clock cases, brass inlay, marquetry and articles made from olive wood, but its most famous product is its artificial pearls which have been made since the turn of the century from beads coated over 30 times with a liquid varnish containing fish scales. They are very realistic and only a jeweller would be likely to know that they had never seen an oyster.

My elder daughter wanted an imitation pearl necklace for her Christmas present, and her sister wanted some earrings; so we went to Perlas Majorica and Perlas Orquidea as both companies have elaborate showrooms offering a huge selection of their pearls and costume jewellery. While there we took the opportunity of joining the tourists and inspecting the factory, looking through glass screens at each stage in the manufacture of the pearls.

From the flat land around Manacor we drove into the pine-covered hills and found ourselves in country where rabbit, hare, partridge and pigeon are still hunted and dwarf palms are grown and dried to provide material for handicrafts including fans. We soon reached Artà which is quite a large town scattered over a hillside with the Oratorio de San Salvador at the top. It is approached by a Way of the Cross rising up between cypress trees and we also visited the Almudaina Castle, a mediaeval fort which is still in good repair.

We continued heading east to Capdepera, an inland village but close enough to the pine-filled coast to have been troubled by pirates. A castle surrounds the early 14th Century town and it is still almost intact. It is roughly triangular in plan with walls between battlemented towers and it embraces the Gothic Oratory of Our Lady of Hope. We walked around the ramparts and enjoyed the fine views from the top.

There is a legend of an attack on the castle by pirates. The townspeople placed a statue of the Virgin on the castle walls in front of the raiders and immediately a fog came down and the pirates fled. This incident is celebrated in the town each December at the *Fiesta de Nuestra Señora de la Esperanza,* the Festival of Our Lady of Hope.

Cala Ratjada is only a few kilometres east of Capdepera. It is a picturesque fishing port, and is very popular as a holiday resort because it has good sandy beaches. Nearby Cabo Capdepera is the easternmost point of the island. It was there that in 1231 King Jaime I went with a small band of supporters and ordered hundreds of fires to be lit to give the Moors on nearby Menorca, who had not yet surrendered to his rule, the impression that he was camped there with a large army. The ruse worked and, when told that the King's forces were preparing to invade them, the Menorcan Moors surrendered without a struggle.

We returned inland and admired the square Torre de Canyamel, pure 13th Century Gothic and battlemented for protection against pirate attacks. It is a prominent feature of the flat countryside and an excellent example of a fortified Majorcan house.

We reached the coast at the Caves of Artà. The entrance to the huge mouth, which yawns at the edge of a forty-six metre drop to the sea, is up a stone causeway. The caves were first explored early in the 16th Century but they were examined in much more detail in the 19th Century by the French spelaeologist E A Martel. The enormous chambers, one as large as Palma cathedral, have descriptive names which include the Chamber of the Thousand Columns, the Chamber of Hell, the Chamber of the Flags (where the stalactites resemble partly unfurled standards), the Chamber of the Fountain, Napoleon's Tomb, the Prince's Grotto, the Peak of Diamonds, and the Hall of Organs.

From there we followed the coast road to Porto Cristo passing the holiday resorts of Cala Millor, Sa Coma, Cala Moreya and S'Illot, most of which have good sandy beaches. Porto Cristo was the port of Manacor and only acquired its present name in 1912. The age of the harbour was proved by the discovery of the wreck of a Roman ship in the sand at the bottom of the port. Nearby is the site where Republican troops landed in 1936 in an abortive attempt to capture the island from the Nationalists during the Spanish Civil War.

Today tourists flock to the Aquarium and the immense *Cuevas del Drach,* the Caves of the Dragon. We had been there previously for a two-hour guided tour; the caves have been called the underground Alhambra and consist of four caverns, the Cave of the French, the Cave of Luis Salvador, the White Cave and the Black Cave which extend in total for about two kilometres. They were fully explored in 1896, on instructions from Luis Salvador of Austria, by the same French expert who re-explored the caves of Artà. Lake Martel, named after the explorer, is a feature of the caves; it is 177 metres long and 8 metres deep and is used as an auditorium with a synchronised show of lights and music played by a trio in a boat.

Just outside Porto Cristo the *Cuevas de Hams*, Caves of Hooks, were discovered in 1906 and explored by Pedro Caldentey but they have only recently been opened to the public. They are named after the hook-like shape of the stalactites in the grotto known as the Angel's Dream. Entrance to the cavern is via a narrow passage leading to chambers called the Imperial Palace, the Circular Chamber of Rest, the Hermit's Desert, the Enchanted City and an underground lake known as the Sea of Venice. Although the water is fresh it is thought to be connected to the sea as it rises and falls with the tide.

Tony and Amanda had suggested that we should reach them in time for a cup of tea before changing for the party. When we arrived Tony was looking rather harassed and said: 'Thank goodness you have come, can you give us a hand in the kitchen?' Without questioning him we quickly took our cases up to our room and when we returned he told us about an incident that had occurred earlier that afternoon.

Tony had borrowed some chairs, tables, umbrellas and checked tablecloths from a local bar and had set them out on a large terrace in front of the house, well in advance in order to have time to assist Amanda with the food and to prepare the drinks. As he was standing admiring his efforts he spotted a large party of cyclists coming up the lane. To his surprise, the leader dismounted outside the house, leant his bicycle against the hedge and seated himself at one of the tables. The rest of the party quickly followed his example until thirty or more thirsty young men were waiting expectantly to be served.

From their conversation Tony realised that they were German and in dire need of refreshment and he had neither the heart nor the linguistic ability to tell them that they were at a private house, so he served them all with beer from the stock he had laid in for the evening. He expected them to be off as soon as they had finished their drinks but they were enjoying sitting in the sun and ordered more, asking if they could also have some food. After a quick consultation with Amanda, Tony carried out the plates of sausage rolls and sandwiches that had been prepared for the party and his 'customers' soon consumed the lot.

The leading cyclist asked for the bill and Tony, not wishing to disillusion him, mentioned the first figure that came into his head. This was paid, plus a generous tip, and the cyclists went away contented. Tony and Amanda were then faced with the need to start once again to prepare the food for the evening and Tony had to go out and get more beer. As he walked to his car some more cyclists appeared; they had met the previous group who had told them that there was a good café just down the road!

18. The Hinterland

Some American friends came to stay with us who knew about the work of Fray Junípero Serra in California and wanted to see his birthplace in Petrá. As they also wished to take some gifts back with them we arranged to take them to Inca market in the morning.

We set off in brilliant sunshine taking the road through Santa Maria, a typical town of the *Pla* devoted mainly to agriculture but also producing cloth with traditional Majorcan patterns, turned, plain and glazed pottery, crocheted baby clothes and liqueurs including hierbas, palo and crema almendra. Being interested in anything of antiquity, our friends were fascinated by the cloister of the 17th Century friary on the south side of the main road inside the town which is very quiet and peaceful with the air of a neglected garden.

We drove through Binissalem and told our American guests about its annual wine festival as we headed for Inca, which is the agricultural centre of this entire region. It comes third after Palma and Manacor in terms of population and produces leather goods of all kinds but especially shoes and clothing. The many potteries around Inca produce dark brown rustic ware which is sometimes decorated in bright yellow.

The market is enormous and we found it rather tiring as we could only shuffle along with the crowd, but eventually we reached the Church of Santa Maria la Mayor which has a 13th Century belfry, although the main building was renovated in the 17th Century in the baroque style. The early 19th Century organ has recently been restored at a cost of over four million pesetas; it was made by Gabriel Thomas and has over 1600 pipes. Our American friends were greatly impressed by the age and scale of the church, and we were very amused when the wife turned to her husband and said: 'Isn't this the cutest little God's box you've ever seen!' The other features of the town include the Convent of San Jerónimo where the nuns still make little cakes known as *concos* which are very hard to resist.

By the time our friends had bought some leather gloves and a large antique copper pot it was time for lunch. The town abounds with old semi-subterranean wine cellars many of which have now been converted into restaurants decorated with huge vats, strings of onions, garlic and tomatoes. One of the most famous of these is called the Celler C'an Amer which specialises in traditional Majorcan food and we had an excellent and slightly unusual lunch in its restaurant below street level.

We headed for Petrá passing through Sineu, a small agricultural centre and market town which is built on a hill at the meeting place of six roads. Its church has a Gothic belfry and we admired an impressive winged lion statue in the square in front of it. The only time Sineu is busy is on a Wednesday when it is market-day.

Petrá is located in the agricultural heart of Majorca. It is a town of stone-built houses which has become world-famous as the birthplace of Fray Junípero Serra on November 24th 1713. Traditionally his birth would have been signified with a branch of laurel hung on the house door – the birth of a baby girl would have been indicated by a sprig of myrtle. He was actually baptised Miquel Joseph Serre (meaning a saw) and became Junípero Serra when he joined the Franciscan order. He was prepared in Palma and received his Franciscan habit at the age of 16 years and nine months.

Twenty years later in 1749 he set sail for California to found missions which were to grow into the cities of Los Angeles, San Diego, Monterey, San José and San Francisco. His statue is in the US State Capitol in Washington.

The modest house that was his original home is open to the public and we were able to see the little courtyard at the back and the small room in the loft which was a bedroom. Close by the Junípero Serra Museum contains an interesting collection of artefacts connected with his life.

Also in the town, the Church of San Bernardino was part of the San Bernardino Monastery which was founded in the 17th Century and was the last to be established by the Franciscans in Majorca. On August 2nd jewellers would go there on *el día de Nuestra Señora de los Angeles*; set up stalls and sell rings, brooches, earrings and decorative buttons. This event was the source of many a wedding ring for the local maidens.

The monument to Fray Junípero Serra in the main square was erected in 1913 on the 200th anniversary of his birth and is the work of Guillermo Galmés, another son of the little town.

The nearby sanctuary of Bon Any (meaning good year and so named to commemorate relief from a long drought) is where Fray Junípero preached his last sermon before departing. It is the object of a *romeria* from Petrá on Easter Tuesday when the people gather at the parish church and, with pennants waving, a statue of St Joseph is taken up to the Sanctuary where there is a picnic of bread, olives, *empanadas* and fruit. From the Sanctuary there is a magnificent view of Petrá with the bell towers of the parish church and monastery prominent above the town.

It was a beautiful evening and the heat of the day was starting to abate, so we continued our tour by driving south to Felanitx, a rather dull town built on four hills with winding crooked streets. It is noted for its cartographers who produced maps and charts including, it is believed, those used by Christopher Columbus. The town once had twenty-five windmills and it still has many pottery workshops which produce traditional ceramics including *gerres brodades,* finely decorated jugs, and *greixoneras,* shallow earthenware cooking pots. Other activities include sausage making, embroidery, enamelled ware, crafted furniture and stringed instruments including violins and guitars. The large Gothic church built in rust-coloured stone dates from the 12th Century but was restored in the 17th and it is approached by a wide flight of steps.

Felanitx is a wine growing area but it has not yet achieved a *Denominación de Origen.* Not far from the town the present Sanctuary of San Salvador is 17th Century, but it was founded in the 12th and is one of oldest Christian sites on Majorca. We entered through a massive gatehouse with a carved wooden representation of the Last Supper and enjoyed a simple meal in the restaurant. The Sanctuary is 600 metres high with a sweeping view of the coast.

We could clearly see Porto Colom, which was the port of Felanitx and played an important role in its wine trade having special links with France. Fishermen there still moor their boats right outside the houses and there are brightly coloured doors on the boat sheds bordering the almost landlocked bay. The scene is made even more attractive by a small sandy beach backed by pines.

To the south of Felanitx on the road to Santanyi, in the middle of almond and fruit orchards, there is a mediaeval fortress in a perfect strategic position 400 metres high overlooking the coast. The present fortification is based on the remains of a 13th Century castle called the Castillo de Santueri. It was constructed by the Moors and has a circular tower above its main entrance. The interior is largely a ruin but the outer walls are still standing. Moorish forces held out here for over a year against King Jaime I and it is one of the oldest fortress sites in Majorca, with Roman associations.

It was getting late and we headed for home, but our friends had been enchanted by the glimpse we had given them of the inland villages that are still unaffected by tourism. This was an aspect of Majorca with which they were totally unfamiliar and we promised to take them to see more of the hinterland the next day.

For a different tour of inland towns, we headed north from Palma and soon reached Alfabia which was originally owned by an Arab called Ben Nabat (also known as Ben-Amet and Benhabet) who converted to Christianity and betrayed his race by assisting King Jaime I with provisions for his troops and who later presented the King's uncle with the estate. The approach is along an avenue of poplars that leads to the baroque-style house featuring a 12th Century Arab ceiling in ebony and olive wood incorporating verses from the Koran.

Alfabia is famous for its beautiful Arab gardens with much use of water including lily ponds, pavilions, romantic arbours, forests of bamboo and a probably more recent rose garden. The house is furnished with prints, paintings and antiques. It is open to the public, but the nearby estate known as Raxa, which has magnificent Italian gardens and which used to be a tourist attraction, is now private.

We retraced our route as far as Bunyola; a town with picturesque tree-lined streets at the foot of the northern mountain range. It was once famous as a centre for the olive oil industry and housed the Royal olive press where, in the early 15th Century, a Royal Procurer measured the oil produced and levied a tenth for the church and state as a tithe. In the 18th Century church there is an alabaster statue of the *Virgen de las Nieves*, Virgin of the Snows, which is almost life size and thought to be of Italian origin. It was brought to the island by the uncle of King Jaime when he owned Alfabia.

Bunyola was the home of the Cabot brothers who continued Fray Junípero Serra's work in California. Fray Pedro Cabot worked at San Antonio and died at San Fernando in 1836 and Fray Juan Cabot is associated with the mission at San Miguel Arcangel.

We then took our American friends for a really delightful drive along narrow winding roads lined with fields where long-legged Majorcan sheep were grazing and woods in which the Majorcans love to come in large parties to enjoy picnics during the summer. After eleven kilometres of twists and turns we came to the very pretty hamlet of Orient, 400 metres high in a tranquil valley. It is no more than a small cluster of honey-coloured-houses and a little church but its single steep winding street offers an opportunity for a photograph at every turn.

We continued to head east through apple orchards and entered a mountainous area where two huge vertical cliffs look as though an enormous bulldozer has sliced a gap between them. On the top of the western cliff, we could just make out the Castle of Alaró. It is 822 metres high and occupies a site which has probably been a fortress since Roman times. The ruins of the present castle date from the 13th Century and a road leads about half of the way up, after which they can only be reached by a ladder-like stairway.

Alaró was the scene of the martyrdom of Guillem Cabrit and Guillem Bassa who remained loyal to Jaime II against his uncle Alfonso of Aragon. They held out when the rest of the island had capitulated to Alfonso who marched his forces there and ordered the defenders to surrender. Legend has it that they sent word asking who was attacking them and the King replied: 'I am Alfonso, the King of Majorca'. The Majorcan translation of Alfonso is Anfos, which also refers to a fish, so they sent a message saying: 'We eat Anfos with sauce'. The furious King asked who had sent such a reply and when he heard the name Cabrit, which means goat in Majorcan, he said: 'Because you are called goat I will roast you like one'. When he had forced them to surrender he carried out his threat and they were burned alive in the square in Alaró.

On hearing of this the Pope was horrified by Alfonso's cruelty; he was excommunicated and the crown was returned to King Jaime II. The remains of the two martyrs are now in the Cathedral in Palma. A small chapel in the centre of the castle is the object of a pilgrimage by the people of the small market town of Alaró on the Sunday after Easter.

From Alaró we drove across flat countryside through the market towns of Consell and Sencelles to Sant Joan; the scene of the fiesta of *Pa i el Paix* which celebrates the feeding of the five thousand, and also the blessing of the animals on the day of St Anthony. It is the birthplace of Melchar Jaume who became a Franciscan friar and took the name of Fray Luis Jaume. He served with Fray Junípero Serra in California and was assigned to the first of the chain of missions at San Diego where he was killed by Indians.

Close to Sant Joan we visited the old estate of Els Calderers, the home of the Veri family. The house dates from around 1750 and it is open to the public as a museum of rural architecture and country life. It is an impressive oblong three storey structure with a flight of steps leading up to its doorway. The estate produced wine until phylloxera struck the island after which it concentrated on cereals.

We entered the large hall off which there was a courtyard with a well. Then we saw a long reception room, an office for the resident priest, a charming small chapel and a wine cellar with wine-making equipment. Inside the rooms are fully furnished as they would have been when the house was occupied.

We were shown a trophy room with weapons and relics of the hunt; a large and comfortable room which was the office of the lord of the manor with books and other items suggesting that he might have had medical qualifications; a dining room seating eighteen; a music room; a room reserved for the lady of the house and a large drawing room. Above were the main bedroom with a sitting room and dressing rooms for the master and mistress; a bathroom; a linen room with facilities for ironing; a nursery and other bedrooms. Outside, attached to the house, were the kitchen and dining room for the workers on the estate; the office of the *Amo*, overseer; a bread oven and a wash house.

The grounds contained an old cart shed with examples of horse-drawn carts and traps, a carpenter's shop and forge, the stables, a slaughter house and pens containing live farm animals. In total the estate provided a very interesting picture of 18th Century rural life in Majorca.

We returned through Montuiri, which looks a little like St Michael's Mount as it rises in the shape of a pyramid from the plane around it. Dina Bowden devotes a chapter to it in her book about Fray Junípero Serra who preached there in 1742 and she describes the festivities on the day of its Patron Saint Bartholomew and the group of dancers known as Es Cossiers about whom she writes: *'The group consists of seven men, one of whom represents a woman, La Dama, who leads the dancers. How curious is their apparel! La Dama is clothed in a white, lace-trimmed shirt and a long white skirt with a wide ribbon sash. The six dancers surrounding 'her' wear white embroidered shirts and short tunics – each a different colour – over voluminous white trousers. These are fastened below the knee by ribbons that are wound spirally around the calves of their white-stockinged legs. Small tinkling bells are attached to these coloured ribbons. The colour that the dancer has chosen for his tunic is repeated in the facing of his large straw hat which, adorned with multi-coloured flowers and small mirrors, is turned up at both sides. The hat of La Dama is smaller, more feminine, its narrow brim being turned down modestly to shade the face. It is decorated with many flowers and a broad ribbon. All wear scapulas. In one hand each dancer carries a large, coloured handkerchief, in the other a nosegay of sweet basil.'*

At the end of Mass two men enter the church in typical Majorcan costume playing the bagpipe and the flute and drum. *La Dama* follows, dancing with leaps and pirouettes, and makes obeisance at the altar, the other dancers follow. When this dance, known as *L'Oferta*, has been completed *Es Cossiers* leave the church and find *El Dimoni*, the devil, awaiting them. *La Dama* is encircled and defended by the other Cossiers and the drama ends with *La Dama* placing her foot on the head of *El Dimoni* as he grovels in the dust.

The American couple were enchanted by Majorca and assured us that they would be urging their friends to include a visit to the island when they were in Europe. They had enjoyed themselves so much that they insisted on taking us out to dinner the night before they departed and asked where we would like to go. Without hesitation we suggested the Restaurante La Gritta at Cala Fornells because there are few more delightful places to eat on a balmy evening than its terrace, high above the water, with the moon illuminating the Isle of Malgrats across the bay.

19. Information and Entertainment

The introduction of satellite TV has eliminated any time barrier in the receipt of news from the UK. In addition to the wide variety of programmes available on BBC and Sky TV, some German stations occasionally show films in English. Spanish TV used to transmit a few films in their original language with sub-titles in Spanish, which suited us very well if they were made in the UK or America, but today they are usually dubbed. Just prior to the widespread availability of Satellite broadcasts, video shops found a large market amongst expatriates; some still prosper but they are fewer in number because many residents now have satellite dishes.

Majorca has two radio stations offering programmes in English. Radio 95.8FM (formerly 106.1 and originally 103.2) is the major operator and broadcasts in English for most of the day. It is financed by advertising and makes no attempt to hide the fact, virtually every advertisement being followed by comments from the disk-jockey giving the advertiser an extra boost. This is rather confusing to those unfamiliar with the system because most of the commercials are made by the same small band of broadcasters who present the programmes and this results in an identical voice being heard 'canned' for the advertisement and then live for the additional comment. 95.8FM is, however, invaluable to expatriates as a source of local news and details of forthcoming events and it is particularly generous in its coverage of any activity aiming to raise money for charity. It transmits news on the hour from the BBC, on the half-hour from CNN, and relays BBC transmissions when it is not on the air itself.

The second station is based in our home town of Calvià and is sponsored by the local *Ayuntamiento* or Council. It transmits in English for one hour every weekday evening on 107.4FM and is hosted by a tremendous personality called Wendy Peters, universally known as Wendy Woo, who has been known to pause for a moment in order to tell her dog to stop chewing the microphone cable. She frequently has interesting guests on her programme and every Wednesday presents a very useful feature on local rules and regulations in conjunction with Kate Mentink who represents *Ciudadanos Europeos* and also the *Instituto de Propietarios Extranjeros* in Majorca. Had we been listening, it could probably have enabled us to avoid the problem we experienced with the late payment of our rates.

With both radio stations it is possible to telephone straight through to the broadcaster while the show is live, though it is sensible to call while a record is being played so that the DJ is free to speak. This facility is much used for birthday and anniversary greetings, and appeals relating to lost people or animals. It makes the service very accessible and we count ourselves fortunate in having two such lively radio stations on Majorca.

The local English language daily paper is the *Majorca Daily Bulletin*. First published in December 1962, it has served the expatriate community faithfully and well and now carries regular colour features. It appears every day except Monday and is prompt in its reporting of international and local news. It is also a rich source of 'howlers' which are understandable when one bears in mind that it is partly typeset by Spanish staff and operates on a fast time-scale, but we treasure recent slip-ups including '*as dusk dawned*' and an account of the difficulty of raising a sunken ship '*thirty metres above the surface*'. Shortly after the new British Consul arrived it reported that '*King Juan Carlos was formally presented to John Blakemore.*'

Two regular contributors to the '*Daily Bee*' as it is popularly known are Gwen D'Arcy with a regular update on local personalities and events in a column headed 'Who's News?' and Ray Fleming who writes excellent musical reviews and also a column under the heading of 'Looking Around' which comments on international matters in a form which is always readable and reasonable but frequently controversial. Other regular features include a page by Riki 'Lash' Lazaar, who prefixes many of his items of local gossip with the heading 'True or False'; he is also very much involved with Radio 95.8FM. The paper has a habit of reporting some interesting events after they happen without having alerted its readers to them in advance, but it has improved in that respect in recent years. Sports fans appreciate its extensive coverage of all sporting events.

The weekly paper in English is called *The Reader* and it also has made much progress recently. Although unable to match its daily rival in speed of reporting, it often covers local news in greater depth and has been responsible for some excellent examples of investigative journalism, not being afraid to quote names when appropriate. It features a lively column of readers' letters and its 'What's On' column often manages to fill in gaps in the details available elsewhere.

For more extensive information regarding future events we mainly rely on the quarterly leaflets in English issued free by the *Instituto Balear de Promocion del Turismo* which can be obtained from any tourist office. These are very comprehensive and cover fiestas, theatres, concerts, sporting fixtures, exhibitions, folk dancing, bullfighting, dog shows and cattle fairs. There are tourist offices in most large towns and at the airport.

Those who plan to spend several weeks on the island have a choice of clubs and associations which they can join in order to meet new friends or participate in sports. The tourist information offices maintain lists of clubs for those interested in archery, athletics, badminton, basketball, billiards, bowls, boxing, bridge, canoeing, caving, chess, clay pigeon shooting, climbing, cycling, darts, fishing, flying, football, golf, gymnastics, horse-riding, hunting, judo, karate, motorcycling, pelota, rugger, scuba-diving, skating, squash, swimming, table tennis, tennis, volleyball, walking, water-skiing weight lifting, wrestling and yachting. They can also provide details of special facilities for the handicapped.

The Institute of Foreign Property Owners was formed to provide a newsletter and advice for those with property in Spain, whether it be a holiday home or a permanent residence. One of its regular activities is the publication of the names of foreigners who have been listed in the *Boletines Oficiales* (Chronicles of Debtors) of the ten areas of Spain most favoured by expatriates, including the Baleares.

The IFPO literature states: '*You may be unaware that you have incurred a debt – a new tax may have been levied; your property may have had a hidden debt attached when you bought it; as town halls do not send out rate bills, you may be unaware of your obligations, possibly your property is affected by new urbanistic planning, or someone who thinks you owe him money has taken you to court.*' Most property owners avoid such problems with the help of a good lawyer but the long lists of names in every issue of the IFPO newsletter shows that some foreigners still find themselves in trouble.

Another area where the IFPO can assist is in questions relating to a *Comunidad de Propietarios* or Community of Owners. All apartment blocks and most urbanisations in Spain are required by law to have such an association to look after the communal parts of the development and charge the cost to the individual owners. In the case of a block of apartments, this would include hallways, lifts, swimming pools, exterior decoration and the maintenance of the grounds. These Communities of Owners are a constant source of problems as some owners only use their apartments once or twice a year and may not be interested in participating, thus permitting unsuitable officers to get elected by default.

The British American Club, sometimes unkindly and unfairly referred to as 'God's waiting room', was formed in 1955. Like most associations of its kind it has had financial problems, most of which have been due to the cost of running its premises, which are situated just off the wide road leading up to Bellver Castle in Son Armadans. In recent years it has thrown off much of its previous image as a parking place for senior citizens, and it now hosts meetings of several other associations, organises bridge classes and tournaments and presents some excellent fashion shows. Its restaurant has about as much ambience as a works canteen, but the food is usually excellent, very competitively priced and available to non-members.

ESRA, the English Speaking Residents' Association has also had its ups and downs in its much shorter life. We were astounded when we attended one of its Annual General Meetings and its Central Council, composed entirely of volunteers who were doing their best to manage a rapidly growing operation, came under tremendous attack from some of the members. This was despite the fact that the modest subscription of £5 per year covered a well-produced magazine, discounts on insurance and airport parking, a careline service to keep an eye on those who were ill or in need, and a programme of social events which included discounted gourmet meals.

We had experienced the difficulties of serving on association committees before we left the UK and had vowed that never again would we expose ourselves to the criticism that those concerned with voluntary work so often have to bear; so we sympathised with the members of the Council who were having difficulty making themselves heard above all the shouting. It all seemed very important at the time to some of those present, but neither of us can now remember what all the fuss was about.

We never lack entertainment and particularly enjoy the many fairs, folk dances and festivals that are held throughout the year. We also like to go to concerts and the ballet but sometimes have difficulty staying awake in the second half as performances often start at ten or later in the evening. In addition to the Teatro Principal and the Auditorium, Palma now has a third theatre, the Teatro Municipal, which is in the Paseo Mallorca in the same building as the *Majorca Daily Bulletin*.

One event we try not to miss is the Chopin Festival held annually in August in the cloisters of the *Cartuja* at Valldemossa. We have been privileged to hear many fine performances there, but one that we shall never forget was given in 1994 by Dame Moura Lympany. It was pure magic from the start when this wonderful lady, erect and looking far younger than her seventy-seven years, came into a circle of light at the junction of the three cloisters where a grand piano awaited her on a dais. Every seat was taken and the audience also extended into the garden where chairs had been set out beside the glassless windows. After she had acknowledged thunderous applause, there was total silence as she seated herself at the grand piano and then the first notes of Chopin's Fantasia-Impromptu in D Sharp Minor sounded clear and pure in the beautiful setting.

From that moment on she captivated her audience who would not release her and demanded encore after encore which she provided entirely from memory with no music to assist her. Her performance was perfect, she never faltered and it was almost impossible to believe that such intricate playing could come from the fingers of a woman who was approaching her eightieth birthday. She was my father's favourite pianist when he was a young man and he had a collection of all her 78 rpm records which were severely worn by being played constantly with a steel needle – that night I understood why.

Other attractive venues where international performers can be heard include concerts held at Son Marroig in an intimate country house atmosphere, even to the extent of sherry being served to the audience during the interval. Concerts are also held in the lovely old church in Deià, La Residencia Hotel, the golf course at Bendinat, the gardens of the Casa March at Cala Ratjada, the impressive circular courtyard of Bellver Castle, and the cloisters of the Santo Domingo Convent in Pollença. A very popular choral concert is held in July at the Torrent de Pareis at Sa Calobra which is best reached by boat to avoid having to use the crowded, winding road down to the sea. In the same area the choir of Lluc monastery, *Els Blauets*, the blue boys, is world famous.

Shortly after a new Chaplain arrived at the Anglican Church in Palma we took him to a performance by Nureyev of excerpts from famous ballets which was held in the courtyard of the large quadrangular building known as *La Misericordia* at the top of La Rambla in Palma. It was being renovated at the time but a stage had been erected at one end and tiered rows of seats were located at the other, while the flat area between was filled with chairs. These turned out to be the most expensive seats and the people who had paid for them protested that they could see far less than those in the raised but cheaper seats behind them; not that anything was really inexpensive as ticket prices started at about £15.

The performance was about to begin when a column of black smoke started to rise from a corner of the building and it grew denser and more ominous until some people started to leave. Amid much confusion it was eventually established that it was caused by a nearby hospital disposing of some rubbish and the audience gradually settled down.

It was a very hot night and tempers had already become a little frayed when disaster struck. The small ballet group were dancing to recorded music and the tape player broke down. Poor Nureyev continued to dance with a male partner but he was obviously in distress. The combination of the heat and tension caused him to perspire to such an extent that, when he performed a pirouette, water spun off him in a spray which, when caught by the lights, made him look exactly like a lawn-sprinkler. The music came back briefly but only served to further confuse the dancers whose mime was by then out of sequence with it. So far as we know, nobody asked for their money back but it was definitely the worst event that we have attended on the island and I would have preferred to remember Nureyev as I had seen him many years earlier.

For light entertainment we are fortunate in having two very lively groups. The Bay Entertainers was formed five years ago and its first performance, which was presented in rather cramped conditions in the Coleman Hall of the Anglican Church, was sensational. We went expecting to see a mildly amusing demonstration of amateur talent and were totally unprepared for their well-rehearsed review which maintained a breathtaking pace from start to finish with good singing and outstanding musical backing. Minor problems, such as the curtains sweeping away the footlights as they closed, were easily corrected by the members of the audience in the front row acting as stage-hands and the evening was so successful that the only question was where and when their next show would take place. Since then they have made their home in the Sala Mozart of the Auditorium, where they present one review and one pantomime each year which are quickly sold out, raising considerable sums for charity. It is difficult to single out one from the many excellent sketches we have enjoyed, but an item entitled *Meow,* enacted to the Cat's Chorus by a very buxom local school mistress dressed in black fish-net tights and little else, and a popular waiter dressed as a tom cat, has never been forgotten by anyone who saw it.

The Pretty Useful Group, the other band of players, also use the Sala Mozart in Palma but they concentrate on revivals of popular plays. Some members are professional actors and we have seen two of their shows, *Blithe Spirit* and *Don't Dress for Dinner.* Both came very close to West-End standards, including the scenery which was excellent considering that the run was for only four days. There was no prompting, the timing was flawless, and we will certainly not miss their next presentation.

Recently, Porto Pi Centro, an American-style shopping mall, opened on the fringe of Palma. Covering 40,000 square metres, it includes a vast hypermarket, several restaurants, over a hundred small shops and an eight-screen cinema showing the latest European and Hollywood releases.

Entertainment of a different kind is provided when a Royal Navy ship docks in Palma harbour. A cocktail party is often arranged on the ship soon after it docks, to enable the local residents to meet members of the ship's company and to reciprocate by entertaining them in their homes. These parties usually end with a short demonstration of drill or a band performance followed by the moving 'sunset' ceremony and the lowering of the ensign. I always find that my eyes are moist on such occasions, particularly when the national anthem is played.

During one such cocktail party, on the large aircraft-carrier *HMS Illustrious,* I was invited to return the following day to be shown around the ship. I was impressed with the controls and navigation equipment on the bridge; I almost understood an explanation of the intricacy of the hydraulic jacks that operate the lift, which takes aircraft from the hanger to the flight deck, and I was then invited to scramble down several almost vertical ladders to reach the engine room. When we eventually got there, all I could see were some grey boxes and I had to take it on trust that they contained Olympus engines like those in Concorde.

On another occasion we were invited to a party on a supply ship which could not dock. We were taken out to it by launch and then transferred to a floating platform, without any side rails, beside which a companion-way ran up to the main deck. Unfortunately it was a very rough night and the visitors, several of whom were in their seventies, had considerable difficulty crossing the platform, waiting until it rose to meet the staircase and jumping onto the bottom step before the raft dropped several feet down in the trough of a wave.

When we left the ship the weather was worse, but all went well until one of the younger women guests went rigid with fear and was totally unable to cross the heaving platform. Eventually two officers had to grip her by the elbows and carry her to the launch. By the time we reached the jetty she had almost recovered but was still very shaken by her experience.

In 1993 a flotilla of Hunt-class minesweepers, *HMS Cottesmore*, *HMS Cattistock* and *HMS Hurworth* put in to Palma while on NATO excercises. On a very cold evening we went aboard the *Cattistock* for cocktails. After having been welcomed by its Captain, we were waiting to be served with drinks when an officer crossed over from the *Cottesmore,* which was moored alongside, and invited us on to his ship. We chatted to him for a moment or two and and then walked across the narrow gangplank to be greeted by the other officers on the ship. As we crossed over my husband turned to me and said: 'Nice chap!' It was quite obvious that he had not recognised the Captain and I had to tell him that it was HRH Prince Andrew, the Duke of York.

It has given us great pleasure to entertain many naval officers over the years including some from *HMS Ark Royal, HMS Brave, HMS Illustrious, HMS Invincible* and *HMS Nottingham* and we find that, after a tour of duty, they seem to enjoy a traditional English lunch followed by a few hours relaxing around the pool. We cherish the memory of the Commander of one mighty aircraft-carrier frowning in deep concentration as he piloted my husband's radio-controlled boat through a minefield of corks across our swimming pool; meanwhile his First Officer tried to swim despite having to dodge both the boat and a marauding model submarine.

The radio-controlled boat has been a very popular toy with our naval visitors. It is amusing to see the care with which they shut down its motor or even throw it into reverse for a moment, in order to bring it gently alongside the edge of the pool. For his birthday, my husband has been given a radio-controlled model hovercraft and he is eagerly awaiting an opportunity to entrust it to some real professionals.

20. Food and Wine

One of the pleasures of life in Majorca is the virtually unlimited choice of restaurants serving dishes from all over the world which are usually sensibly priced because of the intense competition. We occasionally enjoy a Chinese, Indian or Scandinavian meal and, especially in the winter, a traditional British lunch of roast beef and Yorkshire pudding, but we return again and again to our favourite Majorcan restaurants where the quality never seems to vary and the staff take a pride in efficient and friendly service.

Desayuno, breakfast, is little more than a snack for most Majorcans. Tourists usually have breakfast in their hotels which is normally self-service with a choice of fruit juices, yoghurt, cereal, hard-boiled eggs, cold meats, slices of cheese, rolls and butter and coffee or tea. The cafés and restaurants that serve cooked breakfast are usually catering for visitors and almost always have menus available in English.

Almuerzo or more often *comida,* lunch, is served later than in Britain. Shops and offices tend to be open until one-thirty and in Palma they remain closed until four or later, so Majorcans often start lunch at two o'clock. We find that eating out can cost little more than a meal at home if advantage is taken of a *menú del dia* which virtually every restaurant offers at lunch time, although it is sometimes only produced when specifically requested. It is frequently shortened to *el menú* so it is best to remember that the printed menu itself is *la carta* to avoid a request for the menu being wrongly interpreted. There is usually a wide *à la carte* selection which will probably include some international dishes as well as any specialities of the house.

Cena, dinner, is the main meal of the day. Restaurants serve it from around eight but Majorcans tend to eat much later and often arrive after eleven; consequently most cafes and restaurants are open until long after midnight.

Conversation in Majorca soon gets round to food and restaurants. It is not long before a new establishment offering good value is well patronised while one that has allowed its standards to slip soon stands empty. Golf and yacht clubs serve meals to anyone and do not restrict the use of their restaurants to members, while some of the monasteries cater for visitors, thus widening the choice of interesting eating places.

Prior to the tourist boom, Majorcan food reflected the relative poverty of the inhabitants. Main dishes were frequently based on the pig or the harvest of the sea, often bulked out by the addition of bread, tomatoes, peppers, pulses or cabbage and liberally flavoured with garlic. Cooking was based on dry farming with few green vegetables, scarcely any wheat and no beef or veal. Even as late as 1954 we could only buy goat's milk in Deià as there were no local cows.

The pig used to be the prime source of meat, traditionally fed on acorns, bran and figs. From it were produced pork, ham, offal and a wide range of sausages, which are still so popular that an annual sausage fair takes place every year in Sant Joan in October. They include *sobrasada*, which is red and peppery; the almost black *camaiot*; thin *longaniza*; and *butifarrón* which is strongly flavoured with herbs. Locally caught fish, such as the *peix roquer* or rock fish and the *cap-roig* which is Majorcan for red-head, supplemented the diet.

Sopes made an inexpensive but filling meal. The word is often wrongly translated as soup, but it is probably derived from *sopar* which is Majorcan for dinner. It is based on sliced bread over which boiled vegetables, often including cauliflower, are poured; the dish is then left on the fire until the liquid has been absorbed.

When we go to a typical Majorcan restaurant today we are usually first served with bread and olives or, in the better establishments, tasty *tapas* such as *mejillones rellenos*, stuffed mussels; *calamares romana,* rings of deep fried squid, or some other speciality of the house to take the edge off our appetites as we select our first course. There is frequently a wide choice of starters including local dishes such as *caracoles* which are small snails served with garlic butter; *pa amb oli,* literally bread and oil which is flavoured by rubbing a cut tomato over the surface of the bread before dribbling olive oil over it and sometimes topping it with ham; *arroz brut* made with rice and flavoured with sausage and meat, traditionally game; *entreméses* comprising a mixture of slices of cold meats and cheese with a little salad; and *mejillónes marinera* mussels cooked in white wine and onions.

Alternatively we can start with one of the many delicious soups that are popular on the island and which used to be reserved for the evening meal although they are now available at all times. These include *sopa de almendras* made from ground almonds and cream; *sopa de pescadores* and *sopa de mariscos,* the first being based on white fish while the other uses shellfish; *sopa de verduras* a vegetable soup which often includes white beans and *acelgas,* chard. Cold soups are ideal on a hot summer evening and include *gazpacho* made from a blending of tomatoes, green peppers, onions, cucumbers, garlic and bread which is usually served with croûtons and a selection of side dishes of finely chopped cucumber, tomato, green pepper and onion; and *sopa fría de ajo y almendras* comprising stale bread, ground almonds, garlic, olive oil, white wine vinegar, water instead of stock, and a garnish of white muscat grapes.

We find that the main course tends to be very generous and we sometimes follow the example of the Majorcans who often share one starter between two people. This enables us to enjoy the second part of the meal which might consist of *conejo con col* or *con cebollas* rabbit with cabbage or onions; *cabrito,* baby goat; *lechona,* roast suckling pig; *pierna* or *paletilla de cordero,* a leg or shoulder of lamb. The portions can be so large that we often have to ask for *una bolsa por el perro*, a doggy bag, to take the remainder back to Tia Maria who has developed a taste for Majorcan meat and does not object if it is flavoured with garlic or onions.

There is a little restaurant at Orient located in the beautiful fruit-growing country to the east of Bunyola that serves some of the best *lechona* on the island. It is easy to find as it is on the left just as one enters Orient from the direction of Bunyola. On a Sunday in the summer parked cars stretch the length of the village and Majorcans who come late happily wait for a considerable time to secure a table.

We went there with a party of friends and had previously ordered a whole roasted baby pig which was brought for us to admire before it was placed on a serving table behind me to be carved. I had just resumed a conversation with my neighbour when there was some shouting, followed by several bangs, after which a plate virtually exploded on the floor. This is an old Majorcan custom; the meat is very tender and the chef salutes the diners, chops up the pig with the edge of the plate and then smashes it. This has happened since, but I no longer jump out of my skin as I am prepared for it. The same restaurant also offers *tordos con col*, thrushes roasted and served in cabbage leaves, which are a Majorcan speciality.

Other popular meat dishes include *lomo,* loin of pork; *escalope,* which is usually thinly sliced pork unless it is specifically listed as *escalope de ternera blanca* when it will be veal; *solomillo,* filet steak; and *chuletas de cordero,* lamb chops, which are usually small and thinly cut so that one portion may contain as many as five.

Poultry is not widely used by itself in Majorcan cooking although *pollo,* chicken, is of very high quality. However, it is often found in *paellas* along with pork and rabbit. Many *paellas* combine these with shellfish and a mixed *paella* might contain mussels, prawns, thighs of chicken, pork, onions, tomatoes and garlic, all cooked in saffron-flavoured rice. There are many types of *paella* but, as they should be served freshly cooked, it is necessary to order for a minimum of two persons and be prepared to wait for up to half an hour.

Our two daughters are both vegetarians and they enjoy another popular Majorcan dish called *tumbet* which is a mixture of aubergines, red or green peppers, onions and potatoes all fried separately in olive oil and then combined in a sauce of puréed tomatoes. I frequently make *tumbet* and sometimes serve it as a starter; although it contains potatoes it does not seem to suffer by being frozen for use later. Another dish using a mixture of vegetables is *frito Mallorquin* which includes potatoes, leeks and green peppers, but as its main ingredients are fried liver and kidneys it is not suitable for vegetarians.

Some restaurants specialise in fresh fish and offer a very wide choice. Even those that predominantly serve meat will probably include some fish on their menu but it might be have been *congelado*, frozen. Fresh fish tends to be expensive as the Mediterranean is now over-fished and at some restaurants the price is determined by weight. *Rape*, (pronounced rapay) is firm white monkfish which may be served in a *caldereta de pescados*, fish stew, or simply charcoal grilled and served with a salad. *Emperador*, swordfish, is firm and tasty and slightly pink. *Merluza*, hake, is very widely available and affordable as are *bacalao*, cod, *sardinas*, sardines or pilchards according to size, and *salmón* which may be served grilled or poached in a champagne sauce.

More exotic fish include *denton* served whole; *dorada*, gilthead bream; *lubina*, sea bass which is often cooked in a salt crust; *rodaballo*, turbot; *salmonetes*, small red mullet; *cap-roig* with its delicate pink flesh and large bones; *serviola*, which our dictionary translates as amberjack; and *lenguado*, sole, which is often rather small, thin and disappointing compared with a good English Dover sole. *Llampuga*, dolphin-fish is a delicious blue fish which is caught off Majorca from September to the end of November and is not related to the dolphin.

One popular fish dish is Catalan rather than Majorcan in origin. It is called *zarzuela* which literally means an operetta or musical comedy and contains chunks of white fish and shellfish in a rich sauce made with garlic, white wine and saffron. One Sunday in summer we took Beryl Graves to lunch at the beautifully located Restaurante Bens Davall overlooking the sea on the road between Deià and Puerto de Soller and enjoyed the best *zarzuela* we have had on the island.

Nearer to home, we have two favourite restaurants for fish, one on each side of Palma. The one to the east is at Portixol at the far end of the road that encircles the little port; it is a large complex with several dining rooms and a swimming pool and on two occasions when we have been to the main restaurant we have been able to watch guests arrive for a Majorcan wedding reception in one of the banqueting rooms.

Virtually every fish available on the island is on the menu but one evening I decided that I would like a lobster. Shortly afterwards it was brought, live, to our table, causing me to enjoy the meal rather less than would have been the case if it had remained in the kitchen until it was served. I admit that this is pure hypocrisy, but nowadays I ask not to be introduced to my future meal.

Our other favourite fish restaurant is Rififi to the west of Palma on the Avenida Joan Miro at Porto Pi which is smaller and has a more intimate atmosphere. Both are very popular with the Majorcans so it is best to make a reservation.

It is not surprising that *postres*, desserts, hardly figure on most Majorcan menus. The portions of the first two courses tend to be so generous that I seldom have room for a dessert although I find it hard to resist *coco helado*, coconut ice cream which comes in half a coconut shell, when I see it displayed in the cold cabinet. My husband, who has a healthy appetite, likes Majorcan *pudin* which is made in a loaf tin from cake or pieces of ensaimada which are broken up, soaked in caramel, covered with egg custard and then cooked in a *bain-marie* in an oven.

Other typical *postres* include *flan* which is not a tart but what the British would call a caramel custard, and *tarta* which is also confusing because it is cake, often flavoured with almonds or apple. A cheeseboard is rarely seen, but fresh fruit is normally available and *pina*, pineapple cut lengthwise to form a gondola shape is usually excellent. Melon is sometimes offered as a dessert but is more often served with Serrano ham as a starter.

Serrano ham is a subject in itself. It is cured for several months in cool air, served uncooked and cut very thin, almost like smoked salmon, and can be just as delicious. Really fine Serrano ham comes from black pigs, the foot being left on the whole ham to prove that it is indeed from such a prime source.

The majority of the finest Spanish wines are produced on the mainland, mostly in the regions of Penedès and Rioja, but almost every area, including Majorca, makes wine locally. The result is that there is a very wide choice of *tinto, blanco* and *rosado,* red, white and rosé.

Majorca suffered from severe damage by phylloxera, a genus of insects which are very destructive to vines. In 1890 it reduced the acreage of vineyards from around 70,000 to about 12,000 and the total is even less today, but wine is still produced in several areas; the two largest being around Binissalem and Felanitx. Binissalem has qualified for a *Denominación de Origen* which is the approximate Spanish equivalent of the French *Appellation d'Origine Contrôlleé.* It recognises a zone as a producer of wines of exceptional quality and lays down rules such as the maximum amount of wine that can be produced from each kilo of grapes, the grape varieties that can be used and whether or not the vines may be irrigated. In Binissalem, for example, no watering of the vines is permitted and the grapes must be grown within the denominated area, which is protected on the north by the Sierra de Torrellas and includes Consell, Santa Maria, Santa Eugenia and Sencelles.

The main producer in Binissalem is José L Ferrer, a company founded in 1931 and now controlled by the third generation of the family. It produces about 600,000 bottles of wine per year, most of which is consumed on the island. A little is exported to Switzerland and some goes to London, but there is more than enough local demand to absorb its limited output.

When we recently visited his *bodega,* Señor Luis Ferrer explained that Manto Negro grapes, rich in sugar and aroma, account for 85% of his *tintos* and *rosados* while the Moll vine is responsible for a similar proportion of his dry, fresh and fruity *blancos.* Constant efforts towards improvement have been assisted by the introduction of 30,000 litre stainless steel vats in which fermentation can be conducted under controlled conditions. These are desirable because the ambient temperature in Majorca is often well above the 25–29° considered ideal for fermenting *tintos*, while *rosados* and *blancos* require even lower temperatures.

Approximately 40% of the grapes used are grown in the company's own vineyards, the remainder coming from others within the demarcated area. Only a few bunches are allowed to mature low on each vine and, to maintain a good yield per acre, the vines are planted much closer together than is normal. The regulations only permit 0.7 litres of wine to be produced from each kilo of grapes. For a good harvest dry weather is needed during June, July and August; 1994 is expected to produce wines of exceptional quality but, as there is less variation in climate than in areas such as France, 1993, 1991, 1985 and 1984 were also good years. Most Binissalem reds do not improve significantly after five years and their life is considered to be about ten, after which they may start to decline.

The harvest commences in late August or September and lasts for about a month during which over fifty tons of grapes are delivered every day to the *bodega*. When they arrive they have a temperature of about 35° so they are allowed to cool before being lightly pressed and held in the fermentation tanks to convert their sugar to alcohol. *Tintos* ferment for 8–15 days with their skins, *rosados* have the skins removed after 36 hours, but the same grape varieties are used for both. After fermentation the wine is stored in large stainless steel tanks and then in oak casks before being bottled. A *reserva* for example, may spend 36 months in barrel and 24 months in bottle.

The quality and flavour of a wine is determined by many factors. Although the predominant grape for the *tintos* and *rosados* is the Manto Negro, *must* produced from other varieties may be incorporated in the final product; these include the Callet which is an important element in the *reservas*. Similarly the Parellada is mixed with Moll for the *blancos*. The fermentation process is critical, taking several months, and this is followed by the period in barrel which is essential if the wine is later to improve in bottle. Oak casks are employed which were traditionally made of American oak, but French oak barrels are also widely used to provide a different flavour. The French use new 220 litre oak barrels for their Cabernet Sauvignon and Ferrer buy these when they are two years old as they consider that new French oak would give too strong a flavour to their wine.

The minimum storage periods set out for red *reservas* are three years in total in oak barrels and bottles and, for *gran reservas*, a minimum of two years in oak followed by three in bottle. A white *reserva* must spend at least six months in oak out of a total of two years in cask and bottle while a *gran reserva* needs a total of four years, of which at least six months must be in oak. Ferrer keep their better *tintos* in oak for two years and then carefully control storage in bottle, limiting the temperature to a maximum of 19°. They claim that their inexpensive *Crianza*, if stored at such temperatures, would gradually mature to the quality of a *reserva*.

Ferrer pack their better wines horizontally in their cases; which imposes limits on how high cases can be stacked, but is considered important if the wine is to continue to improve in bottle. Even the cork is critical and corks can cost from two to forty pesetas each according to length and quality; conventionally a longer cork is used for the better wines. A good cork will last for up to forty years, the world's largest producers being Spain and Portugal.

The Ferrer range of white wines includes *Vina Veritas*, made from Moll and Parellada grapes; *Blanc de Blanc*, made from the Moll grape, using refrigerated fermentation to bring out the smoothness and aroma, and then stored at 17° to improve its quality. *Rosado* is produced from Manto Negro grapes by a special process in which it is steeped for 24 hours in its own skin before being fermented at controlled temperature. Their red wines include *Tinto de Añada*, which is based on the Manto Negro grape; and *Tinto de Crianza,* which also employs the Manto Negro but includes the Callet, and is aged for 24 months in American oak before continuing to age in bottle.

Other Majorcan bodegas are Florianópolis which is situated on the Andratx to Capdella road producing wines such as *Merlot*, *Cabernet Sauvignon* and *Chardonnay* under their *Santa Catarina* label; and Miquel Oliver at Petrá whose reds include *Manto Negro Reserva* and *Mont Ferrutx Reserva* together with *Muscat* and *Chardonnay* whites.

On his S'Estaca estate near Valldemossa, Michael Douglas is reputed to be producing very small quantities of Malvasia wine. It was known as Malmsey in England and George, Duke of Clarence, the younger brother of King Edward IV, drowned in a vat of it in 1478. The Malvasia grape was once common on Majorca and it usually produces a musky, heavy wine that can be used as an apéritif or to enhance cooking.

Vino de casa, house wine, is available in all restaurants, often unlabelled. It is usually quite drinkable and sometimes of excellent quality. A good restaurant is staking its reputation on its house wine because the choice is made by the restaurant and not the customer, so there is no excuse for an inferior *vino de casa,* but it is unreasonable to expect too much if the wine is supplied as part of an inexpensive *menú del dia*.

The finest *tintos* offered in Majorca mostly come from Rioja and it is generally agreed that 1991, 1990, 1987, 1986, 1985, 1983 were very good years while 1982, 1981, 1980 and 1978 are noted for some wines of exceptional quality. A good *Reserva* or *Gran Reserva* from Rioja will continue to improve for many years.

Majorca produces a liqueur known as *hierbas* which is aniseed-based and green in colour; it usually has actual herbs in the bottle and is available *seca,* dry, or *dulce,* sweet. Another Majorcan liqueur is made from the seeds of the carob tree which grows throughout the island, it is too sweet for some tastes. Tunel in Bunyola produce a range of liqueurs in many flavours including *melocotón*, peach, and *avellana,* hazelnut, which are well worth sampling. Restaurants often serve valued customers with liqueurs at the end of a meal with the compliments of the house when they are known as *chupitos.*

A mixture of brandy, red wine, fresh fruit and juices, called *sangria* is very popular with tourists. It is usually served in a jug to be shared by several persons and, although refreshing at the end of a long sunny day, it is very intoxicating and best avoided by those who will later be driving.

A friend, sadly no longer with us, was a retired RAF Group-Captain, who enjoyed his food and appreciated a good wine to accompany it. After the meal he would settle back in his chair with an appreciative sigh and we knew that the time had come for one of his limitless fund of stories.

One evening he recounted the tale of a man who started a winery and laboured hard with the planting and tending of the vines, picking the grapes at just the right moment and fermenting the wine strictly according to local custom. Eventually the great day came when the first bottle could be sampled, and he invited his closest friend to join him for the momentous occasion. The cork was eased out, two glasses were filled with a rather cloudy liquid and the proud grower awaited the verdict. Instead of immediately pronouncing judgement, his friend asked. 'Where is your winery?' Slightly puzzled, the grower pointed to a converted barn less than half a kilometre down the road. 'As I thought,' said his friend with a shake of his head. 'It is undoubtedly a fine wine, but it does not travel well!'

When we first visited Majorca in the mid-1950's some of the wine merited a somewhat similar description. Producers were more concerned with quantity than quality and their wine was often so cheap that it was not bottled; instead casks were marked *tinto* if they contained an intoxicating red liquid and *blanco* if it was pale yellow. It was quite normal to take one's own bottle and have it filled for a few pesetas. Today Spain produces many excellent wines that can hold their own against any competition.

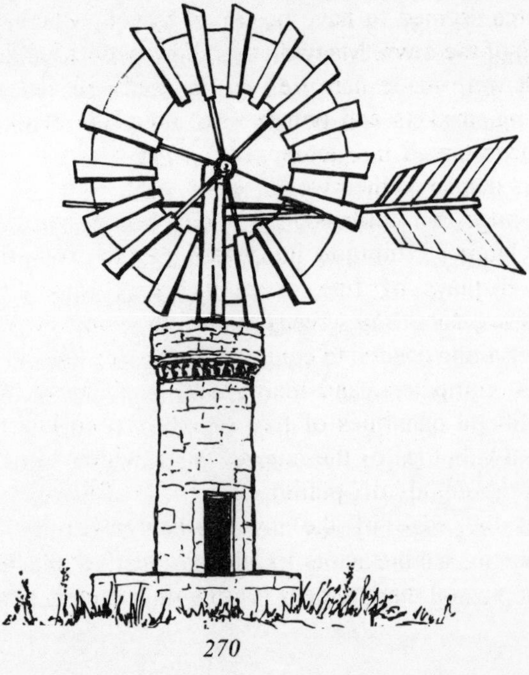

21. The View from Randa

One Saturday in mid-October we were told that there was a fair and dog show at Llucmajor, a small town east of Palma. We thought that this would be similar to the Vilafranca Melon Fair and that it would provide an additional insight into village life and were quite unprepared for what we found. Every car in Majorca seemed to have been parked somewhere within a mile radius of the town. Many thousands of people blocked the streets which were made narrower by hundreds of stalls selling food, clothing, trinkets and pottery. All along the main street houses had been turned into temporary art galleries where painters and potters displayed their work.

A huge tent contained 50 booths which reminded us of the Ideal Home Exhibition in London. Apart from furniture there were displays of fine work in marble and Santanyi stone, staircases, doors and screens beautifully worked in pine, a display of everything needed to equip a hairdressing salon, wood burning stoves, computers, and many food products including cheeses with liberal quantities of free samples on cocktail sticks. There were also bottles of the mineral water which is sold in Majorca under the slightly off-putting trade name of Revoltosa.

On the edge of the town an immense display of farm equipment, from tractors to wind-pumps, covered several acres. Down several streets, pens had been constructed to hold every type of farm animal and they seemed contented to be admired as they stood, immaculately groomed for their big day, awaiting the judges.

We must have walked miles but eventually came to the dog show where there were four rings in simultaneous operation. Five very large dogs of a breed that we could not identify were in one of the rings when we arrived and we watched as they were made to walk, run and then submit to close examination by the judge.

First, second and third prizes were awarded and the proud owners walked off with their pets, but it was obvious that a lady holding the lead of one of the other dogs was far from happy with the result. At one point we wondered whether she might slip its lead and shout 'kill' as she loudly defended its right to be honoured. The judge agreed that it was magnificent, but he had detected a fault in its mouth that disqualified it and he refused to be diverted. Eventually he called a colleague to confirm his decision and the lady was pacified.

We turned to the adjoining ring only to witness another fracas. This time fierce guard dogs were being shown and one had obviously snapped at the judge who had ordered it to be removed; the owner refused and, after a long argument, they came to a compromise with a muzzle being firmly fixed over the vicious mouth. We thought that the judge might have preferred to fit it on the owner, but he got his revenge easily by not awarding the dog a prize.

On a table covered with pink cloth a mass of fur was being combed. It looked like a wig which had been blown off and run over by a passing steamroller. It had a parting down the centre, but both ends were identical with no indication whatsoever of where the head, legs and tail might be. Curiosity overcame one member of the crowd who lifted some fur to be met with a pair of resigned eyes. When we returned half an hour later the grooming was still in progress.

Beautiful scents attracted me to one stall which, I thought, was selling bath salts in small glass jars. The young male assistant was helpful and explained that the essences were medicinal and that the science of curing with scents was known as aromaterapia. I had selected a jar with an attractive aroma which was marked *Ylang-top* and asked what it cured. He looked embarrassed and delved into a pile of literature, finally handing me a leaflet which explained that it '*raises the moral tone, clarifies sightseeing and stimulates sexual appetences.*'

In November, an even larger agricultural show and market is held in Inca known as *Dijous Bo,* Good Thursday, which attracts thousands of visitors from all over the island. Last year the livestock section even included ostriches as well as the customary cattle, pigs, chickens and dogs.

Llucmajor was packed and we decided to get well away before trying to find a restaurant for lunch. We took the road to Santanyi, a conventional Majorcan town which was created by King Jaime II around 1300. As it is only five kilometres from the coast, it was fortified against attack by pirates but only the old *Porta Murada* gate and some old walls remain as evidence. It was from the quarries nearby that stone was taken to construct most of the fine buildings in Palma including the Cathedral.

We drove on to Cala d'Or which offers a wide choice of restaurants. Its white houses attempt to blend with the landscape and are reasonably well-spaced and there are still many pines. It is definitely a tourist area with large hotels, bars and chic boutiques. The small beaches in the rocky indented coastline and the fine modern marina tend to be rather crowded.

After lunch we followed the coast to Porto Petro, which has a natural harbour at the end of a deep inlet. It is still relatively unspoiled and has a sheltered bay with a sandy beach and pines, but we did not linger there as we were eager to get to nearby Cala Mondragó, now a protected area, which also features sandy bays in natural pine woods.

We then drove on to Cala Figuera which has been called the Venice of Majorca. It is built beside a long narrow inlet with steep banks to which the houses cling as best they can. The buildings extend right down to the water's edge where their garages contain boats instead of cars.

Cala Figuera is a lively fishing port and we watched the fishermen working on their nets as fine yachts rode at anchor in the long tongue of sheltered water that widens as it meets the sea.

As we left and turned inland at Cala Santanyi with its large sandy beaches, palms, pines and hotels we looked out to sea and admired the huge rock which is, known as *Es Pontas* because it looks just like a bridge.

We then headed inland to Campos which is famous for pastries and cakes, we stopped at Casa Pomar, which also has a branch in Palma, for some *robiols,* pastries filled with pumpkin jam which the Majorcans call *cabey d'angel,* angel's hair. An annual fair in October incorporates a food week, when the owners of local restaurants explain how to make traditional Majorcan dishes and the Campos Council publishes the recipes.

It was evening, but we drove on to the fishing port and marina at Colonia San Jordi from where we had previously taken a boat trip to the island of Cabrera with other members of the English Speaking Residents' Association. The island is the largest in a group which lies just south of Majorca. It is undulating, mainly barren, but with some pine woods and its highest point, the Puig de la Guardia, is 172 metres above sea level. Its best known feature is its fine natural harbour which is 1600 metres long. Its 14th Century castle was a hotbed of Berber pirates who captured it on several occasions and used it as a base for attacks on

Majorca. The *Cova Blava*, blue grotto, is a cave into which boats can sail to enable their passengers to swim in the clear water and admire the unusual chromatic effects. There is a monument on the island commemorating the French prisoners who were left there to fend for themselves between 1809 and 1814 after the Spanish War of Independence when Spain fought Napoleon and captured them at the battle of Bailen; only 3600 survived out of the original 9000.

The island is a paradise for ornithologists who can see eagles, Aoudouin's gulls, falcons and cormorants. It is also has a herd of wild goats that wander freely over the wild terrain.

A little way along the coast the shadows were lengthening as we strolled on the immense sandy beach of Es Trenc which is bordered by pines. The nude bathers had long since departed and we were almost alone as we watched the sun setting over a perfectly calm sea. Behind us were the salt flats of Ses Salines, much frequented by ornithologists.

Talayots, ancient stone constructions which date from 2000 to 1300 BC, are evidence of human occupation of the district from the earliest times and some historians believe that this area, and not Palma, was the Palmaria of the Romans. Coins and other Roman artefacts have been found here but, because the road from the Roman settlement at Alcudia goes almost as straight as an arrow to Palma, and there is no trace of such a direct route to Colonia Sant Jordi, the evidence points to Palma always having been the capital.

Only a few weeks before this book was due for press I checked the map on the wall of our study on which I had marked off the areas of the island I had already described. One small part remained uncovered which included the coastal strip east of Palma and the little town of Randa, built on the side of a hill with the Sanctuario de Nuestra Señora de Cura at the top. We had been to the town many times, but had never actually visited the Sanctuary or seen the glorious views from its grounds which can extend as far as the islands of Cabrera and Ibiza on a clear day.

We decided to go there for lunch after church on the last Sunday available before this book went to the printer. We had been invited to a cocktail party in the evening but calculated that we would have ample time to take photographs and enjoy a leisurely meal. The evening before a gale blew up and it increased in force until we were awakened during the night by the sound of smashing tiles. In the morning the terrace was littered with shards and a heavy metal chair was lying at the bottom of the swimming pool, while catkins had been blown into drifts in every corner. We had just time to tidy things up a little before setting off for church.

While having coffee after the service we met the British Consul whose party we were due to attend that evening. He was with a visiting Government Minister who had read the lesson and they were about to leave for lunch at La Residencia in Deià. It had started to rain and we sympathised with them because, although it is beautiful at any time, the coast road from Valldemossa to Deià is at its best when the sun turns the sea to a cobalt-blue to contrast with the dark green pines.

On this very grey day we set off in light rain on the road which runs east from Palma beside the bay where the resort towns merge into one another so that it is a little difficult to decide where one stops and the next begins. We drove through El Molinar (the place of the mills) which once produced much of the flour for Palma; and then Coll d'en Rabassa with its enormous Continente hypermarket which sells everything from a double bed to a pot of shrimps.

Continuing along the coast Ca'n Pastilla marks the start of a holiday area that is almost the twin of Palma Nova and Magalluf; it stretches through the Playas de Mallorca to El Arenal where we have enjoyed some very fine meals in the pleasant restaurant at the *Club Nautico*. After this point the density of the development gradually eases off until open country begins at Cala Blava. The sandy beaches, which have recently been widened, and a pedestrian walk lined with the usual mixture of hotels, bars, cafés, souvenir shops and inexpensive boutiques, make this a very popular holiday area.

We turned inland at El Arenal and soon reached Llucmajor which was in its usual quiet form and quite different from when we had visited its fair. It is an old agricultural centre and is also a manufacturing town producing liqueurs, chocolates, knives, pottery, dried flowers, shoes and hand-made furniture. The yellow-gold houses are built on level ground and its 17th Century Convento de San Buenaventura was the seventh Franciscan friary on the island It was from there that Father Mariano Rubi and Father Jerónimo Boscana left to carry on the work of the friars at their missions in California.

After Llucmajor we headed north to Randa. It lies just off the main road and on most days the Sanctuary can be seen for miles from any direction as it is 500 metres high. We pressed on through the little town at the base of the hill; the rain had eased slightly but the cloud was very low and all that was visible were the lower slopes.

Ramón Llull, Majorca's most famous theologian, lived as a hermit in a cave on the mountain where he wrote his *Ars Magna* expounding the philosophical theories which he considered to be his best work. Legend states that after a night spent in contemplation he went outside his cave and found that the leaves of a lentisk bush had unusual markings, like the letters of some unknown alphabet and the shrubs growing nearby are said to still show a different leaf pattern from any others.

We continued up the narrow winding road that twists and turns for four kilometres until it ends at the Sanctuary. The drive was easy at first because the road is well surfaced, but it was not long before we entered the cloud and it was difficult to see more than a few feet in front of the car. We thought that the restaurant would probably be closed because no visitors would be expected on such a foul day, but having got so close we decided to complete the climb and, on entering the car park at the top, were surprised to find that it was almost full.

The Sanctuary of Nuestra Senora de Cura was founded in 1275. It is a large and impressive building, but all that we could make out across the car park was the dim outline of its massive gateway. When we were closer to it we were able to translate the Latin inscription above it which means 'Act in all things in the name of Jesus Christ.'

We entered the large courtyard but could not see across it and had to follow the sound of voices to locate a couple who kindly directed us to the restaurant. We had planned the visit as a highlight with which to end this book and wanted photographs as a base for line drawings but, apart from some steps up to the restaurant and the outline of some old farm implements dimly visible in the mist, we saw very little of the building or its grounds and had to take it on trust that there are usually magnificent views to the coast from its elevated position.

We entered the large restaurant and found that we had arrived only just in time as it was almost full. There must have been about 150 people there, mostly Majorcans, and the noise of conversation was deafening. We had half-expected a small bare room in which we would be welcome to share a humble meal with the monks, possibly in virtual silence; instead we were shown an extensive menu and lunched on superb filet steak with the sound of champagne corks popping behind us.

A large party, which stretched along one entire wall of the restaurant was enjoying a celebratory meal with much laughter and cheering. We had not arrived until two and we had enjoyed a drink and a chat while we waited for the big party to be served, so it was after four by the time we had finished our meal.

We decided that we would soon have to leave in order to change for the evening. It was fortunate that we lingered a little over our coffee, because the obvious leader of the party climbed on to a chair, tapped a wine bottle with a fork to secure silence, and then proceeded to conduct the group as they sang beautifully in Spanish with even the younger children joining in enthusiastically. We asked the waiter who they were and he replied: '*Coro de la iglesia*,' a church choir.

What we thought would be an unrewarding outing because of the dreadful weather, turned into one of those magical moments that are always awaiting those who explore the real Majorca. It was with great reluctance that we eventually left the singing and crept through the cloud, down the mountain and into heavy rain which continued throughout the journey home.

We marked off the last outstanding town on our map, the description of Randa is not what had been intended, but it does at least illustrate how varied life can be on this delightful island.

The next morning I opened the *persianas* to a cloudless blue sky and saw the white ferry from Barcelona, like a painted ship on a painted ocean, passing Santa Ponça on its way to Palma. It was hard to believe that forty-three years had passed since I sailed the same route with the boys on my first visit to Majorca.

Soon Mateo will come to help replace the tiles on the roof, the scum of catkins floating on the pool will be removed and before long I will be able to rise in the morning and have a refreshing dip before breakfast. We will be getting the loungers out and preparing for visits from our family and friends and my husband will replace the batteries in his radio-controlled boats while Tia Maria will abandon the warmth of the utility room in favour of a cool spot on the terrace. In our various different ways we can all truly say that we are enjoying Majorca.

Dates of Festivals and Fiestas

JANUARY

5th (Eve of Epiphany) *Cabalgata de los Reyes Magos*. Procession of the Three Kings.

6th *Adoració dels Tres Reis d'Orient.* The Adoration of the Three Kings of the East, a play in Catalan at Ses Voltes, in front of the Cathedral in Palma.

10th *San Nicanor.* When devils make mischief in towns and villages.

16th *Revetla de Sant Antoni Abat*. Eve of day of St Antonio. Large events in Palma in the Plaza Mayor and at Artà where the ceremony dates from 1719, there are also celebrations in Algaida, Costitx, Pollença, Puerto Pollença, Porreras and Sa Pobla.

17th *Beneïdes de Sant Antoni*. Blessing of St Anthony. Processions to bless animals in Palma, Artà, Puerto de Andratx, Costitx, St Joan, Son Servera and Sa Pobla.

17th *Pi de Sant Antoni.* St Anthony's Pine, ceremonies in Pollença and Puerto Pollença which involve attempts to climb a greased pole.

19th *Revetla de Sant Sebastià.* Fair of Eve of St Sebastian, in Palma.

20th *Fiesta de Sant Sebastià.* Festival of Saint Sebastian, the Patron Saint of Palma. Ceremony in Plaza Cort followed by a cycle ride around Palma.

Also during the month: Display by mounted police in Bellver Woods, the annual interdenominational service at Cathedral and *Alimenta*, a food fair, at IFEBAL.

EASTER-RELATED FESTIVALS.

Thursday before start of Lent *Dijous Llader*, a mock trial ceremony when an effigy is blamed for a town's misfortunes and executed by burning.

Saturday and Sunday immediately before Lent *Es Darrers Dies* carnivals in Palma, Montuïri and other towns for *Sa Rueta*, for children, and *Sa Rua,* a full carnival.

4th Sunday in Lent *Pa i el Peix,* The bread and the fishes, a festival is held at Sant Joan.

Maundy Thursday *La Sang*, a solemn procession in Palma by hooded penitents.

Good Friday *Devallment del Calvari.* The Taking-Down from the Cross, with processions in Pollença and Felanitx. Also procession to church of El Soccoro in Palma.

Easter Sunday *S'Encontrada.* Festival commemorating the resurrection of Christ, in Porreres, Campos and Felanitx.

1st Sunday after Easter *Romeria* from Inca to hermitage of Santa Magdalena.

Easter Tuesday *Romerias* from Selva and Mancor del Valle to Oratorio of Santa Lucia, also from Petrá to Bon Any.

FEBRUARY

2nd Candlemas. Candles are lit in many churches.

Also during month: *Alimenta*, a food fair at the IFEBAL Centre in Palma

MARCH

During month: *Fira del Fang.* Pottery Fair, at Marratxi; also International Organ Week at Santa Maria and Palma Cathedral and Handicraft and Trade Fair at Sant Joan.

APRIL

10th *Festa del Angel.* Feast of the Angel, in Bellver Woods.

During month: *Brocanter.* Antiques Fair, at IFEBAL Centre. Also *Baleares Náutica.* Floating Boat Show, in Palma; Opera season opens at Teatro Principal, Palma.

Index to Festivals and Fiestas

MAY

First Week: *Ses Valentes Dones* in Soller. Includes mock battle against Moors. Also *Fires i Festes de Primavera,* an Annual Spring fair in Manacor.

During month: Book Fair in the Borne, Palma. Many agricultural shows are held during May including those at Campos, Felanitx, Sencelles and Sineu.

JUNE

Corpus Christi. *Ball de les Aguiles,* Dance of the Eagles in Pollença.

13th *Sant Antoni de Juny.* Feast of St Anthony, in Artà, includes *Es Cavallets.*

23rd St John's Eve. Dancing and bonfires in many towns.

24th *Festa d'es sol que balla.* Festival of the sun that dances, at Sant Joan.

24th *Juan Bautista.* The Feast of St John the Baptist. In Muro and many other towns.

29th *San Pedro.* Processions of decorated boats in Palma, Alcudia, Soller and other ports.

30th *Sant Marçial.* In Marratxi, Large event with stalls selling pottery & handicrafts.

JULY

2nd *Romeria a la Virgen de la Victoria.* Pilgrimage and picnic from Alcudia.

16th *Fiesta de la Virgen del Carmen* Decorated boats in Puerto de Andratx, Cala Ratjada, Puerto Pollença and Puerto de Soller.

17th (Approx) Choral concert in Torrent de Pareis.

20th *Es Cavallets.* Little Horses. Dances in Felanitx with cardboard horses.

24th *Es Cossiers.* Traditional dancers, at Montuïri

25th *Sant Jaume.* Patron Saint of Spain. Large procession in Alcudia bearing figure of Christ through the streets. Week-long fiesta in Calvià. *Es Cossiers* dance at Algaida

28th *Carro Triunfal,* Triumphal Cart. Procession for Santa Catalina in Valldemossa.

30th *San Abdón and San Senén.* Inca. Concerts, fireworks and carnival figures.

Also during month: Major classical music festivals at Artà and Deià.

AUGUST

2nd (Approx). *Fiesta de Nuestra Señora de Los Angeles* in Pollença with mock battle.

16th *Es Cossiers* dance in Algaida, also at Montuiri on 23rd and 24th.

24th Traditional Horse Races at Capdepera.

28th *Es Cavallets* dance at Felanitx for festival of San Agustin.

29th Patronal Festival at Sant Joan. With devils, bagpipers and many other events.

Also during month: *Marxa a Peu,* Walk at night from Palma to monastery at Lluc. Fiestas in Santa Ponça including celebration to commemorate landing of King Jaime 1.

SEPTEMBER

1st Sunday. *Processó de la Beata.* Procession for Santa Catalina at Santa Margalida.

2nd Saturday and Sunday *Festas des Meló.* Melon Fair in Vilafranca.

21st *Fiestas de San Mateo.* Festival of St Mathew at Bunyola. Dances etc.

Last Sunday: *Festa d'es Vermar.* Wine Harvest Festival, in Binissalem.

Also during month *El dimoni* and *Els Cossiers* perform at Montuiri.

OCTOBER

1st Sunday. *Torrada d'es Botifarró.* Fair of meats and sausages in Sant Joan.

20th Night of the Virgins, when *Buñuelos* are given to serenaders.

Also during month Annual Fairs at Alcudia, Felanitx, Inca Llucmajor and Porreras. Food week in Campos. *La Beateta.* Procession for Santa Catalina Tomás in Palma.

NOVEMBER

1st *Todos Santos,* All Saints Day. When flowers are taken to graves.

Also during month *Dijous Bo.* Good Thursday. Very large agricultural fair in Inca.

DECEMBER

24th *Cant de la Sibil.la.* Sybil's Song, is sung by a young boy in the Cathedral.

28th *Santos Inocentes.* Day of the Innocents. Spanish equivalent of April Fools.

31st *Festa de l'Estandard.* Ceremony of the Standard in Palma. New Year's Eve celebrations in Palma and most towns.

Also during month *Baleart*, Craft fair, at IFEBAL Centre with displays by local craftsmen. Annual Christmas market in La Rambla with over 100 stalls.

A Brief History of Majorca

5000 BC First evidence of man in Balearics, discovered near Valldemossa.

2000 to 1300 BC Talyots - Boat shaped stone dwellings of copper and early bronze age.

1000 BC Bronze and Iron age. Evidence exists of agriculture and animal husbandry.

406 BC Carthaginian branch of the Phoenicians conquered the island.

123 BC Approximate commencement of period of Roman occupation. The Romans called the island Balearis Major after its stone throwers or slingers.

543 Apolinario, a Byzantine General, conquered the island.

902 Isam el Jaulini was forced to shelter from storm on Majorca while sailing to Mecca. Returned in following year to conquer island which became part of Caliphate of Córdoba.

1014 The Empire of Córdoba disintegrated. The island became part of petty Taifa kingdoms with its capital at Denia in Valencia.

1093 The Island was an unruly outpost of North African nomads.

1113 Ramón Berenguer III sent an expedition of Catalans and people from Pisa, seized the island but withdrew with his booty.

1229 A large force comprising 16,000 men and over 150 ships led by King Jaime I invaded the island and established Christian rule.

1233 Ramón Llull, the theologian and philosopher was born in Palma.

1276 Jaime I died. His son Jaime II was responsible for the initial construction work on the Cathedral. He was powerless to resist King Pedro III's demand for homage.

1285 Pedro III died and his eldest son Alfonso III became ruler of Majorca.

1311 Jaime II died. His first born son Jaime having retired to a monastery, his second son, Sancho became King, paying homage to the King of Aragon.

1324 King Sancho died and, having no direct heir, left the throne to his nephew Jaime III with a regency council. A dispute developed between Majorca and Aragon.

1343 King Pedro IV, the brother-in-law of Jaime III took possession of the island. Jaime III died at a battle at Llucmayor in 1349 attempting to regain control.

1396. King Martin I became King. He sent Hugo de Anglesola to govern Majorca and this brought some stability to the island which had suffered a long period of decline.

1492 Aragon and Castilla united and conquered Granada to form Spain as a nation of which the Baleares formed a part. Columbus discovered America, trade shifted to the new world and Majorca suffered.

1521 Revolt by the Germanies or brotherhoods. Twelve "brothers" formed a ruling council to govern the island. Emperor Charles V sent a punitive force and suppressed the revolt.
1533 Santa Catalina Thomas was born in Valldemossa.
1541 King Carlos I visited Palma in the course of gathering a fleet to attack the pirates who were again troublesome in the Mediterranean.
1550 The Moorish pirate Dragut attacked Pollença and was defeated by Juan Mas.
1561 Corsairs attacked Soller and two were killed by the Casanovas sisters.
1619 A feud raged between two families on Majorca, the Canamuts and Canavalls. Many lives were lost in the dispute which lasted six years.
1652. An outbreak of plague was started from a ship from Spain which arrived at Soller. It spread to Palma and over 15,000 people died.
1700 Felipe V, grandson of King Louis XIV of France, ascended the Spanish throne. The supporters of a rival, Carlos III of Austria, caused the Wars of the Succession.
1713 The Wars of the Succession were settled in 1713 by the Treaty of Utrecht with Felipe V being recognised as King of Spain. Junípero Serra was born in Petrá.
1713. A Bourbon fleet came to Palma to force the island to submit to the rule of Felipe V as agreed in the Treaty of Utrecht, the Viceroy refused but surrendered two years later.
1716 A royal decree appointed a new Government for the island which lost most of its special privileges and became a province of Spain.
1808 An uprising against Napoleon spread to Majorca which supported Fernando VII. The Island was invaded by refugees. Prisoners were sent to Majorca after battle of Bailen.
1812 A severe drought was followed eight years later by plague in Son Servera and Artà. More than half the population died. The next year plague killed 5000 in Palma.
1853 Don Antonio Maura was born in Palma. He studied law in Madrid, rose high in politics and was famous as a writer and orator. (He was elected Prime Minister in 1918.)
1868 A revolt deposed Queen Isabel II. Five years later Spain was declared a Republic.
1874. The monarchy was restored under Alfonso XII, the son of Isabel II.
1902. Old walls of Palma were demolished. The Grand Hotel opened the following year.
1923 King Alfonso accepted General Primo de Rivera as a Dictator. He fell 6 years later and, after much unrest, the King eventually went into exile.
1936 The start of the Spanish Civil War. Majorca was on the Nationalist side and provided Generalísimo Franco's only Mediterranean base. The war ended in 1939.
1966 Robert Graves was awarded the *Premio de los Premios for 1965* in recognition of being the person who had done most for Palma in the previous year.
1975 Generalísimo Franco died. Prince Juan Carlos was sworn in as King the next day.
1977 The first elections for forty-one years took place throughout Spain. Adolfo Suarez became Prime Minister.
1978 A referendum approved a new constitution. The following year the first elections were held under the new constitution and Adolfo Suarez was re-elected.
1982 Felipe Gonzalez became Prime Minister of a Socialist government.
1983 The first autonomous Balearic government was elected. Gabirel Cañellas was invested as the first President of Balearic Autonomous Community.
1984 The Parque del Mar in Palma was officially opened by King Juan Carlos .
1995 Spain celebrated the marriage of the Infanta Elena, the elder daughter of King Juan Carlos and Queen Sofia to Castilian nobleman Jaime de Marichalar in Seville.

INDEX

Age Concern Spain, 231
Alaró, 245, 246
Albufera, 134, 179, 181, 228
Alcudia, 47, 129, 179, 226, 227, 228
Alfabia, 219, 244
Almudaina Palace, 198
Amics de las Tortugues, 181
Andratx, 177, 179, 268
Anglican Church, 116, 129, 225, 228, 233
  25th Anniversary, 131, 136, 138, 206
  Thrift-Shop, 130, 230, 233
Arab Arch and Baths, 204
Archduke Luis Salvador, 17, 60, 238
Artà, 146, 179, 236
As it Happens, TV series, 136
Aucanada, 228
Auditorium, 132, 210, 254, 256
Bailen, Battle of, 275
Bateman, John, 228
Baker, Claire, 9
Banyalbufar, 177
Baroness Aurare de Dudevant, 16
Bars
  Abaco 207
  Benny Hill Pub, 125
  Lady Diana's Pub, 125
  Mucky Duck Pub, 125
  Prince William Pub, 125
  Whispers 136
Bassa, Guillem, 246
Bauza, Mountain, 59, 74
Bay Entertainers, 256
Bay of Alcudia, 228
Bay of Formentor, 49
Bay of Palma, 135
Bay of Pollença, 50, 227
BBC, 249, 250
BCM Disco, 125
Beateta, (Santa Catalina) 152
Bellver Castle, 159, 199, 210, 211, 254
Ben Nabat (also Ben-Amet), 244
Bendinat, 121
Berga Palace, 201
Biniaraix, 219
Binissalem, 161, 177, 209, 240, 265, 266
Bishop John Satterthwaite, 136
Blakemore, John, 251
Borne, 43, 79, 148, 169, 198, 201
Boscana, Fray Jerónimo, 277
Bowden, Carmen, 8, 114
Bowden, Dina Moore, 8, 116, 203, 247
Bowden, George, 8, 114, 115
Branson, Richard, 40, 62
Britannia, Royal Yacht, 202
British American Club, 233, 253
British Consul, 26, 79, 129, 251, 276
British Consulate, 25, 75, 204
British European Airways, 35, 38
Bunyola, 219, 244
Burwitz, Marina, 72
Burwitz, Nils, 72, 133, 138, 201
C'an Barbara, 28
Ca'n Pastilla, 276
Ca'n Picafort, 152, 228
Cabo Capdepera, 237
Cabo Formentor, 49
Cabot Brothers, 244
Cabrit, Guillem, 246
Cala Blava, 276
Cala D'Or, 131, 134, 139, 273
Cala Figuera, 273
Cala Fornells, 56
Cala Major, 119, 140
Cala Mondragó, 273
Cala Ratjada, 156, 237, 254
Cala San Vicente, 225, 229
Cala Santanyi, 274
Cala Tuent, 221
California, 203, 242, 277
Calvario, Pollença, 149
Calvià, 127, 144, 146, 155, 163, 172, 189
Camp de Mar, 62
Campanet, 47, 229
Campos, 179, 274
Camprodon, 199
Cañellas, Gabriel, 56
Canelluñ, 22, 25, 41, 46, 58
Capdella, 27, 58
Capdepera, 236
Cartuja, Valldemossa, 150, 254
Casa March, Gardens, 254
Casa Pomar, Campos, 274

Index

Casino, 125
Castell del Rei, 229
Cathedral, 129, 145, 198, 246
Caves of Artà, 237
Caves of Drach, 238
Caves of Hams, 238
Central Mimbrera, 213
Charcoal burners, 177. 244
Chopin, Frederick, 16, 254
Church of:
  San Antonio, 208
  San Bernardino, Petrà, 242
  San Lorenzo, 141
  Santa Eugenia, 266
  Santa Maria, Inca, 241
  Santa Maria, Manacor, 236
Circulo Mallorquin, 117
Ciudadanos Europeos, 214, 250
Coll d'en Rabassa, 276
Coll de Soller, 45, 219
Colonia San Jordi, 274
Consell, 209, 225, 230, 246, 266
Continente, Hypermarket, 276
Convent of San Francisco, 203
Convent of San Jerónimo, 241
Convent of Santo Domingo, 225, 255
Convento de San Buenaventura, 277
Costitx, 146
Cova Blava, Cabrera, 275
D'Arcy, Gwen, 234, 251
Deià, 17, 28, 41, 53, 78, 254, 276
Devils, 153, 156, 163, 248
Dielh, Adan, 48
Diocese of Gibraltar in Europe, 130, 136
Douglas, Michael, 60, 268
Duke of York, HRH Prince Andrew, 258
Economist Newspaper (The), 33, 36
Edwardes, Bob, 213
El Arenal, 276
El Molinar, 276
El Terreno, 116, 134
El Toro, 126
Els Blauets, Lluc, 255
Els Calderers, 246
English Bridge, 228
English Speaking Res. Assoc., 253, 274
Es Jonquet., 208
Es Pontas, 274
Es Trenc, 275
Escorca, 223
Esporles 59, 66
Estallencs, 62
Felanitx, 149, 168, 177, 207, 242, 265
Ferrer, José L, Bodega, 219, 266
Ferrer, Luis, 266
Firestone Map, 8, 133, 207
Fleming, Ray, 251
Florianópolis Bodega, 268
Folk Dancing, 50, 162
Formentor, 146, 179, 227
Fornalutx, 219
Fundació La Caixa, 201
Galatzo, 59, 74
Galerías Preciados, 87, 144, 208
Galilea, 59, 74
Galmés, Guillermo, 242
Gaudí, Antonio, 200
Gay, Karl, 42, 53, 79
Gelhorn, Martha, 37
Generalísimo Franco, 55, 130
Genova, 231
Golf de Poniente, 126
Gonzalez, Felipe, 55
Gorg Blau, 179, 220
Grand Hotel, 201
Graves, Beryl, 22, 29, 42, 264
Graves, Robert, 11, 19, 22, 39, 53, 79, 149, 199, 207
  Death of, 77
  Letters from, 30-33
Graves, Tomás, 35, 36, 54, 72
Graves, William, 35
Harbour View Nursing Home, 234
Hermitage de la Mare de Deu, 226
Hermitage of Crestaix, 149
Hermitage of Santa Magdalena, 149
HMS Ark Royal, Brave, Cattistock, Cottesmore, Hurworth, Illustrious, Invincible, & Nottingham, 257-258
HMS Grenville, 129
HMS Repulse, 116, 129
Hotels
  Arabella, 212
  Coronado, 56, 74
  Costa D'Or, 28, 31
  Es Moli, 61
  Formentor, 35, 47, 48
  La Residencia, 40, 61, 176, 254

Maristel, 62
Nixe Palace, 119
Punta Negra, 123
Santa Lucia, 140
Son Matias, 140
Son Vida, 212
Trinidad, 140
Villamil, 55
Vistamar, 59
Iberia, Airline, 79
Illetas, 121
Inca, 149, 209, 240
Institute of Foreign Property Owners, 252
Instituto Balear de Promocion del Turismo, 8, 251
Intercontinental Church Society, 140
Island of: Dragonera, 66
Island of Cabrera, 179, 212, 274
Island of Formentor, 50
Island of Malgrats, 126
Island of Sech, 125
Jacobson, Ellis, 207
Jaume, Melchar, 246
Jewish Ghettos, 126, 204
Judd, Forrest, 20, 31
King Alfonso of Aragon, 246
King Jaime I, 7, 121, 126, 166, 209, 229, 237, 243, 244
King Jaime II, 199, 200, 203, 211, 236, 246, 273
King Jaime III, 200, 211
King Juan Carlos, 55, 150, 251
King Pedro IV, 211
King Sancho, 211
La Cartuja, 16, 211
La Granja, 66
La Llonja, 144, 204, 207
La Misericordia, 255
La Rambla, 202, 255
La Sala, 202
Lafiore Glass Factory, 67
Lake, John, 26
Las Tortugas, 43
Laszlo, Stefan, 118
Lazaar, Riki 'The Lash', 251
Lazo de Dama por Merito Civil, 117
Lladró China, 208
Lloseta, 209
Lluc-Alcari, 22, 28, 33, 44
Lluc Monastery, 179, 223
Llucmajor, 152, 211, 271, 277
Llul, Ramón, 203, 206, 277
Los Amigos de Mallorca, 117
Magalluf, 119, 124, 139
Majorca Daily Bulletin, 112, 132, 134, 136, 250
Mal Pas, 227
Manacor, 156, 235
Marineland, 122, 146
Marratxi, 149
Martel, E A, 237
Mas, Juan, 166, 226
Matthews, Tom, Editor, 37
Matthews, Tommy, 11, 19, 22, 27, 37
Mentink, Kate, 214, 250
Mercado, Olivar, 208
Mercado, Santa Catalina, 208
Mercadona Supermarket, 123
Mirador de Ses Pites, 17
Mirador Ses Barques, 220
Miramar, 17
Mola de Planicie, 59
Montuiri, 152, 247
Mounted Police, 159, 167
Muro, 146, 156, 229
Museo Naval, 207
Museums and Galleries:
Archbishop's Palace, 200
Archive of Mąjorca, 204
Junípero Serra Museum, Petrá, 242
Museo Etnológico, Muro, 229
Museum of Majorca, 207
Na Burguesa, 74, 119, 183
Nemo Submarines, 125
Nit de Foc, 163
Night Clubs,
Es Foguero, Palma, 213
Pirates, Magalluf, 125
Son Amar, Palma, 213
Nureyev, Rudolph, 255
O'Hara, Maureen, 21, 28
Oratory de San Salvador, Artà, 236
Oratory of San Pedro, 223
Orient, 177, 179, 245
Ornithologists, 179
Ornithology, 49, 177, 179, 228, 275
Paguera, 58, 175, 217
Palma, 38, 155, 197, 255

Palma Nova, 119, 123, 139, 141
Parque del Mar, 198
Perlas Majorica, 236
Perlas Orquidea, 236
Perpignan, 12, 199
Peters, Wendy, 250
Petrá, 116, 152, 240, 241
Phylloxera, 246, 265
Pla, 47, 177, 225, 240
Pla de Cubert, 220
Playa de la Cuarassa, 227
Playa de Palma Nova, 124
Playas de Mallorca, 276
Plaza Cort, 144, 145, 148, 166, 202, 204
Plaza de la Reina, 148
Plaza de Toros, 24
Plaza España, 209
Plaza Marqués del Palmer, 202
Plaza Mayor, 145, 169, 202, 204, 208
Plaza San Francisco, 204
Plaza Santa Eulalia, 169, 202
Plaza Santa Magdalena, 198
Plaza Vapor, 208
Plaza Weyler, 201
Poligono Victoria, 213
Pollença, 47, 135, 146, 149, 168, 179, 225, 255
Portals Nous, 115, 122
Portals Vells, 125
Porto Colom, 156, 243
Porto Cristo, 235, 238
Porto Petro, 273
Porto Pi, 265
Porto Pi Centro, 256
Posada, 28, 40
Pretty Useful Group, 256
Price, Will, 20, 28, 30, 54
Pueblo Español, 118, 210
Puerta de la Xera, 227
Puerta de San Sebastián, 227
Puerto de Andratx, 131, 146, 156
Puerto de Canonge, 61
Puerto de Soller, 44, 209, 220
Puerto Pollença, 48, 139, 146, 225, 227
Puerto Portals, 122
Puig de la Guardia, 274
Puig de Massanella, 224
Puig des Calvari, 226
Puig Major, 220
Puig Tomir, 47
Puigpuñent, 59, 177
Queen Sofia, 150
Radio 95.8FM, 249
Radio 107.4FM, 250
Randa, 204, 275, 277
Raxa, 244
Reader, (The), 251
Restaurants
  Bahia Mediterraneo, Palma, 210
  Bennett's, San Augusti, 121
  Bens Davall, Nr Deià, 264
  Café Bellavista, Banyalbufar, 61
  Ca na Cucó, Calvià, 127
  Ca'n Matias y Miquel, Palma, 235
  Ca'n Pedro, Genova, 67
  Ca'n Quirante, San Jordi, 213
  Casa Jacinto, Genova, 67
  Celler C'an Amer, Inca, 241
  Ciro's, Palma Nova, 124
  Club Nautico, Arenal, 276
  El Pato, Son Vida 212
  Es Comellà, Calvià, 127
  English Rose, Puigpuñent, 59
  French Coffee Shop, Portals Nous, 122
  Giovanni's, Palma, 207
  Gran Dragon, Palma Nova, 124
  Hoyo 10, Bendinat, 122
  Iska, Palma, 206
  La Gritta, Paguera, 248
  La Residencia, Deià, 276
  La Trattoria Pizzaria, San Agusti, 121
  La Vileta, La Vileta, 213
  Mangiafuoco, Palma, 208
  Maxim, Puerto Pollença, 227
  Meson Ca'n Torrat, Calvià, 127
  Meson Tio Pepe, Son Bonet, 214
  Moderno, Puerto d Andratx, 63
  Portixol, Portixol, 264
  Real Club Nautico, Palma, 206
  Rififi, Palma, 265
  Sa Costa, Valldemossa, 71
  Sanctuary at Randa, 278
  Ses Forquetes, Calvià, 127
  Son Caliu, Son Caliu,123
  Sporting Tenis Playa, Portals Nous, 123
  Terraza Barbieri, Santa Ponça, 126
Roman Remains, 135, 226, 227, 236
Roth, Benjamin, (Benito), 134

Rubi, Fray Mariano, 277
Russell, David, 73, 76
S'Arxiduc - See Archduke Luis Salvador
S'Estaca Estate, 60, 268
S'Hort del Rei Gardens, 198
Sa Caleta, 126
Sa Calobra, 220, 255
Sa Foradada, 17
Sa Pobla, 134, 149, 156, 228, 229
Sa Rapita, 156
Sagrera, Guillermo, 207
Sala Mozart, 256
Salvà, Pere, 199
Salvation Army, 140, 141, 230, 234
San Agusti, 119, 121
San Telmo, 65
Sanctuaries
  Bon Any, 242
  Nuestra Señora de Cura, 275, 278
  San Salvador, 243
Sand, George, 16, 53, 199
Sant Jaume Banda de Música, 164
Sant Joan, 146, 149, 156, 246
Sant Jordi, 213
Santa Ana Chapel, 200
Santa Catalina Tomás, 149, 152, 208, 228
Santa Margalida, 150, 152, 228
Santa Maria, 209, 240, 266
Santa Ponça, 126, 166, 175
Santanyi, 86, 207, 271, 273
Saridakis, Juan, 55
Satterthwaite, Bishop John, 136
Save the Children Fund, 122, 127, 231
Sea Consulate, 207
Segura, Aina, 169
Selva, 225
Sencelles, 246, 266
Serra, Fray Junípero, 8, 116, 203, 240
Ses Lleonès, 201
Ses Salines, 275
Seymour-Smith, Martin, 8, 25, 35, 204
Shelley, Henry, 223
Short, Frank, 79, 118, 129
Sierra de Alfabia, 45, 219
Sierra de Torrellas, 220, 266
Sierra del Teix, 17
Sineu, 152, 241
Sociedad Protectora de Animales y Plantas de Mallorca, 232
Soller, 45, 165, 209, 219
Son Bonet, 51, 214
Son Caliu, 123
Son Marroig, 17, 254
Son Pardo, 232
Son San Juan Airport, 55, 214
Son Vida, 212
Stoba, K J, 177
Stoma, Dr Michael, 108
Suarez, Adolfo, 55
Synagogue, 141
Talayots, 275
Teatro Municipal, 254
Teatro Principal, 201, 254
Ternelles, 146
Thomas, Gabriel, 241
Thomson Holidays, 139
Tia Maria, 69, 73, 79, 80, 111, 179, 215
Torre de Canyamel, 237
Torre dels Enagistes, Manacor, 236
Torrent de Pareis, 221, 255
Torrente La Riera, 43, 208
Tourist Office, 208, 209, 251
Tram, Soller, 45, 46, 209
Tunel, Liqueurs, 269
Un Hiver à Majorque, See Winter in Majorca & George Sand
University of Buffalo, 54
Valldemossa, 16, 71, 149, 204, 254, 276
Veri family, 246
Vilafranca, 159
Vivot Palace, 203
Waters, Neville, 132
Windmills, 47, 177, 208, 242
Winter in Majorca, 8, 17, 53, 72, 199